DEGREES THAT MATTER

DEGREES THAT MATTER

Moving Higher Education to a Learning
Systems Paradigm

Natasha A. Jankowski and
David W. Marshall

National Institute for
Learning Outcomes Assessment
Making Learning Outcomes Usable & Transparent

STERLING, VIRGINIA

Published by Stylus Publishing, LLC.
22883 Quicksilver Drive
Sterling, Virginia 20166-2102

Library of Congress Cataloging-in-Publication Data
Names: Jankowski, Natasha A., author. | Marshall, David W., 1970-
author.
Title: Degrees that matter : moving higher education to a learning
systems paradigm / Natasha A. Jankowski and David W. Marshall.
Description: First edition. |
Sterling, Virginia : Stylus Publishing, 2017. |
Includes bibliographical references.
Identifiers: LCCN 2017008582 (print) |
LCCN 2017032999 (ebook) |
ISBN 9781620364659 (Library networkable e-edition) |
ISBN 9781620364666 (Consumer e-edition) |
ISBN 9781620364635 (cloth : alk. paper) |
ISBN 9781620364642 (pbk. : alk. paper)
Subjects: LCSH: Education, Higher--Aims and objectives--United
States. | Education, Higher--United States--Evaluation. |
Universities and colleges--Curricula--United States. |
National Center for Learning Outcomes Assessment (U.S.)
Classification: LCC LA227.4 (ebook) |
LCC LA227.4 .J36 2017 (print) |
DDC 378.00973--dc23
LC record available at https://lccn.loc.gov/2017008582

13-digit ISBN: 978-1-62036-463-5 (cloth)
13-digit ISBN: 978-1-62036-464-2 (paperback)
13-digit ISBN: 978-1-62036-465-9 (library networkable e-edition)
13-digit ISBN: 978-1-62036-466-6 (consumer e-edition)

Printed in the United States of America

All first editions printed on acid-free paper
that meets the American National Standards Institute
Z39-48 Standard.

Bulk Purchases

Quantity discounts are available for use in workshops and for
staff development.
Call 1-800-232-0223

First Edition, 2017

10   9   8   7   6   5   4   3   2   1

We dedicate this book to all the people doing the work of improving student learning.

"May it be a light to you in dark places, when all other lights go out."

—*J.R.R. Tolkien*, The Fellowship of the Ring *(p. 393)*

CONTENTS

TABLES AND FIGURES

Tables

Figures

ACKNOWLEDGMENTS

This book results from efforts by a great many people who have contributed both directly and indirectly to the emergence of the learning systems paradigm. The paradigm we describe derives from work done in hundreds of institutions and organizations. Many were participants in early pilots of the Degree Qualifications Profile (DQP) and Tuning. Four accrediting commissions, the Accrediting Commission for Community and Junior Colleges, the Higher Learning Commission, the Southern Association of Colleges and School Commission on Colleges, and the Western Association of Schools and Colleges Senior College and University Commission, as well as three national associations, the American Association of State Colleges and Universities, the Association of American Colleges & Universities Quality Collaboratives, and the Council of Independent Colleges, undertook projects that provided us early lessons, for which we are grateful, about the utility of the DQP.

States and organizations also provided us with valuable insights emerging from their work with the Tuning process, among them the states of Indiana, Minnesota, Utah, Texas, and Kentucky, which each undertook Tuning to address various state-level concerns. We would like to thank Norm Jones, Daniel McInerney, and Teddi Safman, from Utah, whose involvement with both DQP and Tuning has demonstrated such remarkable results and from whom we have learned an enormous amount since they first began in 2008. We owe thanks to the Midwest Higher Education Compact for its work in cross-state approaches. Two disciplinary associations, the American Historical Association and the National Communication Association, enabled us to learn about the tremendous potential for Tuning on a national scale. Each has pushed DQP and Tuning in new directions that have informed our work on this book.

These specific acknowledgments leave out the many faculty, staff, and administrators at individual institutions who tackled their particular challenges with DQP and/or Tuning, as well as through other initiatives, such as Pathways and Liberal Education and America's Pathways (LEAP). The reports they have submitted and the case studies they have enabled the National Institute for Learning Outcomes and Assessment (NILOA) to produce have taught valuable lessons regarding the possibilities of using tools such as these.

Additionally, the participants in the NILOA assignment charrettes and various assignment workshops who have shared their own experiences with such initiatives have given us valuable insights.

We are indebted to three other organizations and those who work in them. First, between 2009 and 2015, the Institute for Evidence-Based Change worked on establishing Tuning by facilitating projects with multiple states and organizations. Adina Chapman, Will Dane, Michelle Kalina, Brad Phillips, Shelly Valdez, Marianne Wokeck, and John Yopp each played roles in supporting the emergence of Tuning as a flexible methodology for devising intentional, coherent educational pathways for students in higher education. Without them, David Marshall would have been unable to learn much of what he has contributed to this book.

Second, NILOA has played a pivotal role in documenting and supporting initiatives involving both DQP and Tuning, as well as projects related to them. NILOA's staff and research analysts constructed online reporting systems, collected and sifted through data, and reported findings that form the basis of this book. With their Senior Scholars and DQP/Tuning coaches, NILOA produced documents to support use of DQP and Tuning and developed numerous publications, workshops, and presentations to share findings with others and encourage the construction of intentional approaches to student learning. Pat Hutchings, Jillian Kinzie, Peter Ewell, Paul Lingenfelter, and George Kuh all taught us a great deal in the process.

Third, we are thankful to the Lumina Foundation, whose sponsorship of DQP and Tuning enabled much of the work we document in this book. Holly McKiernan, Courtney Brown, Amber Garrison Duncan, Kevin Corcoran, and Holly Zanville have all advanced DQP/Tuning in the years since 2008. Their vision and diligence in advancing such well-conceived tools for the strengthening of student learning cannot be overstated. Additionally, four individuals working with Lumina need to be recognized for their profound contribution to this book. Cliff Adelman, Peter Ewell, Paul Gaston, and Carol Geary Schneider leave an indelible mark on this book for their own remarkable work in writing the DQP. Their vision of what higher education can be lays at the heart of our work. We are indebted, too, to Cliff Adelman for his work in bringing Tuning to the American context.

Finally, we would like to express our gratitude to colleagues who have enabled us to more concretely conceptualize the argument of this book. David wishes to thank his colleagues at California State University, San Bernardino, in particular, Kimberly Costino, Janelle Gilbert, Joanna Oxendine, and Qiana Wallace, as well as others who have given him opportunities to engage in the kinds of activity this book describes. Without the space they helped to create for collaborative turns toward a full student-experience, his thinking would be much less developed. Natasha would like to thank George Kuh and Stan Ikenberry for providing the space and opportunity to explore and develop the ideas put forward in this book. Without their leadership, guidance, and mentorship, none of this would have been possible.

INTRODUCTION

The rhetoric around higher education in America has been bogged down in an unproductive—perhaps even counterproductive—debate in recent years. That debate has taken up *use* and *purpose* as its keywords and focused on a dichotomy of utility in the economic or political worlds and purity of education for education's sake. The debate has become so prevalent that it has begun to shape, sometimes in dramatic forms, education legislation, policies, and reform initiatives, with legislators decrying "degrees to nowhere" and budgeting money to promote and develop programs in the science, technology, engineering, and math (STEM) fields. Other voices, including academics and educational organization leaders, call for a more civic-minded approach. Still other voices are those of many faculty, who lament the devaluing of knowledge as a worthwhile end in itself.

The driving question: What is the purpose of higher education in America? The question is hotly debated, with an often divisive frame for its answers: the preparation of qualified employees; the development of engaged citizens; or the personal fulfillment of individuals' intellectual, social, and psychological needs. The first, and often the loudest, voice emphasizes the role of higher education in training a workforce that can fill jobs for the twenty-first century and thereby help to advance the American economy. For example, as reported by Kolowich (2011) in *Inside Higher Ed,* in his 2011 speech to the National Governors Association, Bill Gates assumed an educational system geared toward preparing employees. Gates called for a metrics-based self-evaluation of higher education and observed that data can enable campuses to identify the degree to which individual programs live up to subsidies by launching prepared students into the workforce, with STEM and vocationally aligned fields proving of greater value, in his mind, than disciplines in the humanities and social sciences. A year later, *The Economist* argued

> Universities owe it [dealing with their inefficiencies] to the students who have racked up $1 trillion in debt, and to the graduate students who are taking second degrees because their first one was so worthless. They also bear some responsibility for the 17m who are overqualified for their jobs, and for the 3m unfilled positions for which skilled workers cannot be

found. They even owe it to the 37m who went to college, dropped out and ended up with nothing: many left for economic reasons. (Higher education, 2012)

Both arguments revolve around the economics of higher education in relation to the economy at large, with students positioned as education consumers and future employees. It is likely not coincidental that these calls followed the publication of Richard Arum and Josipa Roksa's (2011) *Academically Adrift: Limited Learning on College Campuses*, a book that has been repeatedly cited by critics of U.S. higher education as describing the heart of the issue. Arum and Roksa's (2011) book implicitly calls for accountability in higher education, but that call seems to have been reduced to metrics that focus on employability. Non-STEM or non-vocationally-aligned programs are left with a question of their use and purpose hanging over them and are dismissed as *degrees to nowhere*. In Utah, State Senator Howard Stephenson coined this term, arguing that degrees in the humanities and social sciences put undue stress on limited educational budgets and left students unprepared for careers (Maffly, 2011). Similarly, in Florida, Governor Rick Scott proposed in 2012 a strategy to reduce students in "degrees to nowhere" fields and move them toward STEM fields by differentiating tuition (Alvarez, 2012).

The second voice points to higher education's role in nurturing men and women as individuals who think critically in their personal lives and are active participants in American democracy. Liberal education differs from this more vocationally oriented model of education by its emphasis on a well-rounded education that promotes critical thinking and the so-called "soft skills" that are more difficult to measure. According to the Association of American Colleges & Universities' (AAC&U) website

Liberal Education is an approach to learning that empowers individuals and prepares them to deal with complexity, diversity, and change. It provides students with broad knowledge of the wider world (e.g., science, culture, and society) as well as in-depth study in a specific area of interest. A liberal education helps students develop a sense of social responsibility, as well as strong and transferable intellectual and practical skills such as communication, analytical and problem-solving skills, and a demonstrated ability to apply knowledge and skills in real-world settings. (Association of American Colleges & Universities, n.d.b)

Whereas AAC&U's definition of *liberal education* suggests a broadly applicable use of learning—a point to which we will return later—other thinkers within academic communities assert this position in terms directly opposed to the vocational argument described previously. Martha Nussbaum (2010), for example, makes the following fervent call for a different model, one driven by civic needs:

> Thirsty for national profit, nations, and their systems of education, are heedlessly discarding skills that are needed to keep democracies alive. If this trend continues, nations all over the world will soon be producing generations of useful machines, rather than complete citizens who can think for themselves, criticize tradition, and understand the significance of another person's suffering and achievements. The future of the world's democracies hangs in the balance. (p. 2)

For Nussbaum, higher education's chief contribution is the acculturation of thinking citizens capable of maintaining rule by the people, and the turn she perceives toward education as job training threatens that primary effort. Other writers, often and understandably coming from disciplines in the humanities, think similarly. For example, literature specialists such as Rita Felski (2008) argue for the importance of literature as an avenue to self-knowledge and understanding of others, essential elements to participation in communities. A liberal education that revalues the humanities thus becomes a tool for preparing sensitive, thinking citizens not blinded by rhetoric or numbed by sound-bite media cultures.

Quietly thrumming along, the third and final voice shares its belief in the importance of college and university education in developing knowledge and intellectual growth but rarely does so in public media. A poll conducted by the *Chronicle of Higher Education* and the Pew Research Center (Taylor et al., 2011) suggests that graduates of higher education see the greatest benefits of a college or university degree to be "knowledge and intellectual growth" (74% of respondents rating higher education "very useful") and "personal growth and maturity" (67% of respondents rating it "very useful"); compare this with the rating for "preparation for job or career" (55% of respondents rating it "very useful"). Those statistics will, no doubt, cheer faculty such as David Marshall's colleague who argued that "the minute we engage in the utility conversation, we've lost," because they indicate that graduates value their education for personal benefits. This argument assumes a knowledge for knowledge's sake philosophy that enhances an individual personally.

The problem revealed by the *Chronicle*/Pew statistics, however, is the belief among many graduates that "college didn't teach me anything." Although anecdotal, Natasha Jankowski's (coauthor of this book) experience in conversing with seat partners on airplanes points to a concerning reason for the statistics. When she explains that she works for a research institute that tries to determine how we know whether university students are learning, the most frequent response is "I didn't learn anything in college." In the ensuing conversations, a pattern emerges: Students do not associate their learning in higher education with the kinds of activities and soft skills that they use in their work lives. They associate "learning" with subject content, such as who won the battle of Orange, what marks a scientific genus, or what period of art produced these works. They fail to see, in other words, how their college or university experience developed the abilities and skills that have enabled them to be successful in their work lives. That should be a concern for everyone involved in higher education.

The problem, however, is that this is the wrong debate entirely.

In fact, there should be no debate—at least not in this particular area of higher education. As the debates around the purpose of higher education have continued, fundamental issues have been obscured. Despite the presence of three voices in this seemingly disharmonious chorus, ultimately they combine to form atonal music akin to that of composers like Béla Bartok. Although all singing different lines, all three ultimately ask to what college and university education should be aligned. The economic and civic applications are obvious, but even the fulfillment argument is one of application to personal ends. All three assume a particular end to higher education, and all three see that end as an applied one. In the process of their discordant singing, the parties of these debates have missed one fundamental commonality that obviates the need for promoting exclusive answers. In other words, higher education can and does serve all these ends. The passage from the AAC&U addresses this point directly in its assertion that "liberal education helps students develop a sense of social responsibility, as well as strong and transferable intellectual and practical skills." The term *transferable* speaks directly to myriad possible points of transfer. Students can transfer their learning to economic ends, to civic engagement, and to personal fulfillment.

What has motivated the utility debate? A variety of factors, including the rising costs of higher education, its accessibility, and the effectiveness of its work. Each of these has been rolled under the concern for accountability. These national debates, particularly as they relate to the economic end for education, seek ways of measuring the effectiveness of institutions. For example, in the early considerations of the Obama administration's proposed report card for colleges and universities, employability of graduates arose as a possible criterion for measuring the success of institutions, and debt-to-income ratios continue to receive some support. Historically, accreditation processes have been and remain the primary means of assuring institutional accountability. Although fiscal management and other such factors figure into the evaluation of institutions, student learning often stands as the primary area of interest, at least for faculty, who are responsible for documenting evidence of student learning and, thereby, demonstrating institutional success in the bedrock mission of colleges and universities.

Few things set off frustrated mumbling among faculty more than discussions of accountability and the assessment of student learning. A host of reasons exists. Accreditation, to some, is the imposition of standards from outside bodies. For others, accreditation imports business models into systems that, despite the rise of for-profit institutions, are not organizations to be managed by tried-and-true corporate strategies—apples and oranges, they say. Others, still, bemoan the excessive work that accreditation-driven assessment heaps on them, with the demands to fit data into easily digestible reports and tables. None of these activities, assert these arguments, actually jibe with educators' core mission to teach their students.

The accountability imperative can be recast dramatically if we shift the frame around the debates of higher education's purpose. Rather than being preoccupied with a "what" question, faculty, staff, administrators, and education policymakers would do better to ask a "how" question: How is what students learn in college *aligned* to these three needs motivating higher education? Turning to this "how" question reorients the debate away from ends-based arguments that ossify into exclusive categories toward praxis-oriented explorations of what colleges and universities *do* to assure that their programs are developing the kinds of learning that equip students to make application to each of these three areas. Reorienting in this way encourages a turn away from outward-facing arguments to inward-facing reflection on the strategies used by institutions of higher learning to clarify for students the ways in which the variety of studies in diverse disciplines equips them to be productive employees, engaged citizens, *and* fulfilled human beings. As any faculty member in any discipline will say, their disciplines prepare students for all three arenas. The question is, as we have just said, how?

The "how" question challenges us as faculty, staff, and administrators to examine how we have designed learning experiences for students. If we accept that our institution strives to help students learn for each of these three purposes, then we are led to consider to what extent our institutions have developed curriculum and cocurriculum that enable students to transfer learning to these distinct—but not mutually exclusive—areas. The "how" question leads us to ask a series of more specific, self-examining questions:

- What do we want our students to learn?
- To what extent do our curriculum and cocurriculum encourage students to learn what we want them to learn?
- What other approaches might we employ to ensure that our students are proficient in these areas?

- Who might benefit from being included in our efforts to help students learn?
- Where does student learning get reinforced and developed?
- How are we helping students apply their learning to the different spheres of their lives?
- How—and to what extent—do we see our students succeeding or struggling in their learning?

These are questions that those of us working in higher education are (mostly) accustomed to asking, but in this book we argue that the common answers to date have been constrained by rigid institutional and systemic structures that have hindered the different kinds of productive thinking that are possible. We have witnessed revitalization in institutions that break down those structures to realize the potential of their individual, unique campuses. This book will help faculty, staff, and administrators on college and university campuses try to engage in processes of reflection that seek answers to the "how" question (and the ancillary questions that follow from it) and do so from context-specific considerations of program design, curriculum, cocurriculum, and pedagogy, as well as how each of these aspects have their separate impacts on student learning.

By doing so, institutions and communities of faculty, staff, and administrators can move away from the counterproductive frames that the utility debates have installed. Reorienting practice around student learning and reflective approaches to fostering it has the potential to reinvigorate practice on college and university campuses around a shared mission to improve the lives and futures of students by building coherent curricula and cocurricula that better achieve our desired ends. In the process, the concerns with accountability and accreditation, we argue, will largely resolve themselves by leveraging the kinds of activities faculty and staff already do.

Two Tools for Reflection

This book draws on two recent initiatives in the United States: the Tuning process, adapted from a European approach to breaking down siloes in the European Union educational space, and the Degree Qualifications Profile (DQP), a document that identifies and describes core areas of learning that are (or should be) relatively common among institutions in the United States. Together, Tuning and the DQP have provided faculty, staff, and administrators tools for asking the "how" questions and thinking reflectively about what they do and the ways in which they might do it differently. Many of our examples are drawn from site visit reports, self-reported activities, workshops, and project experience collected by the National Institute for Learning Outcomes Assessment (NILOA) between 2010 and 2016. In that six-year window, NILOA witnessed the use of Tuning and/or the DQP in hundreds of institutions nationally.

Our examples illustrate the kinds of practices the book describes; however, they are not meant to be templates or models. As will become a recurring theme, context matters. We are not suggesting a "one size fits all" approach. On the contrary, what yielded success on one campus may not have the same impact on another. Each institution serves different demographics, has different resources, adheres to different missions, and exercises different curricular models. Those—and other—areas of distinction will shape both the way your own institution may engage with these tools (or any others, for that matter) and the results of those efforts, and they should. What is common, however, are the kinds of questions to be asked and the types of strategies for answering them. That is what this book provides.

The DQP is an outline of agreed-on learning expected at three distinct degree levels—the associate, baccalaureate, and master's. It provides a list of proficiencies in five areas, regardless of degree, and serves as a reference point for what students should know and be able to do, regardless of major, upon graduation. It does not prescribe content or pedagogy but provides a reference point for degree-level learning. Tuning is a faculty-driven process of determining in a specific field of study what a student should know and be able to do upon completion of a degree. Together, DQP and Tuning paint a picture of comprehensive student degree-level learning culminating in a shared understanding of what it means to say one has a degree in X in terms of learning. As tools, they help focus on student learning as opposed to proxy measures such as time to degree or number of courses completed.

The Degree Qualifications Profile

The DQP emerged out of conversations around the need to return the United States to a position of educational dominance in having the highest percentage of college graduates, while recognizing that giving more people degrees is quite easy if the degrees are not of high quality. Thus, it is not enough to have more citizens holding degrees or credentials if those degrees are not of high quality. Even defining what a *high-quality degree* means is not an easy task, because there is not a shared picture of quality in postsecondary education. To address this gap, Lumina Foundation facilitated several discussions in 2009 with U.S. and European educators, association leaders, government officials, and postsecondary administrators. The group, after much deliberation, arrived at an agreement that what was needed was a framework, or a profile, that served to define degrees in terms of learning, but in a way that was distinctively American. Through further meetings, debates continued on the best way to develop such a framework, and a path forward was offered to appoint a small panel with considerable experience in higher education to review various models and frameworks, culminating in a draft document that could be tested in the field.

Released in July 2011, the first draft of the DQP (Lumina Foundation, 2011) was offered to the field of higher education for testing. The document had four authors: Cliff Adelman, a senior associate at the Institute for Higher Education Policy; Peter Ewell, then vice president of the National Center for Higher Education Management Systems; Paul Gaston, trustees professor at Kent State University; and Carol Geary Schneider, then president of the AAC&U. Carol's involvement as an author was key as the AAC&U developed the Liberal Education and America's Promise (LEAP) Essential Learning Outcomes (ELOs), a framework which influenced and helped to align the development of the DQP. The authors were clear that their intentional use of the word *profile* was not only in name but also as a signal that the DQP was not attempting to standardize degrees or limit institutional uniqueness. Instead, the profile allows faculty to explore how specific degrees fit into the DQP, allowing it to act—as one of the authors, Peter Ewell, likes to say—as a universal translator, allowing various groups to talk with each other about how they fit into degree preparation.

The DQP was also intentionally written with active verbs emphasizing what students actually should do to demonstrate learning, through embedded assignments, and it outlined descriptions of what every graduate at a given level of degree attainment ought to know and be able to do. With the release of the draft document, or beta document, various groups initiated institution-led projects to explore the utility of the profile. NILOA was tasked with mapping and tracking the work of institutions using the DQP to better understand the various ways in which the profile could be applied while also gathering evidence regarding what needed to be changed. Feedback was gathered over a three-year period of data collection and study, culminating in a release in October 2014 of the revised DQP document (Lumina Foundation, 2014). The five areas of learning now include the following:

1. Specialized knowledge, what students should demonstrate with respect to their field of study
2. Broad and integrative knowledge, where students apply and integrate learning from different broad fields

3. Intellectual skills, composed of analytic inquiry, use of information resources, ability to engage diverse perspectives, ethical reasoning, quantitative fluency, and communicative fluency
4. Applied and collaborative learning, emphasized by what students do with what they know
5. Civic and global learning, where students engage with and respond to civic, social, environmental, and economic challenges

At present, 780 institutions have used or are currently using the DQP. NILOA collected various points of data on DQP use from 2011 to 2016. In examining the various ways in which the DQP was used, NILOA followed Lumina-funded projects, collected more than 1,000 institutionally completed reports on DQP use and activity, undertook 15 case studies of DQP use, and examined 25 institution-authored examples of practice. NILOA also undertook surveys of administrators and faculty within institutions. It is from this vast collection of data, as well as participation in the project meetings, providing support to institutions on the ground, and developing tools and resources to support engagement with DQP and Tuning, that this book draws.

Because the DQP was a document made without a specific intended use in mind, the following various funded projects that engaged with the DQP took on different approaches to engagement and use:

- The Accrediting Commission for Community and Junior Colleges launched a DQP Project with a cohort of institutions examining the potential of the DQP to enhance educational quality, increase institutional effectiveness, and promote continuous quality improvement in higher education.
- The American Association of State Colleges and Universities (AASCU) worked with three university systems to test the feasibility of the DQP within the unique context of each system.
- AAC&U worked with assessment professionals, faculty, and policy leaders from multiple states in the Quality Collaboratives project, focused on two- and four-year partner institutions and issues of transfer.
- The Council of Independent Colleges (CIC) selected 25 institutions to work as a consortium to examine the usefulness of the DQP to improve student learning as well as the applicability of the document in an independent liberal arts college context.

- The Higher Learning Commission (HLC) used a new model of accreditation referred to as Open Pathways to explore DQP use for accreditation.
- The Southern Association of Colleges and Schools Commission on Colleges (SACSCOC) brought together 22 historically Black colleges and universities (HBCUs) to use the DQP to map curriculum in order to identify strengths and weaknesses.
- The Western Association of Schools and Colleges (WASC) Senior College and University Commission included 29 institutions exploring the use of the DQP as a framework for assisting institutions to assess the quality of degrees or portions of degree programs.

In these projects, the DQP was used to review and revise learning outcomes, map curriculum, align assignments, revise general education, develop new programs, address issues of transfer, and explore alignment of learning outcomes with external expectations. It provided a mechanism by which faculty, staff, administrators, and students could engage in conversations around the "how" of education and explore issues of educational design. The work led to the development of an assignment library and NILOA staff facilitating assignment charrettes, where groups of faculty came together for an intense period of collaborative assignment revision and review (Hutchings, Jankowski, & Ewell, 2014).

Tuning

Tuning predates DQP by slightly more than a year. As with DQP, its emergence derived from concerns over establishing the quality of degrees in light of commitments by both the Lumina Foundation and the Obama administration to increase degree attainment in the United States. Quality emerged as a central concern. Seeking a means of encouraging the quality of U.S. degrees, the foundation commissioned Cliff Adelman (2009) to make a study of Tuning, a process developed by European faculty in response to a program that had resulted in the European Higher Education Area. As a process, Tuning asks faculty to define the essential learning within specific disciplines through collaborative processes. In Europe, it enabled a definition of *learning* that could form a basis for comparability across borders so that students moving from one national system to another would be prepared regardless of where they had studied previously. In the United States, it has been undertaken for a variety of different purposes.

As a process, Tuning in the American context consists of five constituent elements. In Tuning, discipline-specific faculty (a) define learning essential to the discipline in the form of core competencies and learning outcomes; (b) map career pathways; (c) consult stakeholders, including colleagues, institution staff, students, and employer groups; (d) revise the competencies and outcomes in light of consultation and reflection; and (e) implement the results of the preceding elements at a local level. In practice, these elements have rarely taken the form of a step-by-step process (Marshall, 2017). Groups using Tuning have been more likely to work in multiple areas simultaneously—and doubling back through some as the need arose. Local implementation, for example, did not necessarily constitute the fulfillment of Tuning. Rather, faculty would at times incorporate work into local practice along the way or bring local examples to the larger group as a form of input. In short, no two Tuning projects have looked exactly alike.

In different contexts, Tuning has been used to tackle different concerns. Consistently, however, Tuning results in a set of competencies and outcomes that function as a discipline-specific document akin to the DQP, with learning typically described at the associate, baccalaureate, and master's levels specific to a major. Norm Jones (2012) writes that although Tuning is a faculty-led approach, it also involves seeking input from students and employers in the process of developing a shared understanding of what students should know, understand, and be able to do when they finish a disciplinary degree program. He stresses, though, that Tuning necessarily requires conversations that include many institutions, which allows disciplines space to think as a discipline, rather than be subject to local pressures of specific departments.

The impact of Tuning surfaces in several key areas (Marshall, Jankowski, & Vaughan, 2017). First, faculty begin to think more holistically about the shape of their disciplines, shifting away from solely content knowledge to include the epistemologies employed by the discipline as objects of learning. This, in turn, impacts their considerations of curriculum and assignment design. Second, faculty have started to consider the degree to which foundational classes make distinct contributions to general education and, conversely, how courses in majors leverage and develop the learning students begin to attain in general education. The result is a more integrative picture of students' learning experiences. Third, faculty undertake efforts to explicitly help students consider the ways in which disciplinary study equips them to transition into a variety of postgraduate contexts, whether graduate training; civic engagement; or, perhaps most common, employment. Finally, faculty develop greater awareness of how colleagues in other institution types approach educating students, resulting in deepened respect for those colleagues, particularly at community colleges.

Having established through Adelman's work the potential of Tuning to provide clear definitions of *learning*, the Lumina Foundation launched three state-level pilot projects. In 2009, Indiana, Minnesota, and Utah each undertook to "tune" disciplines within their state systems, drawing together faculty in two to three disciplines from both two- and four-year institutions. Transfer tended to be the impetus of these projects for states, and Tuning was subsequently undertaken by Texas and Kentucky for similar reasons. In an experiment in scale, the Midwest Higher Education Compact (MHEC) then engaged in a multistate project that pulled together Indiana, Illinois, and Missouri to examine the impact of "tuning" across state lines. MHEC's motivation, similar to the state-based projects, was to explore outcomes-based transfer of students from state to state.

Tuning then underwent two national-scale experiments, each exploring different facets of the process. The American Historical Association (AHA) determined to use Tuning as a means of establishing essential learning within the discipline of history. Beginning with a small core group who drafted the initial learning competencies and outcomes, AHA convened a larger group of 70, who reviewed the initial documents and made recommendations for revision as they committed to making trials of the outcomes and consulting with stakeholders locally. AHA demonstrated the pronounced impact of engaging in Tuning at this scale in that it motivated faculty to develop reflection and conversations around how best to educate students in the discipline.

Synergism

Following AHA, the National Communication Association (NCA) took up a Tuning project in which they attempted to test the use of DQP within Tuning work. That initiative has seen success equally as dramatic as the AHA project; meanwhile, we have developed fuller understanding about the ways in which DQP and Tuning work synergistically as tools for rethinking how disciplinary faculty can best foster students' learning.

Although reports on the impact of the DQP pilot projects were undertaken (see Jankowski & Giffin, 2016a) and documents to help support institutional use of the DQP were developed (see Jankowski & Marshall, 2014; Jankowski & Giffin, 2016b), we have noticed a difference in the shift occurring within institutions that have worked with both DQP and Tuning. It is this shift that serves as the focus of this book. At the same time, although we use DQP and Tuning as examples of the tools that help facilitate conversations and the paradigmatic shift we argue for in the book, they are two tools of many. We use the lessons learned and examples from our work with DQP and Tuning to provide a framing of the larger argument, but one thing is very clear; there is movement in the field. Multiple approaches are coming into alignment to support the work this book details.

Outline of the Argument

We begin in chapter 1 by considering what has become an exceptionally crowded terrain in the reform of higher education. With the proliferation of initiatives—local, regional, and national—many organizations have sponsored efforts to strengthen student learning in colleges and universities. Yet most are attempting to solve in isolation related issues that are actually connected in nature. The chapter thus provides a means to understand the different initiatives that align with and connect to the work being done in institutions in order to focus on meaningful engagement with assessment and clearly document student learning. Once we examine the connected nature of the various initiatives, we explore the emergence of an alternative paradigm which we term the *learning systems paradigm*. Providing a theory of change and a framework for understanding faculty work, we outline the elements of the paradigm and expand on Barr and Tagg's (1995) efforts to move institutions from an instruction to a learning paradigm. The learning systems paradigm presented in chapter 2 includes four key elements—the work is consensus based, aligned, learner centered, and communicated. Chapter 3 then focuses on developing a theoretical foundation for *alignment*, a word too often tossed around without full consideration of possible meanings and implications. We present a definition of *alignment* beyond Biggs's (1996) focus on constructive alignment at the course level. Instead we suggest a far more encompassing notion of *alignment*, arguing for a definition that requires rethinking the structures that have siloed elements of the higher education landscape. By thinking more holistically, faculty, staff, and administrators can reshape institutional practice in ways that create synergistic, integrative learning in students.

With our learning systems paradigm in place and *alignment* defined, chapters 4 and 5 turn to practice. In chapter 4, we explore the application of the paradigm to the work of curriculum mapping, presenting alternative ways to map and outline the means by which mapping can support a collaborative process of sense-making. We argue that mapping is a way of seeing and, as such, a way of not seeing other areas that support student learning, unless done in a mindful, collaborative manner. Next, in chapter 5 we examine the work of faculty to better align their assignments to assure demonstration of student learning via embedded course-based assessments. The implications of the paradigm for assessment are explored, and we apply the paradigm framework to the work of assignment design and alignment. Yet we would be remiss in not examining barriers to moving the work forward or engaging in collaborative reflection on educational design for student learning. When we are on different college campuses or doing presentations at conferences, we routinely are asked how to get the work started or how to support the approaches we outline. It is for this reason that chapter 6 focuses on barriers to the work and presents ways to start, options for moving around barriers, or ways to conceptualize the barriers in relation to our foundational discussions of initiative connections and paradigm shifts.

In chapter 7, our final chapter, we pursue the implications of our argument. Foremost, given declining confidence in higher education, how do institutions talk about what they have done and are doing? The accountability concerns, we argue, have to do in part with the institutions' struggles to describe what they do to encourage student learning. The concluding chapter takes up this focus, offering strategies for communicating the impact of alignment on student learning.

Taken together, these chapters offer a means of working toward the "how" questions we discussed earlier in this introduction. In short, the chapters that follow challenge you to ask: How do our degrees matter for students, whose learning can help them to become productive employees, engaged citizens, *and* fulfilled human beings? If, as we have argued, education needs to be aligned to the professional, civic, and personal lives of learners, then higher education needs strategies that equip us not only to answer that question but also to work intentionally to foster learning that will enable our students to develop the knowledge and abilities to apply that learning in those different spheres. Doing so requires us to rethink the ways of working among and with faculty, staff, administrators, students, and a variety of stakeholders. Doing so also requires us to consider new approaches to both how we conceptualize where and how students learn, as well as how we engage in activities such as program design, assignment design, and assessment. Taking up the challenge to ask the "how" questions can help to move us away from counter-productive debates about the use and value of higher education; redirect assessment away from compliance toward self-reflection, professional development, and improvement; and advance us toward being able to explain clearly and loudly how our students' degrees matter.

I

LANDSCAPE OF LEARNING INITIATIVES

To say institutions don't change is to ignore the myriad initiatives and projects occurring in the field of higher education. Institutions are struggling with "an alphabet soup of student-success initiatives created across the country," bringing confusion and fatigue along with time and money spent on "boutique reform programs" (C.A. Smith, Baldwin, & Schmidt, 2015, p. 31). The result on many campuses is resistance to undertaking any new initiatives. Activities and acronyms float around higher education, sometimes bumping into each other and other times passing like ships in the night. In some way, they all focus on improving student learning and ensuring successful graduates—but how to do that and what it means depend on which initiative you are participating in. Although some would say this is endemic to higher education, with our history of what Robert Birnbaum (2000) has termed *management fads*, it obscures the fact that there are actual problems these projects and initiatives are trying to address. Yet, as alluded to in the introduction, they cannot be addressed alone or in isolation. To embrace the complexity of the student experience and to ensure student learning we need to employ a wider lens. This means in part we can no longer rely solely on the faculty who are willing to participate in a committee meeting or the same faces we see around the table at the start of various projects. Instead, we need to align our efforts, linking projects and initiatives. Chapter 3 focuses on defining *alignment* in its various forms, whereas this chapter presents a landscape of the field of initiatives by outlining several faculty-led and student-learning-focused projects currently in play. Although we present the evolution of this work as coherent and connected, this has not been the case historically. Our brief landscape portrait highlights the connections those of us on the ground, who are dealing with what George Kuh and Pat Hutchings (2015) have called *initiative fatigue*, so desperately need.

Setting the Scene

When we are in the field engaging with faculty or doing presentations at various conferences, we often lead with one question: Why are we, as educators, doing the things that we are doing? What is the value and purpose of engaging in these activities? But with a cluttered bustle of initiatives, some homegrown, others inspired by regional or national organizations, we often lose sight of the "why." Instead of diving into a "tell me how to do it" mentality, we need a moment to pause and reflect. If we can't answer the "why" questions, then how can we possibly explain to others we may need as partners in our institutions (and beyond) why they should play—and play nicely?

Collectively, institutions of higher education are asked to show the value of attending. We are asked about the return on investment and whether it is worth the cost of attending. We are asked if our graduates are employable. The public and policymakers want assurances that we are offering a quality education—that we really are doing the things we say we are doing. Regional accreditors and specialized or professional accrediting bodies state that it is not enough to have processes in place. According to them, we need to show how we are using various sources of evidence to improve our practice, but we need to do so without letting an accountability-driven environment lead to acting out of a compliance mentality (Kuh et al., 2015). Yet all of these questions about the value of education revolve around one core issue—what does it really mean to earn a degree? What does a degree represent?

So far, our answers to questions about the meaning of a degree in higher education have focused on numbers—seat time, credit hours, grade point averages, clinical hours—or lists of required courses that somehow add up to a meaningful, integrated learning experience. But there are more impactful questions to ask: What do degrees represent in terms of students' actual learning? How does what we are doing in the classroom add up to a degree? How are we ensuring that students are learning what we want? How do we know? And why are some students more successful at getting there than others? In our compliance mentality, however, we tend to disconnect the alphabet soup of initiatives from these questions.

These questions about student learning and degree quality drive the landscape of learning initiatives revolving within higher education. It may be useful, therefore, to understand how some of the most significant initiatives in recent years attempt to tackle these questions. Each frames its answers differently. Each focuses on different elements of higher education. But each attempts to create solutions that speak to what and how students learn as a way of resolving the problems that higher education has encountered. In this chapter we offer an overview of these key initiatives to highlight the particular approaches that have most shaped the recent shifts in how colleges and universities are trying to encourage deeper learning and trying to document that learning to improve practices while simultaneously satisfying policymakers and the public.

To begin conversations about student learning, it helps to have a shared language or understanding of the end goals of higher education. That is what AAC&U focused on in exploring commonalities in liberal education. Working with faculty from across the country and examining institutional statements of learning, they developed a consensus document on ELOs. The ELOs were developed as part of LEAP, a broader initiative launched in 2005. Coupled with the general consensus around essential learning, guiding principles were created to "provide a new framework to guide students' cumulative progress through college" (Association of American Colleges & Universities, n.d.a). States signed on as LEAP states and undertook use of the ELOs. However, a consensus is not enough. Another question emerged: What do the ELOs look like on the ground, in a classroom, with the students we are educating? The question is one of putting the LEAP outcomes into practice.

Addressing questions of learning on the ground, AAC&U (2015a) suggests signature work or signature assignments coupled with authentic assessment of student learning as strategies to realize the ELOs. AAC&U defines *signature work* as a culminating learning experience through a significant project related to a problem or issue that the student defines. The problems are ones where there is no apparent "right" answer, and the goal is to actively connect liberal education with the world beyond the institution. The approach requires students to apply learning as they demonstrate it. In order to develop a consensus around what successful completion of learning might entail as demonstrated through signature work, faculty were again brought together, this time to develop rubrics represented under the title Valid Assessment of Learning in Undergraduate Education (VALUE). A useful resource for a deeper dive into the rubric conversation is Peggy Maki's (2015) report on VALUE, which builds on a philosophy of learning assessment that, as AAC&U (2015a) states in their *LEAP Challenge,* "privileges multiple faculty members' and other educators' expert judgments and shared understanding of the quality of student work through the curriculum, cocurriculum, and beyond *over* reliance on standardized tests administered to samples of students disconnected from an intentional course of study." The VALUE rubrics provide a mechanism by which institutions can assess student learning based on a shared consensus built from the work of students in actual courses. However, using a rubric doesn't answer the questions of the public or policymakers interested in a simpler way to address whether we are assuring quality or being accountable.

To see if it would be possible to use actual student work assessed by faculty using VALUE rubrics to answer the needs of policymakers, a project called the Multi-State Collaborative to Advance Quality Student Learning was born. The work built on assessment of student work from actual courses, making assessment for accountability intricately connected to teaching and learning. It tried to determine whether rubrics could provide comparable information about student achievement at an institutional level. The Multi-State Collaborative focused on faculty assessment of student work using the VALUE rubrics for written communication, critical thinking, and quantitative literacy. In a preliminary report of the work, VALUE is described as breaking "new ground by basing its assessment of student learning achievement on the actual work that students produce in response to assignments from the formal instructional curriculum in whatever institution(s) the student attended" (Association of American Colleges & Universities, 2017, p. 3). Pat Crosson and Bonnie Orcutt (2014) wrote of the experience that "there is a growing sense among many faculty members and academic leaders that we need to understand better what is happening in classrooms and an increasing willingness to rethink curricula and instruction to better achieve learning objectives that go beyond the course level" (p. 26). The Multi-State Collaborative project focused on policymakers' interests, intending to prompt policy-level questions (Association of American Colleges & Universities, 2017) but did not explore how we, as faculty, know what we did to get students there. It left questions about what impact we, or our curriculum or educational experiences, have on student learning as a collective, beyond individual assignments. To answer the question of how we are preparing students for success, several other initiatives emerged, including high-impact practices, guided pathways, and the various support services students need in order to be successful.

High-Impact Practices

High-impact practices (HIPs) were identified by George Kuh (2008) as teaching and learning processes and activities focused on improving learning and sustaining student engagement. That focus has made them a popular strategy for understanding how particular types of pedagogical and curricular practice actually nurture student learning. They include the following:

- First-year seminars
- Common intellectual experiences
- Learning communities

- Writing-intensive courses
- Collaborative assignments and projects
- Undergraduate research
- Diversity/global learning
- Service-learning/community-based learning
- Internships
- Capstone courses and projects
- ePortfolios

HIPs were identified from years of research that indicate "student development is a cumulative process shaped by many events and experiences, inside and outside the classroom" (Kuh, 2008, p. 13). The research also pointed toward the variability of beneficial effects among students from the same educational programs and practices. Kuh (2008) argues that "when done well—some programs and activities appear to engage participants at levels that elevate their performance across multiple engagement and desired-outcomes measures such as persistence" and that such "deep approaches to learning are important because students who use these approaches tend to earn higher grades and retain, integrate, and transfer information at higher rates" (p. 14). HIPs, importantly, address issues of equity in higher education. According to Kuh's research, students historically underserved by higher education benefit *more* from engaging in HIPs, making them a mechanism to ensure that *all* students are successful in attaining educational goals. In administrative interviews conducted by Hart Research Associates (2015a), respondents stated there is value in HIPs "both in supporting higher rates of persistence and higher levels of achievement of learning outcomes" (p. 3) and that student demand for such experiences is quite high.

HIPs are effective, in part, because they require students to devote considerable amounts of time and effort to specific tasks while interacting with faculty and peers and receiving frequent feedback on their performance. As part of a "coherent, academically challenging curriculum" (Kuh, 2008, p. 15), students are able to see how what they are learning connects with and applies to different settings on and off a college campus. Kuh suggests that students participate in at least two HIPs, one in the first year and one later, within the major. An important point of the HIPs literature is that the activities are part of a coherent, integrated, and intentional curriculum—one in which connections between activities and learning outcomes are made clear and in which students have opportunities to apply their learning in multiple scenarios and settings. In a commentary piece regarding national evaluations of student success projects, Ashley Finley (2016) looked across the various findings and concluded that campuses need to make commitments to student engagement with experiences that are connected over time, where engagement is pervasive and expected and doesn't take the form of a "one off" experience. Thus, it is not enough for institutions of higher education to offer students the opportunity to participate in such activities; they need to be an integral part of the lived educational experience of *all* students in order to see the highest impacts.

Pathways

To help facilitate coherent curricular experiences for students, some campuses have turned to developing curricular pathways. Why does this matter? David Dill (2014) argues that research on students in the United States indicates that student subject knowledge and cognitive development are "significantly associated with the pattern and sequence of courses in which they enroll, with program requirements that integrate learning across courses, and with the frequency of communication and interaction among faculty members in the subject field" (p. 55). The problem Dill's research addresses is that students have been left on their own to make meaning or find coherence within the curriculum, leaving, as he argues, too much learning to chance. In an article on general education at James Madison University, Sanchez (n.d.) observes that students struggled with a curriculum they felt was disorganized. Sanchez recounts Dean of General Education Linda Halpern's sense that "a freshman seminar that allowed faculty members to choose what they wanted to teach left 'students furious' based on what she called the 'roommate effect'—everyone's roommate had an easier or more enjoyable course." Changing this situation required conversations among faculty across the campus about what students should know as opposed to what programs needed to do or change. By beginning with the question of what students should know, faculty were able to restructure the program around revised goals and embedded assessments. The effect was that connections in the curriculum were explicitly unpacked for students.

Other types of pathways projects have emerged, too. Some pathways projects have focused on specific course sequences where students struggle, such as developmental math. The Mathways Project (Rutschow & Diamond, 2015) undertook a revisioning of math requirements and their place in the curriculum in Texas, coupled with intentional learning strategies to help students develop math skills. New courses were developed in alignment with necessary math skills. The courses helped students understand why they were learning particular skills and what they could do with them in life and in careers. Results of such pathways are encouraging. Indian River State College in Florida, which participated in the American Association of Community

Colleges Pathway Project, saw a 90.6% success rate for students in rede-signed developmental math courses (A.A. Smith, 2016). Other pathways have focused on building exposure to future career options and the active integration of academic and technical skills (Jobs for the Future, 2014). For instance, a 2-year, 10-state effort led by the Center for Law and Social Policy (CLASP), sought to identify criteria for high-quality career-oriented path-way systems. The work, organized by the Alliance for Quality Career Path-ways, found that career pathway systems needed to include an intentional sequence of learning, ongoing formative assessments, proactive advising, and supportive services for students, including childcare and transportation. The goal of the effort was to develop "well-articulated sequences of quality educa-tion and training offerings and supportive services that enable educationally underprepared youth and adults to advance over time to successively higher levels of education and employment in a given industry sector of occupation" (CLASP, 2013, p. 9). Despite this, meaningful employer engagement has been indicated as a common challenge in career pathways along with a lack of understanding on the part of students regarding labor market knowledge and skill requirements (Jobs for the Future, 2014).

At the community college level, AAC&U undertook a pathway project to develop a Community College Student Roadmap. The project, begun in 2010, tried to engage students as active partners, foster collaboration between academic and student affairs, and integrate the various initiatives underway at community colleges into a seamless educational experience for students. Tia McNair (2013), writing about the community college roadmap project, notes that the goal is to create an integrated and proactive academic program coupled with social support for students and aligned with expected learning outcomes. The work focused on aligning HIPs with student supports in the curriculum and cocurriculum in ways that were sensitive to the particular context of the institution and its students while actively engaging students in the process. Student engagement was vital because the roadmaps did not assume that students continuously enroll; thus, roads needed to be built for students to step in and step out (Long, 2013).

AAC&U took the work of guided pathways at the community college level and distilled elements into a guided learning pathway in which faculty define *learning outcomes*, design learning experiences that scaffold students toward meeting them, and require all students to participate in HIPs and signature work along the way. Taking these principles and in light of com-plaints against general education programs being organized like "an *a la carte* menu of disconnected survey courses" (2015b, p. v) leading to fragmented and incoherent learning experiences, AAC&U initiated the General Educa-tion Maps and Markers (GEMS) project. GEMS used the DQP to reflect on

the purpose and design of general education programs as well as their connections to majors or specialized learning programs beyond the community
college context. The pathway, here, is through the typically incoherent terrain of general education.

But pathways are not initiatives that can exist in isolation from other campus offices. In a case study of how guided pathways have been implemented,
researchers found that administrative support and leadership, along with
ongoing communication mechanisms, were vital to move success from pilot
projects to systemic change. Scaling these projects has proven an approach
that helps students who had been unclear about how to progress through
programs with too many course choices and a limited understanding of program requirements (Community College Research Center, 2015). What we
learn from this is that implementing guided pathways requires collaboration
(Bailey, Jaggars, & Jenkins, 2015a). Once sequences of courses are established, the courses need to be implemented as intended, and faculty and staff
need to work together to support students as they make progress through the
pathway. As the implementation guide for guided pathways states, "Faculty
must also collaborate to assess students' mastery of learning outcomes and
to improve instruction across programs, not just within individual courses,
so that students build skills as they progress through the curriculum" (Bailey
et al., 2015a, p. 1). This curricular and pedagogical strategy of sequencing
experiences and building knowledge and skills over time depends on alignment of learning outcomes to assignments that are intentionally designed to
indicate whether students are building the knowledge and skills identified
in outcomes. Thus, pathways work involves faculty collectively scaffolding
learning over time, providing opportunities for intentional integration across
courses, working in partnership with support services, and explicitly communicating to students the connections in the curriculum with intended
learning.

Documenting Learning

Even if we can move students through a curricular pathway designed by
faculty and supported through connected courses, and even if we can incorporate student support services within the integrated curricula and applied
learning experiences, how do we document it? That question is yet another
motivator for recent initiatives in higher education. Our traditional transcripts have been limited in presenting the academic experiences of students
without incorporating the world of work, prior learning, and the cocurriculum. In other words, they have underrepresented what students do and
learn. In an effort to present a comprehensive student record, Student Affairs

Administrators in Higher Education (still called NASPA from its former name, National Association of Student Personnel Administrators) and the American Association of College Registrars and Administrative Officers (AACRAO) have worked together to jointly develop transcripts reflective of learning in and out of the classroom (American Association of College Registrars and Administrative Officers, n.d.). Pilot institutions have experimented with technology as a means to better capture and report more comprehensively the breadth of the student learning experience. In addition, the work of the Center for Adult and Experiential Learning (CAEL) has provided information on documenting prior learning through their work with online portfolio assessment (CAEL, n.d.). These efforts have made progress in improving recognition of the breadth of student learning experiences and reflecting them in the documents that record them. Developing portfolios of student work along with providing means to capture that learning in alternative transcripts helps support the notion that learning happens in multiple places and every instance should count.

Nevertheless, even if we document student learning in all the places it happens, our students are mobile and there is no guarantee that other institutions will accept our conclusions. In an effort to resolve that problem, the Western Interstate Commission for Higher Education (WICHE) developed their Interstate Passport (WICHE, n.d.). The Interstate Passport provides a framework for transfer based on learning outcomes in general education as a collective whole to facilitate block transfer. The effort focuses on what students know and can do as opposed to the specific courses they have taken (Ewell, 2016). The project began as a grassroots effort in 2010 by chief academic leaders in the West who wanted to assist transfer students and avoid loss of credits and repeated courses. The passport entails learning outcomes, referencing the LEAP ELOs described earlier in the chapter, along with criteria indicating how a student demonstrates proficiency in specified learning outcomes. The project developed out of a recognized need to facilitate transfer across state lines, since 24% of transfer students cross state lines according to a study by the National Student Clearinghouse (Shapiro, Dundar, Wakhungu, Yuan, & Harrell, 2015). Faculty members at passport institutions provide students with learning opportunities to address learning outcomes, assess student proficiency, and then award the passport to students who have earned it.

Competency-Based Education

Transcripting projects have made strides, despite certain unresolved conflicts, toward a richer documentation of what and where students learn. Thinking about where learning happens, how it can be supported, and its relation to seat time and credit hours, a report on the Carnegie Credit Unit claimed that "decades of outcomes-based accountability demands are coming to a head, pressuring institutions to be more transparent about how much and how well students are learning, not just how many hours of coursework they have clocked" (Silva & White, 2015, p. 69). One approach focused on learning regardless of time is competency-based education.

In a competency-based education program, credits are awarded based on student learning as opposed to time spent in class. Competency-based education enables students to move at their own pace through materials, placing the educational experience in partnership with students' lived experiences (Baker, 2015). Wolk (2015) states that competency-based education helps students by focusing less on where, when, or how students learn and more on their ability to demonstrate their learning in relation to high standards. Thus, for students in a competency-based education program, learning is fixed whereas time is variable, with an emphasis on demonstration of learning rather than the process of learning. Those features can enable programs to grant credit for prior learning (Porter & Reilly, 2014). But competency-based education programs are not for everyone. In an examination of the student experience with competency-based education programs, it was found that programs needed to clearly communicate to students how the program approach might or might not be a good fit and tended to target specific groups of students who would be successful in the format as opposed to students as a collective whole (Baker, 2015).

According to McClarty and Gaertner (2015) in their piece on best practices for assessment in competency-based education, such programs need to have clearly defined competencies that are aligned to assessments of student learning, but the efforts need to be integrated and coherent. They argue for the use of evidence-centered design, in which the designers of the assessments connect the intended claims about what students know and are able to do with actual evidence that a student would need to support such claims. In effect, they encourage the design of assessments that elicit such evidence so that students can document their own learning. Writing about best practices in competency-based education, a piece by Mathematica Policy Research (2015) states that competency-based education views instructors as mentors, helping to facilitate student learning through coherent programs of study aligned to academic and industry standards. In some ways, then, competency-based education programs design learning experiences to facilitate student integration and transfer of knowledge in a way that is mindful of the variety of learners in higher education today.

What Are the Lessons to Be Learned From This Collection of Initiatives?

The various initiatives presented in this chapter require those within higher education to start with students and what they need to be successful as learners, a point raised by Peter Ewell (1997), who goes as far as saying that such an approach "requires all members of the institutions to fundamentally rethink what they do" (p. 54). For these efforts to be effective, the "change must be systemic" (p. 55) and those involved need to consider not only how different isolated efforts might contribute to the end goals but also how different parts of the institution are related to one another in helping students reach them. That is why each of the initiatives are faculty based and curriculum embedded—they are fundamentally about teaching and learning. They also utilize approaches that involve students' lived experiences or explore application of skills and content to help students see the utility of what they are learning and ways their learning may be employed. Moreover, these initiatives all attempt to create connections through coherent, intentional learning experiences that scaffold and build over time with regular feedback given to students on their learning as it progresses.

At this point, you may have noticed that a sizable majority of what is ongoing within institutions of higher education is not new. Most efforts revolve around learning outcomes approaches, which have been with us for, literally, decades, and we in higher education have been broadly familiar with outcomes for 30 years. These initiatives, however, emphasize program-level and degree-level outcomes, which orient thinking away from isolated classes. Building from conversations around outcomes-based education in K–12, the focus is not so much on which courses students take but on what they can do when they leave (Brandt, 1993; Spady & Marshall, 1991), which, as noted previously, is the driving point of the WICHE Interstate Passport and efforts generally of competency-based education. But these initiatives do not simply push degree- and program-level outcomes; they attempt to address the structures we build to help students reach them. Bill Spady (1994), writing on K–12 outcomes-based education, calls for careful attention to incremental outcomes—basically the unpacking of the elements in educational experiences that we design to "get students there" by scaffolding their learning. A focus on getting students successfully to completion is at the heart of pathway work, too, with its emphasis on transparency, connections, and scaffolded student learning.

Another example addressing the adaptation of programs to address the diverse needs of learners is that of competency-based education. Before the onset of competency-based education as we know it today, Spady argued in an interview with Brandt (1993) that for students to achieve mastery of learning, time needs to be variable instead of constant. In other words, individual students should work at the pace best suited to their mastery of learning—an argument made by the competency-based education community today. Although such work raises questions about the role of the Carnegie Credit Unit and ease of transfer, within competency-based programs a focus on learners and scaffolded learning environments has required a radical rethinking about how instruction is delivered to various student groups in colleges and universities.

In addition, outcomes-based education has led to increased thinking about the integration of learning within higher education. Remember the student experiences of à la carte course menus within general education as stacks of seemingly unrelated courses disconnected from learning in majors. Designing educational experiences with an end goal in mind and expanding the ways students learn and demonstrate their learning require that outcomes are woven throughout a set of learning experiences and not the purview of a single course (Brandt, 1993). As Tom Angelo (2014) regularly states at assessment conferences, "A well designed course is a clever learning trap, from which students cannot escape without demonstrating they have mastered the intended learning outcomes at the required high standard" (para. 5). That jumble of initiatives we have described in this brief landscape all point to the need for students to encounter, in multiple formats at different times, the learning we, as educators, want them to develop by the time they graduate or transfer. That shift, however, requires a turn away from a "my classes" mentality to an "our curriculum" view in which faculty and staff across a campus think more collaboratively about the shape of their students' learning and the supports needed to help students advance.

Why Is All of This Work Important?

So what? Why does all this work even matter for faculty and staff? The answer is fairly straightforward and hits at the heart of what educators *do* on a daily basis: teach. Pedagogy is an important element implied by most, if not all, of these initiatives. As Kuh (2008) argues in his work with HIPs, "At institutions with better-than-expected graduation rates, faculty members are more likely to use engaging classroom pedagogical practices" (p. 21). But equally important, what faculty think about students and what they value also makes a difference. Related to HIPs, an increase in the importance faculty place on an activity corresponds to "about a 20 percent increase in student participation" (Kuh, 2008, p. 21).

The fact that actively involving students in their learning and building from their lived experience fosters deep learning is not new. Kolb (1984) addressed the importance of experiential learning in the 1980s. From a neuroscience perspective, Voss and colleagues (2011) indicate that

> volition control [i.e., active learning] is advantageous for learning because distinct neural systems related to planning/predicting, attention, and object processing can be updated in an iterative fashion via communication with the hippocampus, such that . . . behaviors become more finely tuned to the most critical environmental information. (p. 120)

In other words, deep learning occurs when we actively engage students in the learning process. But this begins to hit at the dynamic interplay of educational structures within institutions and the classrooms, labs, and other spaces where learning happens. In other words, pedagogy and curriculum are linked. Creating curricular coherence is important because "students deprived of a general education that is transparently purposeful, substantive, clearly aligned with their personal goals, and expressive of explicitly defined institutional learning goals are far less likely to remain motivated, to strive for excellence, and to make a compelling case for themselves to potential employers" (Gaston, 2015, p. 5). What we see, then, is a need to consider how curricula are structured to advance student learning and how courses within curricula are linked to help students make connections, transfer learning, and reach the goals we set for them in learning outcomes (Jankowski, 2017).

A large portion of the efforts presented in this chapter seek to address fragmented coursework and disparate learning experiences and move toward more sequential, aligned, integrated, and coherent learning trajectories (Achieving the Dream et al., 2015). Peter Ewell (1997) writes that learning occurs best in the context of a compelling "presenting problem," basically a problem that a student wants to solve and has the capacity to solve—much like the signature assignment work championed by AAC&U and the work of the assignment library associated with the DQP. He goes on to state that although students often do not see direct use or application of what they are learning, that is due in part to having few opportunities to try things out in different settings. It is introduced in one course but not picked up in another. Or potentially more confusing, it is assumed that mastery of a complex learning outcome can be met in a single course.

The end to which these initiatives strive is developed from projects that have sought to determine a consensus on what learning matters most from faculty in higher education (e.g., the work of the LEAP ELOs or the DQP). In an exploration of shared design elements of competency-based education programs, Public Agenda (2015) found that 93% of faculty adopted competencies from national norms or other credible tools such as the DQP and AAC&U ELOs. In the vein of student-centeredness, 95% had processes in place to listen to and learn from students, and 97% provided curriculum with multiple and varied opportunities to develop and demonstrate learning (i.e., integration). Further, Wax (2015) has found that 100% of surveyed competency-based education programs measured not only learning but also transfer of learning across multiple contexts through frequent formative and summative assessments, with 100% indicating they were learner centered.

The problem is not that we, in higher education, do not have outcomes. In a survey of 325 chief academic officers, nearly all indicated that they have a common set of learning outcomes for all undergraduate students (Hart Research Associates, 2016). Rather, students don't have a good understanding of the goals for which they should be aiming. Further, only 44% indicated experiencing a coherent sequence of courses and/or educational experiences and 67% wanted more emphasis on integration of knowledge, skills, and applications for students (Hart Research Associates, 2016). In an employer survey (Hart Research Associates, 2015b) 80% of employers wanted demonstration of application of knowledge and skills to real-world settings and preferred cross-cutting over discipline-specific knowledge and skills; nevertheless, a survey of chief academic officers found that only 23% required all students to participate in such significant learning projects (Hart Research Associates, 2016). Institutions struggle with how we currently communicate the learning we want students to achieve, and this interferes with our ability to communicate clearly the intended design of educational experiences to students and employers.

Creating not only coherence but also collaborative, collective, shared understanding of learning is important for the mobile students for whom we strive to provide learning opportunities. In a report from the National Student Clearinghouse, researchers indicated, "Of the 3.6 million students who entered college for the first time in fall 2008 over one-third (37.2%) transferred to a different institution at least once within six years. Of those, almost half changed their institution more than once (45%). Counting multiple moves, students made 2.4 million transitions from one institution to another from 2008 to 2014" (Shapiro et al., 2015, p. 3). This trend is not new. A 2012 report from the National Student Clearinghouse Research Center found that transfer patterns "reflect the complexity of postsecondary student enrollment, transfer, and persistence across all sectors of higher education. The results suggest that the linear view of college access and success that focuses on the initial institution attended often fails to address the realities on the ground" (Shapiro et al., 2012, p. 6). At that time, one-third of all students transferred at least once within five years, with the most common point of transfer occurring in the second year. Student mobility is not a within-state issue either, as nearly one in five transfers of students starting in two-year public institutions and nearly a quarter of transfers from four-year institutions crossed state lines. Also, transfer isn't necessarily one way, meaning it is not the community college's responsibility to work with four-year institutions to align their efforts unidirectionally or create a one-way pathway. The National Student Clearinghouse report points out that two-year public institutions are the top mobility destination for students who start in four-year institutions, with 51% of students transferring from public four-year institutions (and 40% from private four-year institutions) to two-year institutions. The report concludes that in order to serve the reality of students today, institutions *collectively* need to work together in order to smooth transition points and reduce hurdles for students.

But does it matter if we make a more coherent sequence of educational experiences that allows students to move about, either within a single campus or from one campus to another? Research suggests that it does. Terry (2015) investigated the proposition that linked courses help student learning. Surveying students about their perceptions of integration among three courses and their application of knowledge in them, along with a survey directed toward students in a nonconnected curriculum experience, yielded indirect evidence that program objectives were being achieved. Institutional Research compiled 10 semesters' worth of data from linked classes and also compared the fall 2011 and 2012 survey data from both linked and nonlinked classes. The results indicated that, "overall, students in the linked sections perceived themselves to have a better understanding of how the courses were connected and to have benefitted more from relationships with their classmates" (Terry, 2015, p. 2). A 2013 study by the Alliance for Excellent Education of two New Hampshire high schools implementing competency-based education focused on increasing coherence found "significant declines in the dropout rate, school failures, and disciplinary problems, and increases in student engagement and learning" (Wolk, 2015, p. 30). In addition, students claimed that they understood why they were being asked to do what they were in their classes, which led to more rewarding interaction with teachers (Wolk, 2015, p. 30). Finally, an exploration of the relationship between instruction and student outcomes points to five areas in which faculty instruction impacts student retention, learning, and graduation, including the need for transparency of design and alignment of learning experiences into a coherent whole (Jankowski, 2017).

With All This Activity, Why Haven't We Been Successful?

Given all these different initiatives and activities, why isn't it working like we might hope? In part, our efforts may not have worked because it is a difficult challenge "requiring an analysis of every facet of higher education structure and delivery. Indeed, success demands the sober recognition that we must reinvent centuries-old institutions to help ensure the success of students who have rarely succeeded in the past" (S. Jones, 2015, p. 28). Peter Ewell (1997) argues that change initiatives fail in large part because they are implemented without an understanding of what collegiate-level learning means and/or what can be done to promote it. He positions learning as a creative act, where every student learns with and despite us. According to his argument, students are constantly learning, as we all are, in different places and in different times, regardless of whether or not there is a "classroom" in which it takes place. Higher education may not recognize it, or validate it, but learning is constantly occurring. Lave (2011) has argued that most theories of learning are often merely theories of teaching, and there has been a lack of focus on learners within our approaches to learning. Building from the assumption that knowledge is produced in universities by "elite knowledge producers who engage in created research" (para. 2), teaching becomes positioned as a matter of transmitting knowledge from one group to the other. Instead, Lave positions teaching as a complex social phenomenon, inherently dependent on context that emerges from our understanding of learning. Only learners can learn; faculty cannot do it for them. Thus, teaching in Lave's view is a "complicated activity" focused on "fostering an environment in which students learn" (para. 5). The unpacking of our assumptions around students in terms of how they learn, what they can learn, and how capable we think they are is a vital part of internal exploration within any of the ongoing initiatives focused on improving learning in higher education. Within each of the initiatives presented in this landscape, there are implicit assumptions about how the work will impact students to improve their learning. They each have their own inherent theory of change as well as a theory of learning.

Alternative Models for Enhanced Student Learning

It is important to note that one should not view any of the various initiatives as a silver bullet that on its own will lead to success. As Methvin and Markham (2015) state, "The power to develop a truly 'student-ready' institution rests in institutions' ability to identify the proper combination of solutions for their student populations and to integrate the solutions across what are often institutional dividing lines" (p. 55). Each of the various initiatives we have described involves collaboration, alignment, redesign, gap closing, and a focus on every student—work that necessarily requires bridging offices that often operate in isolation from one another. It also requires an understanding of each initiative's approach to enhancing student learning.

For instance, Tom Bailey and colleagues (Bailey, Jaggars, & Jenkins, 2015b) at the Community College Research Center state that the idea behind guided pathways is that students are more likely to complete a degree in a timely fashion if they choose a program and develop an academic plan early on. The argument is that if students have a clear outline of the courses they need to complete as well as receive ongoing guidance and support along the way, they are more likely to be successful. The pathways approach is an alternative to the "cafeteria model" or a laundry list of possible courses from which students select their own path through to completion without any clear indication of how courses connect together into a coherent experience (Ashford, 2015). Although the pathways approach focuses less on the intended learning and more on the curricular requirements needed to complete a degree, it does present "courses in the context of highly structured educationally coherent program maps that align with students' goals for careers and further education" (Bailey et al., 2015b, p. 1). Having a clear pathway for students who choose to take it helps to simplify student decision-making (Ashford, 2015) and is part of a larger "comprehensive approach entailing a systemic redesign of the student experience from initial connection to college through to completion" (Bailey et al., 2015b, p. 2). Guided pathways efforts involve a questioning of the

> traditional paradigm that we have been operating under with our students for at least decades, and perhaps centuries. It requires a hard look at the values and beliefs on which our systems are based and demands we explore whom the traditional system was designed for and for whom it currently works well. (Johnston, 2015, p. 3)

Simply put, however, the underlying assumption with the pathways initiatives is that if we make clear sequences of courses for students, they will finish more easily. Perhaps that is true. Perhaps there are other factors in play, but that assumption provided the impetus for this kind of project. These kinds of assumptions need to be unpacked. Failure to do so can lead to ill-informed initiatives driven by poorly thought out theories of change that do not align well to the needs of students.

To highlight the importance of how an unclear examination of assumptions can negatively impact the learning environment, consider the following example. We were working at an urban campus with a high commuter population of students. Suddenly one semester, students started coming to class 10 minutes late. The faculty complained: "How can we be expected to teach students who aren't motivated to learn?" They were assuming that if students cared they would show up to class on time. Yet no one in the institution asked the students about the sudden change in behavior. Through student focus groups we discovered that the city bus schedule had changed—with the high commuter population, a vast majority of the students took the bus to campus. Instead of the issue being a lack of readiness to learn or willingness to engage in meaningful ways with the curriculum on the part of students, it was a matter of the administration needing to work with the city to address the bus schedule. Yet the easy fix was not noticed because of the existing assumption about the current student population—that the students weren't interested in learning in the first place—so the sudden change in behavior was not questioned but was seen as another example of their supposed lack of interest. Without fully understanding the students we strive to teach, how can we possibly think our initiatives will be successful?

Without being clear about our assumptions and our underlying theories of change regarding why we think doing things in the way that we are will benefit students or enhance their learning, there is little chance that we will actually be successful. In part, we need to fully undertake the shift that has been championed by Barr and Tagg (1995) to move from a teaching to a learning paradigm and position ourselves fully in an improvement paradigm over an accountability-driven one (Ewell, 2009)—an issue taken up in the subsequent chapter.

What Role Do the DQP and Tuning Play?

The DQP and Tuning are tools that have helped faculty explore assumptions, unpack theories of change, and begin to make paradigm shifts associated with the various initiatives presented in this chapter. Institutions that have participated in DQP- and Tuning-related projects were involved in multiple initiatives at the same time, with the DQP serving as a mechanism to bring them all together (Jankowski & Giffin, 2016a). Together, DQP and Tuning provided what others argue is needed for sustainable change in higher education—that it must "be built on meaningful, collaborative projects that [foster] a common language and a shared vision for student learning through repeated, intentional, formal and informal interactions" (Ferren, Dolinsky, & McCambly, 2014, p. 31). Much of the work entails holistic redesign. Additionally, engagement with DQP and Tuning led to reimagining of our work in "those conversations with our colleagues that made the 'groundlife shudder under [our] feet' through shared intellectual exchange" (Brakke et al., 2014, p. 8). When we speak with faculty about their work with DQP and Tuning, the first and most poignant mention is the importance and value of the conversations they have engaged in with colleagues about the value and purpose of learning. They highlight the importance of the DQP in providing a common language that allows for meaningful dialogue across disciplinary lines.

For instance, the Quality Collaboratives projects by AAC&U were focused on transfer between institutional pairs through application of learning and the creation of clear, easy-to-navigate pathways for students. Debra Humphreys, Heather McCambly, and Judith Ramaley (2015) explain:

> On the whole, what the Quality Collaboratives project demonstrated is the benefit of a common set of reference points for quality. As project participants developed and experimented with highly various approaches to aligning curricular designs, assessment methods, and transfer policies—all within their own unique campus contexts—their work was anchored by the Degree Qualifications Profile. Different though the policy environments and interventions were, the Degree Qualifications Profile enabled project participants to form a community of shared learning and innovation. (p. 34)

Faculty participants in the Quality Collaboratives work found a need to rethink general education, program courses, the role of electives, and pre- and corequisites in part because the DQP served as a useful tool to facilitate alignment conversations by providing a common ground for participants to explore how their pieces intersected (Rhodes et al., 2016). In work with transfer partners, "every dyad reported a significant positive change from preconceived notions about partner institutions to more accurate and positive understandings" (G.R. Brown & Rhodes, 2016, p. 7). The work of the two-year and four-year institutional teams helped create a shared understanding and reframe values around the work being done by building on and enhancing existing relationships and joint efforts. Through faculty collaboration, campuses in the Quality Collaboratives explored sequences of courses and intentional assignment designs. In their report on the initiative, Gary Brown and Terry Rhodes (2016) note the following:

> When faculty fully engage in assessment through the Quality Collaborative project models, the conversation focuses on the quality of the attributes of student work, the assignments that elicited the demonstration of proficiencies, and, finally, the teaching strategies used to develop the competencies. The conversation can then turn to the development and sequencing of

assignments and the way assignments are scaffolded to help prepare students for the more advanced levels of performance expected for capstone projects, for successful transfer, and for completion of degree programs. (p. 14)

A lesson learned from AAC&U's Quality Collaboratives project was that working with the DQP changed the kinds of conversations faculty and staff were having about student learning (Dolinsky, Rhodes, & McCambly, 2016). The DQP allowed space for conversations between different institutions to listen to each other and appreciate each other's values and experiences, a point that was salient to the finding that all change is local (Dolinsky et al., 2016). As Paul Gaston (2015) writes, neither the ELOs nor the DQP outline specific approaches. Instead, they raise questions about twenty-first-century college education in ways that are consistent with the mission and needs of a particular institution's student body. They offer a paradigm shift, a changing of the lens through which we, as educators, view both our work and how we have organized ourselves around enhancing student learning—a topic explored in the following chapter.

What differentiates DQP and Tuning from the other initiatives in our landscape is the profound flexibility they offer in facilitating the kinds of collective and collaborative reflection that many of the initiatives require. DQP, as a set of inert statements of expected student proficiency, implies a process of working. Tuning, as a flexible methodology for working, implies some end result. Institutions and institutional partners are thereby enabled to identify for themselves what both their processes and end products will be, both of which are dependent on their particular contexts. Because both DQP and Tuning encourage collective and collaborative reflection on what students learn and where they learn it, some campuses have found that work with DQP and Tuning has helped faculty and staff draw together various, sometimes competing, campus initiatives into a coherent whole, whereby DQP and Tuning actually become an antidote to initiative fatigue (Jankowski & Jones, 2016).

Concluding Thoughts

We know that one of the hardest things to do is help students integrate and apply their learning across different settings and points of time (Huber & Hutchings, 2004)—basically, recognizing that what they learned over here is applicable over there. Yet Mary Huber and Pat Hutchings (2004) argue that even the basic structures of academia work against connection, with courses seen as isolated requirements needed to complete a degree or occurring within a semester and having no connection term to term. Gerald Graff (1991) adds to this discussion, arguing the following:

> The classes being taught at any moment on a campus represent rich potential conversations between scholars and across disciplines. But since these conversations are experienced as a series of monologues, the possible links are apparent only to the minority of students who can connect disparate ideas on their own. (p. 48)

The efforts of these different initiatives involve a desire to move away from letting students make connections on their own to helping students learn through intentionality and integration (Huber & Hutchings, 2004)—the keyword being *intentional*—on the part of educators. Such an approach avoids the experience Huber and Hutchings (2004) claim "can be a fragmented landscape of general education courses, preparation for the major, cocurricular activities, and the 'real world' beyond the campus" (p. 13). At the end of the day we are trying to create a curriculum that intentionally builds in integrated learning opportunities with formative feedback over time for students to apply and practice as well as transfer their knowledge and skills through assignments, in and out of classes.

Can we do it? Although not yet at scale, an issue this book seeks to address, there are clear instances of this work having an impact on students and their learning in various settings. Steven Pollock (2014) provides an example from the sciences of how to move from lecture-based teaching in a large introductory course to a student-centered pedagogy with insight on how to scale the work for deeper learning in junior-level classes. Karen Singer-Freeman and Linda Bastone (2016) provide an example of what is possible when a large general education course integrates evidence-based pedagogical practices, active learning, and embedded assessments. This approach avoids what Shireman (2016) refers to as "artificially created measures" or "gibberish and the insane curriculum map database" because it keeps student work at the center.

Learning outcomes statements can, as Ewell (2016) argues in an essay in *Inside Higher Ed,* "articulate collective faculty intent about the desired impact of curricula and instruction." However, there is the following problem:

> When the assessment bandwagon really caught on with accreditors in the mid-1990s, it required institutions and programs to establish SLOs [student learning outcomes] solely for the purpose of constructing assessments. These statements otherwise weren't connected to anything. So it was no wonder that they were ignored by faculty who saw no link with their everyday tasks in the classroom. (Ewell, 2016)

They also weren't written for students. They were written for us, for purposes of compliance, and rarely involved the fostering of a shared understanding of the outcomes as written. We wrote them because we were told to write some. Now, the various efforts presented in this landscape seek to bring meaning to the work that reconnects it with teaching and learning—the mechanism by which this occurs is alignment, the basic building block of the shifting paradigm. But what is the paradigm and what role does alignment play? What does it look like? And how do we get to it? Chapter 2 provides a description of the paradigm shift, followed by a theoretical framework from which to understand better the notion of alignment, a concept unpacked in chapter 3.

2

SHIFTING PARADIGMS

As the various initiatives presented in the previous chapter have unfolded, they have worked in similar spaces and with similar approaches but have remained disconnected and, as a whole, incoherent. They have been so because no paradigm has existed to encompass the nature of the work. Higher education has lacked a cohesive theory that brings the disparate elements together. An explicit theory of change is one necessary element to remedy this problem; the other is a paradigm derived from that theory, a paradigm that can encompass the vision presented by the collection of initiatives and the work put into them. We employ Kuhn's definition of *paradigm* as a comprehensive model of understanding that provides rules and viewpoints on what the problems of a specific field are, along with how we are to solve them. Kuhn (1996) states, "Paradigms gain their status because they are more successful than their competitors in solving a few problems that the group of practitioners has come to recognize as acute" (p. 23). So what are our problems and how are we to solve them? As mentioned in the previous chapter, a smattering of issues includes curricular incoherence, students who report they aren't learning, employers who indicate graduates are not meeting their needs, and faculty who feel burdened by reporting and compliance mandates divorced from teaching and learning. To arrive at a clear explanation of the paradigm, however, we first need a theory of change.

The different initiatives in higher education have often been undertaken with only an implicit theory of change. Rarely have those who launched them or the practitioners responsible for "doing" them articulated the theories of change behind them. How we solve various issues requires unpacking the theory of change underlying our efforts; otherwise, we work under assumptions that may not hold or that need to be tested. The work around the DQP and Tuning have demonstrated strong results, but what is the theory of change behind them? What these efforts have brought that others lacked are tools to help align degree requirements with expected competencies and outcomes in ways that have allowed those within higher education to communicate the value of their degrees, respond in meaningful ways to accountability demands, make the implicit explicit for students, and add coherence and intentionality to programs of study. But how and why have they been successful in their approach? We begin by outlining a theory of change.

A Developing Theory of Change

Theories of change are the underlying assumptions about why we think doing certain things will move us from point A to point B (G.R. Jones, 2010; Ployhart & Vandenburg, 2010); in our case, how we think doing certain activities will solve the problems we encounter in higher education. Theories of change provide a means to outline causal pathways by specifying what we need to do to achieve our desired ends (Carman, 2010). Of note, in our exploration of a theory of change, we are not employing a linear, lockstep view of causality. Jacobson and Kapur (2012) state that "causality, full or conditional, is merely the idea of relating effects to their causes that may be one or many, sequential or simultaneous" (p. 310). Our exploration of a theory of change, therefore, is focused on unpacking relationships and exploring root causes. An analysis of root causes examines not only *that* something happened but also *why* it happened the way it did (Rooney & Heuvel, 2004). Examination of root causes provides a lens to move beyond apparent surface-level problem identification to examining the underlying assumptions at play in order to prevent or avoid reoccurrences (Taitz et al., 2010). Thus, the connection points between a theory of change and root causes provide the rules and viewpoints that encompass a paradigm by outlining what our problems are and how we go about addressing them.

In the field of higher education, there are various theories of change that crop up with regularity. A plethora of "how-to" guides claim that, if followed, "you, too, can have a successful program." Typically, however, they lack theoretical or empirical framing and are built on unquestioned assumptions. For instance, consider the following example of coverage of content. A department learns that students are struggling with writing and so decides to add a course on writing to the curriculum. The underlying idea is that students learn in courses; if they haven't learned something, then there needs to be a course on it, and once students complete the course they will have acquired the desired outcome and writing will improve. The root cause for the lack of learning is believed to be the absence of a course focused on writing, and the theory is that students learn in courses; thus, adding a course will address the learning need in writing. In this instance, the theory of change is also a theory of learning.

Consider another example regarding opportunities and support. Student writing in a course is not reaching the desired level of mastery, so faculty alert students to the availability of the writing center as a mechanism to offer support. The assumption is that once students are aware of the support available, they will make use of the service and writing will improve. The root cause is a lack of awareness about existing support, and the theory is that students, once aware, will know they need to use the services; will actively make use of the services having been informed and empowered through information; and, upon making use of the support about which they had previously not known, will improve their writing. In this instance, the theory of change is also a theory of student agency.

Yet another example is that of transparency. The idea here is that once students are aware of the ends they are striving to achieve, and once they see the connections between what they are doing and the learning goals, they are more likely to engage, learn, and complete. The root cause in this example is a lack of transparency or communication about the goals of programs of study, and the theory is that once students see where they are going they will be motivated to get there by seeing the value in the steps along the way. In this instance, the theory of change is also a theory of organizing for learning.

These three examples are intentionally simplistic and bracketed. The majority of decisions made regarding curricula that support student learning will involve a combination of responses. The point is that at times we employ each of these solutions, and many others not offered in this sampling, without proper exploration of why we think making the change will enhance student learning. We forget we are operating within a paradigm. None of the examples are right or wrong—they are theories about how students learn, involve assumptions about our role as faculty or staff in the process and the role of students in relation to their learning, and identify what is thought to be causing the problem. Within each of the examples are beliefs about root causes in terms of why students are not learning or meeting a specific outcome along with the mechanism by which students should be able to succeed. In the work of DQP and Tuning, we have watched faculty engage in different conversations, with a different set of questions and end up in a different paradigm from the one in which they started, all by exploring and unpacking hidden assumptions. To present the alternative paradigm we need to examine what the problems are and how we are to solve them.

The various initiatives presented in the previous chapter address multiple issues facing higher education, including the following:

- Lack of a shared understanding, language, or consensus around learning outcomes within and across institutions, with students, or with employers

- Lack of an ability to communicate the value of various educational experiences to ourselves, students, and other audiences
- Lack of understanding about what a degree means or what students who attain a degree know and can do regardless of discipline
- Lack of consensus within disciplines about what a degree in X indicates in terms of knowledge and skills
- Disjointed and increasingly fragmented curriculum wherein students do not see the relevance or coherence of their program of study
- Increased mobility of students and growing availability of decentralized learning opportunities with varied validation approaches
- Gaps in the success of students from various backgrounds and population groups

Signs of the problems abound and include the routine faulting of higher education by employers. In a recent survey, 11% of business leaders considered college graduates to be prepared for the workforce, whereas 96% of chief academic officers in colleges and universities did (Lumina Foundation, 2016). Further, students report a disconnect with the world of work; only 35% say they feel prepared to enter careers following college and university (Tyszko & Sheets, 2016). Employers claim that higher education does not produce students who are able to "think critically" or "work in teams," yet there is little consensus on what these outcomes mean or may look like (Hart Research Associates, 2013; "Role of Higher Education," 2013). The National Network of Business Industry Associations report (2014) indicates, "While employers rely on employees to have the same basic skills, they do not always talk about or label them the same way. This makes it difficult for prospective employees and educators to know exactly what it takes to be ready to succeed in any career path in any industry" (p. 2). This problem is not solely a "higher education issue" because, as Jason Tyszko and Bob Sheets (2016) argue, employers need to work collaboratively to better communicate their needs. Higher education should be responsive to employer needs, but there must be a clarification of terms and creation of common language and shared understanding prior to curricular changes or alignment efforts. Within our departments and our institutions, as well as outside of higher education, little shared understanding exists regarding the knowledge and skills students will acquire through their program of study. Tools such as the DQP and LEAP ELOs, along with processes such as Tuning, provide a means for higher education to respond as a collective voice—a voice that does not fall into vocationalizing the curriculum.

The need for a shared understanding of the knowledge and skills for which we are striving is not solely an issue of communicating with employers.

We need agreement not only on knowledge and skills along with how to get students to achieve them but also on ways to communicate them to students that allow for portability. Let's take one of the most dramatic examples as a case in point: transfer of students to and from institutions. Multiple pathways through the varied educational landscape are vital, because our institutions serve many types of students with very different interests in pursuing degrees. The traditional graduating high school senior is actually in the minority of American higher education students, with a host of other types of students making up the majority, including returning adults, veterans entering college after service, and individuals seeking retraining. That diversity of intent means we need multiple ways for students to move in and out of higher education. One way students move through the educational system is transfer. Hossler and colleagues (2012) found that roughly one-third of all entering college students in 2006 transferred schools, with public 4-year universities being the most likely destination overall. Monaghan and Attewell (2015), in their nationally representative sample of community colleges, found that just over 40% of students at 2-year institutions transferring to 4-year universities lengthen their time to degree due to earned credits not being recognized. Often, this is due to a near-complete absence of understanding about what learning was achieved in courses earning those credits. Instead, mismatched course descriptions and transcript notations create the impression of misalignment.

Pathways focused on learning, as opposed to syllabi or articulation agreements of specific courses, have the greatest opportunity to be beneficial when they are utilized as a means to reach shared consensus, scaffold learning opportunities, and make connections across systems based on students and their learning. The DQP's focus on degree-level proficiencies aimed at increasing levels of degree attainment provides a means to think differently about student learning, transfer, and how degrees and credentials build on each other. Shared understanding of learning as a scaffolded, recursive process, then, is one piece of resolving these issues, but there are other pieces that need to be put in place, too. In the dizzying array of learning opportunities available to students, clear communication becomes essential if students are to understand why we ask them to move through our curricular learning experiences as we do. Pathways through the curricular maze become important to help bring learning together for students and for faculty, who have worked in curricular systems (particularly in general education) that have grown over time in ways that erode coherence. The work of curricular coherence also has implications for transcripts that are adaptable and reflective of learning from an array of educational pathways and learning experiences. All of these different pieces point to the necessity that work we have seen with DQP and Tuning (or similar tools) need to be faculty driven, collaborative, and built on an understanding that educational activities are part of interrelated and connected processes that function as a coherent learning progression. When that has happened, benefits accrue to everyone.

A different theory of change emerges from the problems higher education is addressing and the kinds of approaches that DQP and Tuning encourage, one that requires connections and involves collaboration with others both inside and outside institutions of higher education. For instance, a department discovers through review of senior capstone projects that graduating students are struggling with finding proper references to support their work; in other words, their evidence base is not matching the disciplinary standard and their information literacy is lacking. Upon examination of the program's curriculum, the faculty decide to provide students with more opportunities to engage in locating discipline-specific references. They decide to cover the topic frequently in multiple classes and provide assignments and feedback regularly in various settings. The idea is that if students hear about information literacy more often and are asked to practice it more through class assignments, they will be better prepared in the capstone to demonstrate their knowledge in that area. The department also partners with the library to provide supplemental support for students in the search process and works with the departmental student association to bring in field-specific authors who talk about their process of literature review with students. In addition, the department explores connections between general education and the major related to information literacy and finds areas for reinforcing student learning and bridging general education and discipline-specific approaches to locating valid and reliable resources. The difference between this example and those previously noted is akin to the shift from providing instruction to producing the type of learning for which Robert Barr and John Tagg (1995) argue. Our example, however, extends beyond their distinction. It operates within a different paradigm entirely, not only because of the reasons that department members have identified as different root causes but also because of the reasons why faculty think that undertaking joint approaches will encourage meaningful change in student learning. The example, by the way, is not hypothetical. We have taken it from the field.

Shifting Paradigms and Emerging Theory

Barr and Tagg (1995) outline a shift from viewing college as an institution that exists to deliver instruction to one that nurtures learning, a move away from viewing instruction as an end to producing learning by whatever means works best. They write:

We've witnessed reformers advocate many of the new paradigm's elements over the years, only to see few of them widely adopted. The reason is that they have been applied piecemeal within the structures of a dominant paradigm that rejects or distorts them. Indeed, for two decades the response to calls for reform from national commissions and task forces generally has been an attempt to address the issues *within the framework of the Instruction Paradigm*. The movements thus generated have most often failed, undone by the contradictions within the traditional paradigm. (p. 14, italics in original)

The work of shifting from a teaching to a learning paradigm requires altering different parts of the organization in alignment with a vision for the whole; additionally, that work positions students as coproducers of learning, where the institution strives to create environments and learning experiences that bring students together to construct knowledge for themselves. Within the learning paradigm, institutions encourage knowledge construction by focusing institutional conversations on a different set of questions and possible responses. In effect, Barr and Tagg (1995) suggest that this shift of lenses avoids "educational atomism, fractionation, without understanding of the larger context into which they fit and which gives them meaning" (p. 22). Yet, although a useful lens and an important step, the learning paradigm is a *pedagogical* paradigm.

Tagg (2003) refers to the *learning paradigm* as an organizational paradigm of theories-in-use "consisting of the framework of examples, models, and rules that define the boundaries of the organization's proper activities" (p. 15). He posits that learning, as opposed to instruction, is the responsibility of the institution and that a student lens is needed for the work. The learning paradigm focuses on pedagogies as the vehicle for advancing learning, but, although a vital element of the process, we must also be mindful that learning can happen in all sorts of places at all sorts of times. The work of DQP and Tuning has opened up discussions of learning to the varied places that learning may happen. Initiatives using DQP and Tuning have also examined providers of learning who may be outside the traditional academic curriculum—providers that might include advisers, student clubs, community engagement offices, and even the world of work. Those working with DQP and Tuning, in other words, have shifted from thinking about the pedagogies that produce student learning to thinking about the relationships within the organizational systems in which pedagogies are situated. The shift is from a learning paradigm to the learning systems paradigm.

To make that shift we need collective agreement on learning within disciplines and at different degree levels. Such work necessarily hinges on consensus and alignment, a key element of the learning systems paradigm we will present in the following chapter. Our paradigm does not negate Tagg but incorporates his learning paradigm into a larger system. Tagg's (2003) emphasis on supporting students in pursuit of their goals and requiring frequent student performance in the form of assignments coupled with regular and ongoing feedback are both important elements. Working with learning frameworks such as the DQP and those developed from Tuning also reinforces the point of authentic connections, where students see that what they are asked to do in courses is relevant to their own educational goals. Working with DQP and Tuning, faculty make connections between courses and other elements in an effort to produce self-reflective learners. Thus, DQP and Tuning serve as two tools for institutions and organizations "interested in analyzing student learning outcomes, curriculum, pedagogies, and outcomes assessment" (Jankowski & Marshall, 2015a, p. 1) without specifying what is taught or how content should be delivered. As tools, they push back on the idea that completion of courses or accumulation of credit hours can serve as a meaningful proxy for learning (Jankowski & Marshall, 2015b). Instead, they require all students to demonstrate that they have achieved faculty-determined levels of proficiency by integrating learning that includes "general proficiencies in specialized programs; consideration of disciplinary contributions to general education; and a clearer definition of relationships between educational segments" (Jankowski & Marshall, 2015c, p. 79). But how does working in the ways encouraged by DQP and Tuning do such things? And how much structure and scaffolding of student learning over time is needed (E.M. Nussbaum, 2012)?

Norm Jones (2012) argues that most reforms fail because they impose a "why" that means nothing to faculty in classrooms. He states, "Any vision of assessment that ignores our vision of our professional responsibility will fail because we will dismiss it as untrustworthy and as an enemy of our professional mission" (p. 53). In the case of Tuning, disciplines as broad communities use dialogue to find common language and shared vision regarding disciplinary degrees. In all the DQP and Tuning projects, the most important element has been the conversations that have emerged in the process. The NCA Tuning project, Learning Outcomes in Communication (LOC), viewed the developed disciplinary outcomes as starting points for conversation, as reference points that were neither exhaustive nor prescriptive (National Communication Association, 2015). The documents serve as a mechanism by which educational communities are able to jointly make meaning. NCA (2015) further writes that the process is most productive when undertaken as part of collective reflection "regarding not just *whether* but *how* a program is or is not constructed to support student attainment of learning" (p. 3). The process of reflection and dialogue provides building blocks for examining how programs and educational experiences are designed and built to encourage student learning, and how each of the various elements are aligned. The idea is that for educational design, clear articulations of learning are necessary for building intentional learning. Such design is vital because we know that students struggle to transfer their knowledge from one setting to another (Toomey Zimmerman & Bell, 2012); what they can do here in this experience or course they need to be able to do over there as well.

The process outlined in Figure 2.1 presents the means by which institutions and those within them have worked with DQP and Tuning to undertake meaningful change (Jankowski & Giffin, 2016b). It involves collaborative review and revision of learning outcomes in relation to disciplinary and degree-level learning, alignment of learning and mapping of educational experiences, revision and redesign of curriculum and learning experiences, revision and alignment of assessment activities, and revision of

Figure 2.1. The process of working with learning frameworks.

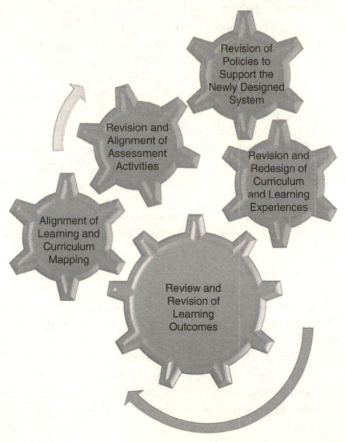

policies to support the newly designed system. In essence, the process helps to create student-centered learning environments that "facilitate student- or self-directed learning by enabling students to productively engage complex, open-ended problems that are aligned authentically with the practices, culture, or processes of a domain" (Land, Hannafin, & Oliver, 2012, p. 3). Student-centered learning environments are thus designed to support individual efforts of meaning-making through authentic activities that students construct or design.

The learning systems paradigm widens the lens of Tagg's pedagogically focused paradigm from colleges to include any learning environment, within or outside of a course. Pedagogical reforms within Tagg's learning paradigm include problem-based learning, collaborative learning, service-learning, and others. The learning paradigm "attends to students" (2003, p. 31) but does not actively involve them beyond in-course approaches to teaching. The work of DQP and Tuning, on the other hand, requires that we actively involve students without solving the issues of education for them or on their behalf. In a re-envisioning of student and faculty partnership as meaningful collaboration, Cook-Sather, Bovill, and Felten (2014) argue for respect, reciprocity, and joint responsibility for learning, including in the design of curriculum. They define *respect* as valuing what others bring to an encounter and claim it only works when it is reciprocal, flowing in both directions from faculty to students and from students to faculty. They define "*student-faculty partnership* as a collaborative, reciprocal process through which all participants have the opportunity to contribute equally, although not necessarily in the same ways, to curricular or pedagogical conceptualization, decision-making, implementation, investigation, or analysis" (Cook-Sather et al., 2014, pp. 6–7, emphasis added). That's a stark contrast to students as consumers to please or vessels to teach. The idea of students as partners begins to move toward a student-centered learning system, one that is not bound within a specific institution or specific courses. The openness of a student-centered learning system is important for this paradigm, because DQP and Tuning highlight the importance of fostering success for *all* students at any given time. That emphasis recasts every encounter students have on our campuses as potential learning opportunities. Everyone that students interact with may help them to succeed or reinforce notions of failure—all moments are educational and every interaction can make or break a learner, whether the interaction occurs with advising staff, librarians, facilities staff, faculty, or parking attendants.

Although working with DQP and Tuning has helped institutions, colleges, and departments move from an instruction to a learning paradigm, it has also added a few key elements to the mix—consensus, alignment, communication, and learner-centeredness—that expand Tagg's paradigm to the learning systems paradigm. The student-centered approach strives to clarify for students the learning outcomes of educational experiences along with the connected nature of the curriculum. The focus on undertaking assessment as something done with students as opposed to something that is done to them permeates the work. The idea that in every educational interaction it must be clear to students what we are asking them to do and why, what additional value these elements add, and how they all fit together through course-embedded opportunities to apply and integrate knowledge and skills is central to the work of DQP and Tuning. Of note, the focus is on individual learners—ensuring that every student is learning, not that the institution is accountable by having a robust number of graduates who are placed into jobs, but that every student learns and we know that they have. Table 2.1 provides an outline of the learning systems paradigm that extends on Barr and Tagg's (1995) shift to a learning paradigm by moving the focus from the institution to the student and expanding beyond the pedagogical to the educational environment.

Students, as opposed to institutions, are at the center as the unit of analysis and focus of learning. The shift to student-centered learning environments is intended to serve as a point of conversation for faculty, staff, administrators, employers, policymakers, and others. It may be used as a tool to help outline shared goals and identify how various groups may contribute to or advance the movement toward a student-centered approach to learning. As our learner population becomes increasingly diverse and mobile, with the ability to learn anywhere at any time, designing systems to help foster reflective and active learners who are successful inside and outside of higher education is vital.

TABLE 2.1
Shift to a Learner-Centered Learning Environment

Institution Focused	Learner Centered
Learning assessed for a sample of students	Learning demonstrated for every student
Normative approach	Responsive approach
Summative	Formative
Structured (seat time)	Adaptive/flexible offerings
Implicit outcomes and connections	Explicit outcomes and connections
Individual courses	"Our courses"
Silos/territories	Integrated and collaborative
Learning occurring in the institution	Learning happening everywhere

The learner-centered addition to the learning paradigm involves making learning outcomes more transparent to all stakeholders, ensuring the quality of degrees across institutions, aligning and integrating general education and the major, communicating to students enhanced curricular coherence, and embedding opportunities to apply and integrate knowledge throughout learning experiences. Thus, we create learning experiences that are responsive to student needs, provide regular feedback that students are able to act on, allow for adaptive and flexible offerings of courses and alternative learning environments, and make explicit the outcomes of interest and how student learning builds toward their attainment over time. It also involves an acceptance of the tenet that learning can happen everywhere and that we are able to demonstrate learning at the individual student level.

A picture begins to emerge of a learner-focused environment. Education Design Lab (2016) describes 12 promising nontraditional pathways to attainment for students and indicates that when looking across the list of various initiatives, the most exciting theme is the "creative problem solving on the part of learning institutions to meet students where they are"—in part an unyielding focus on learners by putting them at the center. If we start with students and what they need to be successful learners, all members within an institution begin to rethink and reposition what they do around that shared focus. Curricula must be built in a manner to consistently, connectedly, and intentionally develop student learning both horizontally and vertically. Integration at a horizontal level for Ewell (1997) involves the application of knowledge and various skills in different settings, whereas a vertical approach involves the scaffolded development over time of specific knowledge and skills.

When examining the work of faculty in relation to DQP efforts, we see a marked shift from conversations about "my course" to "our courses" and an awareness of the need to work together with different departments but also different units and constituents within and outside of institutions (Jankowski & Giffin, 2016a). In addition, the DQP has provided a common language and reference points from which to share with learners how specific courses and/or assignments fit into a larger, comprehensive whole. It has allowed different parts of the campus to come together to talk about how they contribute to a coherent whole (Jankowski & Jones, 2016).

As Norm Jones (2012) states, curricula do not exist in vacuums, but we can make an intentional, coherent system of preparation for learners. Through Tuning, participants were able to create tighter relationships between general education and the major where the core learning experiences serve to prepare students for the major that then moves a student to a degree. The focus on student movement also served to enhance transfer and articulation. Jones (2012) argues that built into Tuning is the concept of levels, much like the DQP, that provide benchmarks of performance at various points in the educational journey. Thus part of Tuning a discipline successfully is understanding what students entering a major should know, understand, and be able to do, while also alerting students to experiences that are supportive outside of the department in preparation for success within the major. Points of connection raised by Jones (2012) include not only general education but also the library, academic advising, career advising, K–12 systems, alumni, employers, and university staff. The clarity of how things fit together provides a means to make learning outcomes apparent to students and gives them a vocabulary to talk about their learning. The LOC project was also more than a clear definition of learning within the discipline, implying a process of alignment of programmatic curricula and pedagogies to the statements of learning. The National Communication Association (2015) states, "In LOC curricular activities, program faculty compare their own outcomes to the LOCs and then analyze the degree to which curricula and pedagogies are structured to enable students to learn and demonstrate learning of the individual department's particular iteration of the LOCs" (p. 3).

The Learning Systems Paradigm

The student-centered learning environment coupled with alignment helps faculty to make a shift from an institution lens to a student-centered approach to learning that is built on consensus around learning outcomes that are clearly communicated and aligned throughout educational experiences. The assumption is that such design will lead to a more equitable, coherent, and integrated educational experience for all learners. Once students are aware of the various courses they are being asked to take, why they are being asked to take them, what each adds to their knowledge and skills, how what they are learning in the course is applied in the real world, and what career paths the various learning opportunities build toward, then students have multiple pathways into and out of education that are flexible, transparent, and responsive to student needs. Further, designing educational systems for learners helps to foster reflective, active learners, able to effectively discuss their knowledge and skill sets with employers.

George Kuh anticipated this idea in an article written for *Journal of College Student Development* in 1996, advancing an image of higher education and guiding principles for what he called the "seamless learning environment" (Kuh, 1996a, p. 11). For Kuh (1996b), "the concept of seamless learning implies that undergraduate activities and experiences traditionally assumed to be unrelated—such as course and out-of-class activities and off-campus experiences—can be intentionally arranged to be mutually supporting, thereby promoting higher levels of student learning" (p. 11). Clear connections among courses, cocurricular experiences, learning outcomes, and career paths help to engage students in their education, and when engaged, students are more likely to persist and graduate. You may have noticed that we just outlined a theory of change. Figure 2.2 presents an image of the four elements of the theory of change which compose the learning systems paradigm that has emerged from work with DQP and Tuning.

Consensus based focuses on faculty-led conversations as well as reflections and explorations with employers, alumni, and others to develop a shared understanding and consensus on learning outcomes. This shared understanding serves as the foundation for revising outcomes for enhanced clarity and designing educational experiences. Robert Birnbaum (1988) states that "real consensus . . . arises when discussion is possible and expected, when participants feel that they have had a fair chance to state their position and to influence the outcomes, and when people are comfortable about supporting the chosen alternative even if it was not their first view" (p. 89). It is in part about reaching an agreement on the nature of reality

Figure 2.2. The learning systems paradigm.

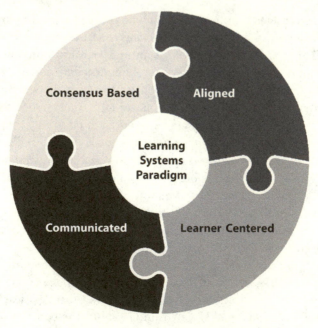

and, through reflection, allowing participants to unpack assumptions, a necessary step because assumptions often entail untested notions about cause and effect that may lead to action which exacerbates instead of resolves an issue (Birnbaum, 1988). Consensus takes time and ongoing conversations but is necessary in part because institutions generally operate with vague and ambiguous goals and little shared agreement as to what they mean or entail (Baldridge, Curtis, Ecker, & Riley, 1974). It will be impossible to align elements if we can't agree to what we are aligning. Discussions among faculty, students, administrators, and staff are also necessary to reach shared understanding on what the curriculum and other educational elements are attempting to achieve. William Tierney (2008) writes of the cultural focus of curriculum as "an ideological statement that derives from the organizational participants' understanding of the curricula" (p. 4)—an understanding that is only reached via dialogue.

Once consensus has been reached, educational experiences are *aligned* by faculty and staff throughout the institution for intentional integration, coherence, and fostering of multiple pathways. Alignment involves curriculum mapping, scaffolding, assignment design, delineation of career pathways, and cocurricular engagement. Having a shared understanding of learning outcomes does not mean that there is agreement on how to achieve them. Developing a shared understanding of the nature of reality, what each of the elements is designed to do and how they all actually operate in support of the larger educational system, allows people to see how they each need to revise practice to accommodate a collective understanding of education. Alignment is further explored in chapter 3, and applications of the learning systems paradigm to curriculum mapping and assignment design as practical examples are discussed in subsequent chapters. Here, for an example of alignment within a learning system, we offer a comment received during a presentation at the Assessment Institute in Indianapolis, Indiana:

> We have a student population that is often working, highly digitally engaged, increasingly from more diverse backgrounds, and focused on engagement and action more than on listening, reading, reflection, and contemplation. We are re-designing our general education curriculum to provide more authentic, active, integrative, and intentionally scaffolded learning opportunities. We are also trying to be more directly responsive to who our individual students are and providing them the support they need through enhanced faculty and peer advising, academic coaching, supplemental instruction, and an institution-wide commitment to student learning.

Even if there is consensus and efforts are aligned, if the work has not been *learner centered* there is likely to be little payoff. The design efforts in the example are focused on the students actually attending the institution. Keeping a learner-centered view means that educational systems reorganize educational experiences around *all* students and their learning. Taking a student view includes consideration of issues of equity, learning-focused transfer, alternative delivery models, flexibility in offerings, integration of prior learning assessment, ensuring stackable credentials, and building multiple pathways. It requires an exploration of students within a specific educational experience, including who they are and what they need. It involves not designing educational systems with good intentions but actively engaging with the learners to design them together. It further entails exploring the assumptions that we have on what our students can and cannot do, how they learn, and where we think learning occurs—even if we have not been the ones who have validated it.

Collaboration with students and other audiences through transparent discussions around outcomes works to make the implicit explicit, *communicated* throughout the educational system and outward from there. Communication involves exploration and integration with advisers, alternative transcripts, admissions, and employers. We can have a shared understanding or consensus on the learning outcomes of interest, and from that consensus we can build and redesign our educational experiences to be in alignment with them; we can even have included learners in the design and have facilitated understandings of who students are, but if we do not communicate about the intentional design or the learning outcomes, how are learners and others to know? Communication with the various constituents is key and has implications for orientation of new employees as well as for conversations with employers. Advisers need to understand the educational design to support students in the process, career services staff need to be aware of how to communicate learning and design to employers, and we also need to rethink how we document learning in the form of transcripts.

We hope the reason for naming this paradigm the *learning systems paradigm* is now clear—because, once the work begins, the entire educational system is involved. One of the findings from the impact study of work with the DQP was that the longer an institution engaged with the DQP, the more people were involved and brought into the process (Jankowski & Giffin, 2016a). The practice of using the frameworks also mirrors well the elements in the paradigm with revision and alignment of learning outcomes occurring through conversations, changes to the assessment system, mapping of curriculum and learning experiences, and policy all changing to support the consensus reached on what we are all trying to *collectively* achieve. It is also fits well with work that has occurred outside of DQP and Tuning, such as that of the Competency-Based Education Network (C-BEN), in the development of quality standards for competency-based programs. The draft standards include elements such as coherent curriculum design, clear and meaningful competencies, intentionally designed and engaged student experience, collaboration with external partners, and transparency of student learning (Competency-Based Education Network, 2016). Each of those elements are considered and discussed within the learning systems paradigm.

Of note, issues of equity are an integral part of the learning systems paradigm, not as a step in the process, but as an embedded element of learner-centered education. Embedding equity throughout both the paradigm and the praxis it prompts shifts the focus that places "responsibility for student success on the very groups that have experienced marginalization, rather than on the individuals and institutions whose responsibility it is to remedy that marginalization" (Witham, Malcom-Piqueux, Dowd, & Bensimon, 2015, p. 2). According to *A Summary of "Best Practices" for Recruitment and Retention of Students of Color* (Minnesota State Colleges and Universities System, 2002), university programs that "expressed support for improvements in minority student recruitment and retention at the highest administrative levels" used community outreach, "summer bridge," "academic and cultural support," and inclusionary programming to create successful outcomes across a wide swath of diverse institutions. Yet programs such as Upward Bound, or summer bridge, are generally targeted to small numbers of students, have an underrepresentation of males, and are difficult to scale up to the entire institution (Bial & Gandara, 2001). In sum, although the programs are impactful, they do not, and possibly cannot, go far enough on their own to close gaps in the equity of opportunity. Thus coming together across the educational community in an effort to focus on learning and building systems that are equitable can help us collectively advance student learning. The idea is that if we create pathways of learning for students based not solely on course sequences, include applied and problem-based approaches with HIP opportunities for every student, and have it all occur within a system that is built around diverse opportunities for students to demonstrate learning, then students will succeed.

Concluding Thoughts

Moving toward the learning systems paradigm includes a number of approaches whereby institutions and educational communities refocus and alter processes and approaches in terms of institutional policy (e.g., tenure and review) and how learning is organized and supported throughout the educational environment along with how curricular programs are designed and delivered. Yet it is impossible for an institution to work on each of these areas at once. It is more beneficial for an institution to focus on one of the pieces that relates to a current ongoing initiative or a question of concern from the campus, beginning with work that the institution already identifies as needed. Beginning with an ongoing project is helpful for integration, buy-in, and sustainability (Jankowski & Giffin, 2016b). For instance, institutions involved in efforts to create transfer pathways can build on the work because elements of successful transfer redesign include clearly defined goals and mapping of academic pathways (Soricone, Pleasants McDonnell, Couturier, Endel, & Freeman, 2016).

Intentional redesign of educational experiences necessarily includes broad stakeholder engagement and regular communication. Sharing, both internally and externally, success stories; using cross-functional teams; and taking the time to foster dialogue and reflection are points raised in various change efforts (Jankowski & Giffin, 2016b; Soricone et al., 2016). In order to begin, those involved need to be clear on the value and purpose of the work and how it can help students succeed, but they also need to be aware that as the work unfolds it entails shifting lenses from one paradigm to another or uncovering an existing paradigm that has never been questioned. The questions we ask about structures begin to shift such that we are no longer asking how this one assignment operates within a specific course, but how all of the pieces fit together in supportive roles to achieve intended learning at the desired level. Woven throughout the conversations are issues of pedagogy, support, design, and assessment. The next chapter unpacks the paradigm's critical element of alignment. Alignment is key to all of the efforts, the glue that holds the pieces together, and something that emerges as colleagues shift from one paradigm to another.

3

ALIGNING FOR LEARNING

As we said in chapter 2, the learning systems paradigm emerged from work done with the DQP and Tuning, though the paradigm connects with the work of the various initiatives outlined in chapter 1. Four elements work synergistically to comprise the paradigm: It is consensus based, aligned, learner centered, and communicated by and among stakeholders. Together, these four elements have had transformative impacts in programs and on campuses around the country, because they move our frame from our classes and what we do in them to a more holistic understanding of student learning in and across learning experiences. As our frame broadens, we recognize opportunities for partnership and collaboration that escaped our view previously. As institutions have taken up DQP and Tuning or as they have participated in the different initiatives we related in chapter 1, each has identified starting points particular to their local needs. Although each has attended to pieces of the paradigm (to varying degrees), alignment has proven to be the major area of concern, one that is ill-defined but supports the other elements of the paradigm. In this chapter we offer a definition of *alignment* that moves from the conceptual to the operational. In the process, we show how other elements of the paradigm emerge as necessary components of building aligned educational experiences for students.

What Is Alignment?

By now, the term *alignment* may already feel well-worn, as it has been tossed around in nearly every corner of education. At the K–12 level, we hear about the Common Core State Standards as being aligned to both workforce and higher education readiness (Conley & Gaston, 2013; Tepe, 2014; U.S. Department of Education, 2012), with the standards stacking and reinforcing over time to achieve that end. In higher education we hear similar calls for curricula to be aligned to the needs of the economy, for external learning frameworks (Public Agenda, 2015), or for our community colleges and transfer institutions to be aligned for smoother transfer from one to the other (Humphreys, McCambly, & Ramaley, 2015). The idea of *pathways* through higher education has proliferated in recent years, though whether the pathways are to employability or through the higher education system (Brau et al., 2013) or through general education remains fuzzy, given all the different uses of the term. Others write about academic alignment in terms of ensuring college readiness (Ajinkya, Brabender, Chen, & Moreland, 2015), remediation (Achieving the Dream et al., 2015; Methvin & Markham, 2015), or alignment of the educational pipeline for student completion (Ewell, Jones, & Kelly, 2003).

The core problem is how higher education has tried to establish alignment. At the level of transfer from institution to institution, alignment has been assumed based on the degree to which course descriptions at the starting school match the course descriptions at the destination school. Faculty and registrars analyze language that tends to be oriented around reductive descriptions of course content that rarely reference the areas of learning students will experience. Within single institutions, alignment is assumed around shared membership within the teaching community. Faculty within a department who share responsibility for teaching students depend on common investment in their discipline as the basis of alignment—we are all English teachers or psychology teachers or applied health teachers. At the degree level, institutions rely on seat time or credit accrual as an indication that students are moving successfully through curricula that align to institutional degree expectations. None of these is actually alignment, because in each case alignment is assumed and not based on intentional design of student learning experiences. Course descriptions conceal intended learning more than they reveal. Shared disciplinary membership ignores the sometimes deep differences in how disciplinary experts understand the inquiry in a given subject field and the methodologies used to conduct that inquiry. Seat time and credit accrual are only proxy measures for student learning; they say nothing about what students have learned while sitting in their seats or in the process of accruing their credits. In each case, the assumption of alignment forecloses meaningful efforts to think critically about the basis on which we say our institutions are aligned.

The turn to outcomes-based education implies alignment, for sure. As W.G. Spady (1994) notes, outcomes-based education implies that educational systems are organized around the desired endpoint of students within the system, much like the backward design approach addressed by Wiggins and McTighe (2005). Outcomes express the endpoint and faculty develop programs of study that lead to the demonstration of learning, but in practice we often assume that the kinds of instruction and the modes of assignments we give students are inherently aligned to what we expect of students. Alignment of outcomes and learning experiences, therefore, is often assumed but may not actually exist. Unclear ideas of what *alignment* means only compound the problem.

That lack of clarity is an important problem to note. For all the talk of *alignment*, there has been little effort to define what the word actually means. This haziness of meaning is a big problem for anyone working in higher education, because pressure increases to create aligned programs. Aligned with whom or to what? *Alignment* implies, rather obviously, multiple elements of a desired structure or system working in conjunction; however without a clear definition of what those elements are, the odds of attaining that end are slim. Aligning for smooth reentry into higher education by military personnel is a far different task from aligning for transfer from community college to university. To align for career readiness may be quite different from aligning for integrative learning. Without a clearer definition of *alignment,* all the effort put into this process may achieve very little.

You may have noticed by this point that alignment hinges upon exploration of relationships. Within the learning systems paradigm, alignment becomes geared toward defining the relationships among all the elements of the learning system. First, the various elements of the learning system need to be identified. Second, through discussion, reflection, and consensus, the relationships and connections among the elements need to be explored and made explicit. There are various ways in which alignment, or relationship exploration and definition, may occur, including within a specific course.

Approaches to Alignment

In the scholarship of teaching and learning, John Biggs (1996) has offered a clear definition of *alignment*, at least one type, by coining the term *constructive alignment*. Biggs ties together two key concepts. First, using constructivist theory, he observes that students create meaning in the processes by which they learn. Second, he notes that teachers align their learning activities to their assignments, which likely seems, by now, an obvious point, even if not always well practiced. Constructive alignment, then, proposes that teachers create pedagogies and activities for students that enable them to create the learning that is stated in the learning outcomes established for a class. Norton (2004) argues that constructive alignment can remedy issues he finds in outcomes assessment. According to Norton, outcomes assessment, if not handled critically, can result in students concentrating on evaluative criteria strategically and focusing on meeting evaluative criteria in superficial ways rather than engaging in activities intended to help them develop their learning. Constructive alignment, the generation of assignments that engage students in tasks by which they construct learning, can alleviate that superficiality to promote the deeper learning that we intend for students. Doing so requires careful construction of learning experiences and intentional, reflective design of assignments to yield this deeper learning.

This type of approach speaks to the shift away from the educational models that foreground delivery of content to the learning-centered approach described by Tagg (2003) and discussed by Wang, Su, Cheung, Wong, and Kwong (2013) in relation to their comparative study of the impacts of constructive alignment of curriculum design and student learning. The students in a constructively aligned course, in contrast to those in a nonaligned course, recognized "the expectation of the instructor and the learning priorities" in a course that built up "links between course intended learning outcomes, teaching and learning activities, and assessment tasks so that they understand why they needed to take the course and how the course was related to other courses and even the programme goals" (Wang et al., 2013, p. 487). By contrast, students in the non-aligned program found it disconnected and experienced a gap between the assessment criteria and their perceptions of the learning objectives. The end result was "a negative perception of the learning environment" and a reduction in student engagement.

But negative results go beyond student experiences. Anderson (2002) makes the prescient observation that poorly aligned curriculum results in our underestimating the effect of instruction on learning. Given the ubiquity of outcomes assessment as an integral component of accreditation processes, programs and institutions evaluate their efficacy in instruction based on assessment results. Where students seem not to demonstrate learning in relation to outcomes, we may be concealing the impact of our instruction. If our teaching and learning activities, including modes of instruction and assignment design, are not aligned to the goals we set for our students, we are unable to demonstrate the excellent work in teaching that we do (Jankowski, 2017). We may be hiding our light under a bushel. Intentional efforts toward alignment may remedy that by providing us with a better description of how our instructional activities facilitate and encourage student learning.

The type of alignment we are suggesting builds on this notion but expands Biggs's (1996) scale from the classroom to the learning system. Institutions of higher education are places that contain multiple sites of learning, not just individual classrooms. Students learn in general education and in majors or minors. They learn in labs, internships, cocurricular activities, and student employment. Each of these different learning sites can function as another piece of a constructively aligned learning system. The DQP and Tuning are tools that we find particularly useful for working on this type of holistic alignment, because they cut across the principles of dialogic approaches, collaborative perspectives, and intentional design that we've just described. There are, no doubt, other tools, as indicated by the various initiatives described in chapter 1, but DQP and Tuning have consistently offered frameworks and strategies for faculty thinking about an institution, its structures, curricula, cocurricula, and desired ends for students in a frame of constructive alignment.

Although constructive alignment offers a conceptual foundation for holistic alignment, this type of alignment has its own defining features. In the broadest terms, holistic alignment differs from the smaller-scale model of Biggs's (1996) constructive alignment in that it does not work only in assignment relationship perspectives bound to a course. Constructive alignment posits that course-level outcomes are the superstructure that governs the pieces of assignment design. In this model, each individual assignment within a specific course hits on particular course outcomes in a vertical relationship; the learning expressed in the course outcomes is related to the assignments, and expectations for course-embedded assignments are related to course activities that allow students to develop learning prior to assessment. That kind of bounded, course-specific, linear-progressive model tends to direct how alignment is conceptualized in higher education. The scope is largely bidirectional, moving up and down, with emphasis put on assuring that classes develop the outcomes without looking for connections beyond the specific course in question. The lateral relationships among courses and other educational experiences are often deemphasized. Scaling up, the lateral relationships among *programs* or curriculum and cocurriculum are often ignored.

In holistic institutional alignment, the lateral connections are given equal weight. In a program, the relationships laterally among courses are considered. The relationships between general education and majors are reflected upon. The complementarity of academic curricula and cocurricular engagement are examined. The result is a more complex picture of learning. Rather than being linear-progressive, with discrete, rarely intersecting vertical lines of relationships, holistic institutional alignment recognizes that lateral relationships thread those vertical lines together. A horizontal-progressive understanding appears much more like a web, representing the way that students learn in so many different contexts across the learning environment. To be clear, we are not suggesting that every element of the learning system should be integrally linked. That would be an impossibly tall order. As Weick (1976) observes of tight and loose coupling in organizations, different parts of the institution might have tight alignment, such as the relationship between a course-learning outcome and an assignment designed to elicit student demonstration of that learning outcome. However, the vast majority of students' learning experiences are marked by loosely coupled relationships among various curricular elements and other experiences such as the cocurricular or employment. Recognizing the different degrees of alignment relationships and identifying which need to be tightly coupled and which loosely coupled is an integral part of the alignment process.

Beyond this broad distinction, the kind of holistic alignment encouraged in work with DQP and Tuning can be addressed through four different lenses or approaches that discuss relationships, some of which are more applicable for specific types of institutions or learning experiences. They are scaffolding, reinforcing, integrating, and embedding. Each is driven by the principle that, because students learn in multiple places on, across, and beyond our campuses, our structures and practices should not just promote learning in each of these spaces but also equip students to make connections across their experiences in them. By doing so, institutions encourage students to learn skills and content, integrate their learning, and apply it to an infinite number of potential purposes. That rationale foregrounds students as active in learning, not just as collectors of knowledge but as producers and users of knowledge. In short, within this perspective, we *empower students to learn*, effectively intensifying Tagg's (2003) ideal of the learning paradigm.

Scaffolding

Biggs's (1996) constructive alignment illustrates the scaffolding of learning within a given course. As noted previously, Biggs would advise faculty to define what learning they intend students to develop, represented in current practice by course-level learning outcomes. Assignments are then designed to enable students to demonstrate that learning, but students are also given opportunities to develop knowledge and skills through activities both in class and out. Those activities scaffold learning, allowing students to practice in discrete areas of the course's outcomes, which are assessed in larger course assignments. Students, in other words, have an active, iterative experience in which learning builds from smaller units into a larger whole, which they demonstrate in their assignments. Although this example is course-specific, this is the basis of scaffolding in holistic alignment.

Scaled up, scaffolding recognizes that institutions designate overarching learning goals—institutional learning outcomes. Theoretically, all learning leads to the development of these outcomes, so general education and major program outcomes align to the outcomes of the institution. Similar to

Biggs's model, with smaller elements stacking toward larger learning goals, a scaffolded institution situates learning sequentially and iteratively, so that as learners progress through their courses, proficiency builds over time. For instance, what students learn in their first year provides the foundation for developing that learning in subsequent years. In the final year students are provided opportunities through capstone courses, signature assignments, or other such culminating experiences to demonstrate the sum total of their scaffolded learning. The principle holds whether students embark on a two-year program or a baccalaureate degree or even a graduate degree. DQP and Tuning explicitly encourage thinking in these terms. A look across the table of DQP proficiencies demonstrates this. Across the five proficiency areas, statements describe what learning looks like at the end of associate, bac-calaureate, and master's degrees. Learning at the baccalaureate level assumes learning at the associate level is in place, and so, too, with the master's. Tun-ing, in its focus on defining essential learning within disciplines, often results in discipline-specific documents that describe learning in the same kind of structure. Scaffolding, then, recognizes that learning builds iteratively over time. By now, most institutions have recognized this in theory, but tend not to recognize the practical ramifications, which will be discussed later in this chapter in terms of alignment being embedded.

For now, it is worth observing that the benefit for students of scaffolded learning is a coherent, iterative learning experience, particularly in general education. As Paul Gaston (2015) describes it, "In order to be inviting and compelling, clear curricular pathways leading from cornerstone to capstone must offer increasing, carefully ratcheted levels of challenge. Otherwise, there is the risk that general education, following a superficial once-over, will continue to offer 'merely requirements to be fulfilled and checked off a list, one course in lonely isolation at a time.'" (p. 27). All too often, students con-front a buffet of options that provides little rationale for choosing one over another. They often comment that courses are irrelevant to them. On one hand, this may reflect their own lack of understanding regarding how our curricula encourages broad-based learning in which they can situate a major. On the other hand, this response may indicate lack of explicit discussion by faculty with their students about the purpose of general education and its particular shape.

One problem, however, may be that there is little meaningful rationale for the structure of a general education program. Historically, general edu-cation has developed with new courses being added as options over time until the size of general education programs bloats. We may have lost sight of the purpose and value of general education due to a host of factors, includ-ing faculty desires to teach particular topics or budgeting models that tie departmental funding to full-time equivalent student numbers. The budget challenges leave departments, particularly small ones such as philosophy or anthropology, in defensive positions that permit little movement in revisions of general education. Another problem may be that scaffolding can be thwarted by student enrollment. The most well scaffolded curriculum will fail to provide students with the developmental, constructivist, iterative learning experience we design if students do not move through it in the ways we intend. Understanding the role of prerequisites and working in partnership with advising become essential.

The same is true of major programs. In recent years, the phrase *murky middle* has grown in use to describe the problem of curricula that establish foundational courses and culminating experiences but fail to consider the means by which students advance from one to the other. What do students need to know as they enter focused study of a discipline? What does their learning look like at the end of the second year? How does that build in later educational experiences? Although learning happens recursively, the idea here is that major programs can construct curricula that scaffold learning, either through increasingly difficult content or through increasingly difficult or complex application of the learning established from one experience to the next. Conley and Gaston (2013) argue that work with the DQP explicitly supports the move of higher education toward greater intentionality, explaining that "the unambiguous higher education outcomes set forth in the DQP offer a structure to guide curricular planning at every level—the college degree, the major, the program, the course" (p. 5). Work with DQP and Tuning promote, in other words, the kind of reflection about what differentiates one learning experience from the next in leading to better-scaffolded learning experiences that provide increasingly challenging opportunities for students to develop and demonstrate their learning.

Reinforcing

Just as alignment may occur through scaffolding, it can also occur through reinforcement. Reinforced learning begins to thread together the individual, linear paths of learning by making connections across learning experiences and by finding opportunities to help students develop their learning through cocurricular experiences. The idea is, as Newman, Carpenter, Grawe, and Jaret-McKinstry (2014) explain, that

> the intellectual skills at the heart of a liberal arts education must be developed in, and then applied across, multiple contexts—in different courses, in a variety of disciplines, using a range of modalities. Just as students do not learn to become effective writers by taking a single "first-year comp"

course, they will not learn to be numerically, visually, and culturally proficient unless these skills are modeled and reinforced throughout the curriculum. Students will not really appreciate the power of quantitative reasoning
if they think it only matters in their math classes; so too if they think visual
learning is only for the artistically inclined. . . . These exercises in integrative learning encourage students to reflect on how and why they should
learn these skills, as well as how they might apply them in novel contexts.
(p. 14)

Their explanation most obviously applies to the kinds of skills that predomi-
nate in most general education outcomes, things like quantitative fluency,
critical thinking, communicative fluency in both written and oral forms, and
the area of the DQP labeled Intellectual Skills; their example of composition
courses reflects what may be the best model.

College and university campuses often see a periodic complaint that goes
something like this: If students have taken first-year writing, then why can't
they write when they get to my [insert discipline] class? The assumptions that
underlie this complaint are that first-year writing classes can prepare students
to write in any genre for any discipline in any context and that writing is an
ability that can be honed and perfected in a single academic term. Neither of
these assumptions is correct. Regarding the latter, students require opportunities to apply their learning in new contexts to develop greater proficiency.
Remember, transference of learning is the greatest challenge. Moving from
the writing classroom to the philosophy or the business or the sociology
classroom requires students to be sensitized to the applicability of their writing class to these new contexts. Regarding the former, foundational classes
establish exactly that, foundations on which students can build as they move
through their educational experiences. Without intentional reinforcement
of what they learn in their foundational classes, they are left to make connections on their own and are far less likely to transfer the learning that we
intend for them.

The same is true within major programs, a point that returns us to murky
middles and the often ill-defined distinctions among 200-, 300-, and 400-
level courses. Although scaffolding learning can "ratchet up" challenges to
develop students' capacity to apply early learning within increasingly complex
situations, the lateral connections across each stratum offer an opportunity to
reinforce what students learn in a given year. Susan Elrod (2014) provides an
example of supporting quantitative reasoning laterally across the curriculum.
As faculty at California's West Hills Coalinga College found in their work
with the DQP, examining the ways in which proficiencies could be addressed
both vertically through the curriculum and laterally across the curriculum
resulted in a shift of focus among the faculty (Accrediting Commission for

Community and Junior Colleges, 2015). Rather than being concerned with course completion as a measure of student progress, they emphasized the attainment of learning through intentional connections within curricula and across discipline-specific and general education.

Reinforcement of learning need not be limited to academic programs. Cocurricular programs can contribute, too, particularly if we accept the premise that ultimately we want to prepare learners who can transfer and apply their learning in new contexts and situations. Cocurricular programs provide students with new contexts in which to recognize opportunities to utilize their learning and to continue developing their proficiency, particularly in the intellectual skills that make up the heart of so many general education programs. DePauw University recognized this possibility when they undertook an effort to map cocurricular activities to the university's general education outcomes (Kirkpatrick, 2014). The result was a set of conversations around the roles that the cocurriculum can play in helping students to develop the learning we encourage. We would anticipate that a psychology club could do the same for students majoring in psychology.

The same principle extends to leveraging campus spaces that rarely receive attention as sites of learning. The Iowa Grow program, for example, reveals the connections that can be made between student learning in academic programs and work experiences (University of Iowa Vice President for Student Life, 2017). Students, when asked about the relevance of their studies to campus jobs, rarely see any applicability—at first. The Iowa Grow program prompts students to reflect on how their employment enables them to apply what they learn in their classes. Although they initially struggle to see the relevance, over time participating students begin to make connections and see the relevance of their learning in these unexpected places. Iowa Grow, thus, encourages student employment to become a site that reinforces the learning that develops in academic spaces.

Integrating

A careful review of the DQP and its proficiency statements reveals the overlapping and interconnected nature of each of its proficiency areas. Specialized knowledge encourages application, whereas learning expects use of intellectual skills; this is true across areas. Were it to be represented pictorially, DQP might resemble a web in which discrete areas of learning weave together, not only to reinforce learning but also to integrate learning across a student's educational experience. We might think of this kind of cross-cutting as intensifying the challenge of transferring knowledge discussed previously. Integration, if we view it in this way, asks students to transfer disparate areas of knowledge toward a single focused end. In the process they might apply intellectual skills (learned in foundational classes and reinforced elsewhere), different disciplinary epistemologies (or "ways of knowing and doing"), and content knowledge to a particular problem. Problem-based learning approaches that make use of "wicked problems" are one common pedagogy that positions students to pull together the breadth of their learning into a single, coherent whole (Teater, 2011).

Faculty who participated in the AAC&U's Quality Collaboratives project found thinking about educating students integratively required a reorientation of their own pedagogical focus. As the AAC&U report on the project observes, "Partners need to be motivated by an interest in questions that extend beyond the usual discourse about a particular discipline or profession. Faculty in the [Quality Collaboratives] project discovered that they need to think about general education, major program courses, and electives, as well pre- and co-requisites" (Rhodes et al., 2016, p. 13). This kind of reorientation should not be confused with an end to study within disciplines. After all, to integrate learning, students need to have learning to integrate. To pull disparate areas of learning together, students need to have some grasp of those disparate areas. That may begin with becoming versed in the various ways in which differing areas of learning produce knowledge, the kinds of questions that they ask, and the strategies they use to answer them. This is why the DQP proposes that students be conversant with a couple of disciplines in addition to their majors.

Reorienting ourselves around integrative learning experiences does require a shift in our approach to pedagogy. Ferren and Paris (2015) observe, "Integrative liberal learning requires connections that are logical and transparent to students within the curriculum, between the curriculum and cocurriculum, and with larger communities" (p. 4). Historically, U.S. higher education has assumed that students will make these kinds of connections across fields of study and areas of application, but that assumption has been repeatedly proven untrue. Cutrufello's (2013) work in this area demonstrates that students experience the typical general education course list buffet, separate from the major and cocurriculum, as disjointed, leaving them to go through the motions of learning without taking much away. Ferren and Paris (2015) make clear, though, that students benefit from educational approaches that explicitly connect various learning experiences, particularly when the assignments they complete develop those connections through reflection and feedback.

The turn to integrative learning tracks well to faculty beliefs about how our institutions can best prepare students. As Ferren and Paris (2015) note, "Faculty believe that sharply separating general education and specialized study makes it less likely that there will be coherence, intentionality, and integration in a student's coursework and less likely that students will gain all that they might from their undergraduate education" (p. 1). As we know from our own experience, moving through the world requires a constant integration of what we have learned, whether we are considering how to vote on a particular issue, determining whether we should lease or buy a car, or completing a project for an employer. As faculty, our values are clearly in keeping with the need for helping students work integratively in areas like these. Where we have struggled is in actualizing pedagogies that can help us help learners get there, a point we will return to later while discussing embedding.

Integrative learning can also occur in cocurricular spaces of our institutions. Think back to the Iowa Grow program, with its goal of making campus work experiences educationally meaningful for students. As we have already noted, employment often requires nimble and flexible use and application of learning to complete job duties. That feature makes the workplace a space in which students might be challenged to reflect on the ways in which they apply and integrate the different areas of learning. The same is true of student clubs and organizations. The average fraternity or sorority, for example, comprises students from majors that sweep across a campus's administrative units. Community service programs are another place for students to reflect on the integration of their learning and draw lessons about not just what they have learned but also their own capacity to deploy learning to some productive end.

Newman and colleagues (2014) point out, "Our experience has reinforced one overriding lesson: integrative learning is as much about pedagogy as about curriculum, as much about the culture of learning and collegiality as about specific programs" (p. 15). The "culture of learning and collegiality" is an important point to underscore here. Institutions are organized around the different broad epistemologies employed by disciplines, with natural and physical sciences clustered in an administrative unit, social and behavioral sciences grouped in another, arts and letters in yet another, continuing education and extension offices in another space, career and technical education separated as well, and business and other professional-focused programs in their own additional administrative group. Those administrative divisions can tend to be pedagogical divisions, too, with little passing, for example, between faculty in physics and philosophy. The all-too-typical loss in this organization is collaboration across these divisions. Newman and colleagues suggest that we may need to consider ourselves as colleagues in practice, not just employment.

A variety of community colleges that participated in the Accrediting Commission for Community and Junior Colleges (Accrediting Commission for Community and Junior Colleges, 2015) project around the DQP undertook this kind of culture change to varying degrees and found tremendous benefit. The College of the Marshall Islands found differentiation of general education courses from courses in the major for assessment of degree-level learning outcomes was not useful and moved to include the DQP areas of learning across the entire degree program of study. Riverside City College decided to view the degree in its entirety, not with general education as separate, and wove the DQP outcomes throughout. They found that, "when viewed as a coherent program of study leading to a degree, the combined general education component and discipline-specific requirements could better be considered for how all areas of learning were being addressed in the curriculum" (Accrediting Commission for Community and Junior Colleges, 2015, p. 37). Pasadena City College observed the following from their experience:

> The DQP is a valuable tool to prompt deeper thinking about the nature and value of learning outcomes and their potential to link disciplines around solving real world problems of human need. The flexibility and generalizability of the model makes it highly adaptable and easily communicated. The strength of the DQP as an independent system that acknowledges the essential qualities of life-long learning, along with a structured learning framework, creates a common currency across disciplines and institutions that deepens educational engagement by both faculty and students alike. (Accrediting Commission for Community and Junior Colleges, 2015, p. 66)

Embedding

Each of the first three aspects of holistic alignment emphasizes the importance of alignment being embedded in practice. One principle remains constant: Educating is something we do *with* learners, not *to* them—the learner-centered portion of the learning systems paradigm. Think for a moment about Tagg's (2003) distinction between the teaching paradigm and the learning paradigm. In the former, as he argues, the institution focuses on performing activities that transmit learning to students, rendering students passive recipients of knowledge. In the learning paradigm, students are active agents in their own learning. They ask questions. They develop answers. They confront challenges. They create solutions. Students in the learning paradigm are engaged participants in the give and take that defines faculty/learner interactions in and out of the classroom. Having an aligned institution, therefore, depends on actualizing the curricular and cocurricular structures designed to scaffold, reinforce, and integrate the pedagogies and activities students encounter directly. In other words, if pedagogy and activities do not manifest and enact the intended alignment, there is no alignment, because alignment is practical.

Pedagogy in holistic alignment emphasizes a mindfulness of the strategies we use to encourage students to be actively involved in producing their own learning. Although we addressed this topic previously in our discussion of scaffolding, it is worth pointing out that if we strive to enable students to become active learning agents, then our understanding of what pedagogy looks like may need to expand. Ferren and Paris (2015) argue the following:

> Faculty leaders understand that integrative liberal learning requires reconceptualizing the faculty role from designing the learning experiences to constructing the learning as a coach and co-learner with students. In this co-learner role, faculty ask meaningful questions about complex issues; encourage students to use multiple ways of knowing; suggest relationships, patterns, and alternative perspectives to inform understanding; and support students as they struggle with ambiguity, uncertainty, and unanticipated conclusions. (p. 16)

Understanding the need to reconceptualize and knowing how to enact that in our own classrooms, however, are two different matters. A host of literature exists to help, on strategies such as problem-based learning, project-based learning, flipped classrooms, experiential learning, and service-learning models. But this, too, is where the expanded frame of the learning systems paradigm is important. If we conceive of student learning in our classrooms as one piece of a larger set of coherent learning experiences, then we can work collaboratively to identify pedagogies that, although different from teacher to teacher, build on one another. The exchange of ideas about how we facilitate student learning fosters our own development as educators.

The implications of embedding alignment within faculty practice are significant for assessment of student learning, too. Activities and assignments are the means by which we help students to develop and demonstrate their learning, and they are, therefore, the best indication of student learning. If evaluation of the degree to which students are learning is the end goal of assessment, then assignments are the logical means of making that evaluation. Rooting assessment in assignments completed for classes leverages the work faculty are already doing to facilitate learning and avoids the kinds of add-on approaches that campuses have turned to in an appropriate distrust of grades as valid measures of student learning. When common rubrics are used to focus grading of student work, that distrust can be neutralized and valuable insights can be gained into how well students learn. Because this work occurs within the core activities of the learning system, assessment has, for many undertaking work with DQP and Tuning, become meaningful in ways that far surpass expectations. We are better able to see the patterns of strength in student learning as well as the patterns of struggle. We can better relate those patterns to the various elements of the student learning experience and respond by developing strategies for addressing them. In other words, within the learning systems paradigm, assessment is integrated into what we are largely doing already, a topic we will take up later in chapter 5.

Building Aligned Learning Experiences

If we accept defining *alignment* as exploring relationships among the various elements of the learning system to support shared ends, the importance of another element of our paradigm becomes clear: The learning system is consensus-based. Alignment, as we have described it and as may already be apparent, depends on different parts of the learning system, whether departments and divisions on a campus or feeder institutions and destination institutions, accepting a shared understanding of essential learning for students and designing learning environments and experiences for them that will best facilitate that learning. Work with DQP and Tuning demonstrates this. In Utah, for example, Tuning was used to bring together discipline-specific faculty from community colleges and four-year institutions to identify the essential learning specific to those disciplines and to describe what that learning looks like at the end of two years or an associate degree and again at the end of the baccalaureate. (Other states, including Indiana, Minnesota, Texas, and Kentucky, worked similarly.) Regular, ongoing meetings of faculty within the state have enabled conversations that carry forward the shared understanding of what learning programs foster in students so that beginning juniors, whether coming from a university or from a community college, have the same learning under their belts even if their particular learning experiences have been different. A useful resource developed by two Utah faculty members, Norm Jones and Daniel McInerney (2016), provides questions that faculty can use to dicuss how the various pieces of the educational experience fit together.

On a larger scale, both AHA and the NCA took up Tuning to identify essential learning in each discipline, again describing what that learning looks like at the end of an associate degree and again at the end of a baccalaureate degree. Participants in each project engaged in collective reflection, discussion, and debate to make those determinations, vetting their thinking with colleagues across the country in a consultative process of consensus-building. The results for each organization have included ongoing discussions about how the first years of study within the discipline lay foundations for upper-division work, as well as about how lower-division courses in the discipline contribute distinctively to general education while facilitating student learning around general education outcomes. These conversations encourage alignment of lower-division learning and upper-division study in the major while encouraging horizontal alignment across general education and the major.

These examples illustrate the degree to which alignment of student learning experiences happens only when those who create those learning experiences—be they curricular or cocurricular—are working together intentionally and explicitly. Alignment, in other words, is inherently dialogical and collaborative. Without different members of the educational environment talking to each other, alignment cannot be achieved, and alignment is not successful when it becomes an administrative task, because it requires those who directly foster learning to explicitly work in aligned ways. Remember, alignment is essentially practical even if it has a conceptual basis.

Dialogue is fundamental to building aligned learning experiences, as the previous examples indicate, because alignment depends on consensus. If faculty responsible for academic programs and staff responsible for cocurricular programs do not agree about what learning is essential, then alignment cannot occur, because the practical nature of alignment requires praxis among colleagues to become apparent to learners. Consensus, however, requires work and a collaborative spirit. As Birnbaum (1988) notes, "Real consensus . . . arises when open discussion is possible and expected, when participants feel that they have had a fair chance to state their position and to influence the outcome, and when people are comfortable about supporting the chosen alternative even if it was not their first view" (p. 89). That means alignment begins with dialogue aimed at building consensus.

Consensus-building typically moves through an organic process, which can be described with Bruce Tuckman's (1965) stages of teaming. Tuckman explains a "developmental sequence in small groups" that, when small teams are organized, goes through four key stages: forming, storming, norming, and finally performing. Forming is a process of knowledge building by individual members of the team who must become informed about projects and challenges. When they move to the storming stage, participants, according to Tuckman, confront conflicts of personality and may challenge the leader of the team, though Tuckman's data suggest that many teams do not experience this stage. Norming engages team members in a process of establishing working relationships that enable them to move forward, though he notes that the concern about potential conflicts may prevent completely open conversation. When teams move to performing, they make the decisions with which they are charged. Consensus-building poses a challenge, because team dynamics are inherent in the collaborative approach necessary to it.

Stasis theory (Brizee, 2008) offers another frame for thinking about building the consensus necessary to alignment. Although its ancient origins with Aristotle and Hermagoras encourage a process of questions for conducting analyses, its application to working toward consensus can be highly productive, particularly if we think about its use in Tuckman's forming stage. Stasis theory in consensus-building asks participants to work through four levels of agreement:

1. Facts: Participants must agree about the facts of a particular issue, including whether or not it exists, its origins, changes in circumstances, and what aspects of the issue can be changed.
2. Definition: Participants must agree about the nature of the issue, the type of problem before them, and the different parts of the issue.
3. Quality: Participants must agree about the seriousness of the issue, its impact on stakeholders, the ramifications of inaction, and costs (not necessarily monetary) of taking action.
4. Policy: Participants must agree about whether or not action should be taken, who should take action, what actions should be taken, and what else needs to occur to solve the problem.

In a process of consensus-building for alignment, stasis theory can provide a helpful structuring device, because it focuses dialogue toward working systematically through a process of seeing existing educational structures, considering implications for students, and devising approaches to strengthen those structures to better facilitate student learning. Figure 3.1 relates stasis theory to the different points of discussion that often emerge around alignment as a series of questions that advance from identifying problems, to describing them, to determining how to address them.

The scale and scope of dialogue around alignment is important. Institutions of higher education are complex learning spaces, as we noted in chapter 2, that include faculty in academic curricular programs (both general education and discipline-specific majors, minors, and certificates); staff in cocurricular programs that include community engagement, student clubs, athletics, and student work-study; and staff and administrators in financial aid, housing and residence life, facilities services, and campus safety. Each of these different constituent parts may have a role to play and ideas to offer for achieving an educational environment in which students construct and apply knowledge across the campus and its divisions. Eisenmann, Brumberg-Kraus, Gavigan, and Morgan (2014) explain that their own collaborative

Figure 3.1. Stasis theory applied to alignment.

Stasis Theory	Alignment
Facts	To what extent are our educational experiences for learners aligned? What activities, events, or changes on our campus or among campuses might impact the coherence of our students' learning experiences? What elements of our learning environment might we change?
Definitions	To what extent are outcomes aligned? To what extent do we agree about what the outcomes mean? How might curricular structures contribute to the lack of alignment? How might learner course-taking patterns contribute to their experience of incoherent learning experiences? How might pedagogies or assignments be contributing to the problem?
Qualities	How do these issues impact our students' learning experiences and learning? How do these issues affect faculty and staff responsible for facilitating learning? What are the consequences of making no changes? What are the costs (labor, time, money) of taking action or taking no action?
Policies	What action should be taken? Who is best positioned to undertake that action? How should that action be taken? Whom should we inform about this action? How shall we inform them?

efforts resulted in "an important recognition: our campus has frequently presumed that learning occurs only in classrooms under the guidance of faculty members, often ignoring the contributions of staff who support students in cocurricular and applied settings" (pp. 17–18). Higher education, moreover, looks beyond its own confines to larger contexts. We strive to prepare students for future careers and for lives as citizens active in their communities. These arenas draw other stakeholder groups into our orbit and create opportunities to engage in dialogue with them, too. All these players pose the challenge of knowing with whom to begin dialogue, so identifying potential sites of dialogue may be helpful.

Within Programs

Within programs, as we have said, faculty often assume that shared participation in a discipline and its conventions constitutes alignment of student learning experiences. If faculty share similar training, they must be working in a coherent fashion. Often, however, faculty discover that reviewing outcomes reveals different conceptions of what outcomes mean. Although not inherently a bad thing, these differences can create confusion for learners if we are not aware of these differences. For faculty within programs, therefore, alignment consists of arriving at consensus around the meaning of outcomes, considering how curricula might best be constructed (including determining pre- and corequisite classes), and creating a relationship between general education and programs of study in ways that provide learners with the recursively progressive learning experiences that enable them to discern the coherence of their studies.

Among Programs

Among programs, we rarely consider the degree to which we are working in alignment with colleagues in other programs. To what extent, for example, are the foundational writing lessons in first-year writing programs or the initial lessons in critical thinking often established in general education philosophy courses being leveraged so that learners can apply those lessons in new contexts? How, in other words, do discipline-specific programs build on prior learning in general education by explicitly referring students back to that learning for specific purposes? Moreover, the DQP prompts reflection on whether students can integrate learning from one discipline with other disciplines. Because we do not often identify opportunities with our students to make those kinds of connections, their learning can become insular. Without dialogue among colleagues across programs, we constrain our own ability to help students integrate their learning.

Across Divisions

Because learners participate in campus lives outside their courses, they have opportunities to make connections between academic learning experiences and the learning experiences provided by a host of other activities. Doing so requires an awareness among faculty and staff of how they support student learning. As Ferren, Anderson, and Hovland (2014) note, "Although faculty typically claim sole ownership of the curriculum, the initial campus inventories also pointed to important roles for professional staff in connecting classrooms to cocurricular requirements, community projects, and work experiences—all opportunities for integrative learning" (p. 6). DePauw University undertook a strategic process of mapping the university's general education outcomes to cocurricular activities to identify the ways in which the cocurriculum reinforces the learning students construct in their academic experiences. Further, the work on comprehensive student records between student affairs and registrars serves to document and validate learning from various activities and experiences. This kind of cross-divisional collaboration endeavors to provide students with opportunities to apply learning in new contexts in a process of recursive development.

With Stakeholders

Given the larger context in which higher education works—preparing citizens and members of the workforce—alignment with these spaces equips colleges and universities to help learners make smoother transitions beyond the institution. To be clear, we are not advocating a vocationalized institution. Career and technical education programs in community colleges have an obvious alignment to the world of work, but even here, understanding the degree to which students are ready for that transition requires reflection and discussion among partners. AHA's work with Tuning has led to initiatives that involve engaging employers and employer groups in a two-way conversation in which historians explain the kinds of knowledge and skills that history majors develop while employers explain the ways of working within the world of work. These kinds of dialogues put both sides in an informed position.

With Learners

Learners may seem a surprising group with whom to think about collaboration, but they are our chief partners in education. The collaboration we are describing across multiple constituencies ultimately stands to benefit learners. Ferren and Paris (2015) observe that in "collaboration across organization and intellectual boundaries . . . students draw together their life experiences and aspirations with classroom, cocurricular, and community opportunities" (p. 20). However, that only becomes fully possible if we are working with students to understand not only how the plurality of their experiences accrues learning for them but also how we actively and intentionally foster their development as learners. If learners are active agents in the construction of knowledge, then engaging with students as collaborators in building our learning environments enables us to provide learning experiences that address who they are, where they are, and what they do.

Concluding Thoughts

You might think that trying to align so many different pieces of the learning environment results in a house of cards. Remove one piece and the whole structure crumbles. Remove one of a house's four walls, and it, too, will collapse. True, there are both load-bearing and non-load-bearing walls, but recall the distinction between tightly and loosely coupled alignment discussed previously. The goal of aligning our learning systems is not to create a tight alignment of every piece. Alignment, as we have described it, is an intentional effort to see the complex learning system in which our students are constructing and applying knowledge and to unpack for ourselves the relationships among the pieces in ways that allow us to communicate to others the educational design. Only by seeing that complexity can we hope to help learners move through their experience in ways that facilitate scaffolded, reinforced, and integrative learning.

Achieving holistic alignment requires three key emphases. First, alignment must be faculty led. Although learning can happen in all sorts of places and nonacademic programs tend to have learning outcomes, meaningful change will not happen at scale if faculty are not leading the conversations around relationships within the learning system. As those responsible for academic programs and their expression in curricula and pedagogy, faculty are best-positioned to lead these efforts. Second, holistic alignment only happens in collaborative processes. If different participants in the learning environment are not aware of one another, they cannot align their pieces of the system. Third, conversations regarding alignment need to explore relationships beyond those of vertical, programmatic pipelines of learning. Students move horizontally through our learning systems, too, so our alignment conversations need to be mindful of that. Rather than envisioning learning experiences as pipelines, we might better imagine them as spirals in which learners move vertically and horizontally through experiences that are scaffolded vertically, but also reinforced and integrated horizontally.

The most important caveat is this: Alignment happens within a specific local context. Every institution is distinct in the students it teaches, the communities it serves, the problems it faces, and the resources (including faculty and staff, as well as physical and monetary resources) it possesses, among a host of other spots of potential idiosyncrasy. Alignment is never a process of bringing an individual campus "into line" with comparable institutions. It is a process of asking questions collectively and collaboratively built from local context in order to develop a specific institution's own meaningful answers.

4

APPLYING THE PARADIGM
TO CURRICULUM MAPPING

Mapping is a procedural tool that has demonstrated tremendous impact on building consensus, aligning educational systems, encouraging a learner-centered approach, and even fostering communication with a variety of parties in and out of institutions, showing its relevance to each different element of the learning systems paradigm. The idea of a map is, obviously, a metaphor, invoking cartography. Consider, for a moment, the use of maps on trips. Those old paper maps that were easy to unfold but were never quite so easy to fold back up depicted large areas of terrain, lined with red, green, blue, and white roads. Until global positioning systems (GPSs) took over the job, maps never plotted out a particular route for getting from one place to another. Rather, the various lines of different types offered the navigator a variety of possible options for getting from a starting point to a destination and provided information surrounding the route possibilities. One might take an interstate part of the way before exiting to double back on a rural route to some desired locale. From there, the trip might continue on through small roads or back onto a different highway until, through the various options, the navigator arrives at the destination. Which route a navigator chooses to take enables a variety of opportunities to see a multitude of different things along the way. On other journeys between the two places, other routes might be taken to see other things, stop for lunch in a state park, or visit a landmark of interest. Maps, in other words, provide diverse possible ways of understanding paths from one place to another. All those lines offer many different options for connecting or relating the destination to the starting point. Mapping within higher education works similarly. There is not a single way of seeing the path to or through an institution or among institutions.

In work with learning frameworks like the DQP and those produced in Tuning, a typical process has emerged. The initial step in exploring the relationships between learning frameworks and local learning outcomes has been to review and revise for alignment between the two (Jankowski & Giffin, 2016a, 2016b). This is not a uniquely U.S. experience, as shown by Zayed University in the United Arab Emirates, for instance, which has formal policies on alignment with the Qualifications Framework Emirates and its own internal learning outcomes assessment processes. Once learning outcomes have been reviewed in relation to an external reference point and subsequently revised, the second step undertaken by the majority of institutions has been mapping learning within and across learning experiences. Work with DQP and Tuning has led to mapping a variety of learning experiences in part because neither tool limits learning to that which occurs in courses (Jankowski & Marshall, 2015b). Curriculum mapping, the approach to mapping invoked by the majority of institutions in DQP and Tuning efforts, is a practice occurring in a variety of different contexts, not solely from engagement with DQP and Tuning but more broadly as a focus solely on the curriculum. In a survey of C-BEN member institutions (2015), 88% stated that they had developed curriculum maps. After having written elsewhere about approaches for curriculum mapping from DQP and Tuning work (Jankowski & Marshall, 2014), in this chapter we apply the four elements of the learning systems paradigm to curriculum mapping by exploring what happens when curriculum mapping becomes consensus based, aligned, learner centered, and communicated. After exploring the framework as applied to mapping of the curriculum, we broaden what it means to map, suggesting additional paths that use mapping processes to develop a deeper conversancy with the terrain of and among institutions and their contexts.

A Curriculum Mapping Primer

There are a variety of ways to map curriculum—as well as other aspects of education that can be mapped beyond just the curriculum. For instance, Silva and White (2015) discuss the mapping of credit hours to competencies for determining equivalencies in dual-reporting systems for competency-based education programs. And mapping can happen in many places. For instance, Queen's University in Kingston, Ontario, has developed maps of majors for each undergraduate program, outlining the skills students develop that are complementary to a degree such as those within the cocurriculum, including learning experiences such as community service (White, 2015). Outlining these connections between curricular and cocurricular learning launched a campaign called "It All Adds Up" to help students understand what the various activities they participate in mean. Others have used Broad's

(2003) approach of dynamic criteria mapping which builds from student work to explore with faculty their shared values. Dynamic criteria mapping allows for dialogue among faculty about what is valued by carefully reviewing student work and nominating valued characteristics that are present in the work as well as mentioning those that are missing (Johnson & Schuck, 2014). The developed criteria are then placed onto a visual map of evaluative criteria that can be revised over time. And others, such as registrars and student affairs professionals (American Association of Collegiate Registrars and Admissions Officers and NASPA, 2016), are investigating how to document learning from a variety of places through comprehensive student records. Thinking broadly about mapping is important because students bring with them prior learning, taking many paths in their learning journeys and experiencing different learning opportunities throughout. However, the majority of mapping experiences have focused on the curriculum and have not been overly fruitful or collaborative.

Curriculum mapping *can* foster dialogue aimed at better aligning educational experiences for learners, but to use maps in this way requires a different perspective on how we produce and use them. By now, assessment personnel and faculty responsible for program assessment activities are familiar with curriculum maps. Typically, and in their most simplistic form, they take the form of a two-dimensional matrix with outcomes listed across the horizontal axis and courses listed down the vertical axis, as Table 4.1 shows. To show which classes develop learning in a particular outcome area, a mark is placed in the boxes formed by the intersection of courses and outcomes. Table 4.1 represents a typical curriculum map.

TABLE 4.1
The Typical Curriculum Map Matrix

	Program Outcome 1	**Program Outcome 2**	**Program Outcome 3**
Course 1	X	X	
Course 2		X	X
Course 3	X		X

Sometimes the mark is simply an *X* to designate that relationship. Other times, levels of challenge are indicated with a taxonomy such as *I* for introduced, *D* for developed, and *M* for mastered, as presented in Table 4.2. Sumsion and Goodfellow (2004) offer six indicators that can be used on maps beyond the basics of introduced, developed, and mastered:

1. Assumed (students are assumed to have acquired this skill prior to the unit)
2. Encouraged (students are encouraged to gain/practice/refine this skill in this unit)
3. Modeled ([behaviors are modeled] for students in this unit)
4. Explicitly taught (to students in this unit)
5. Required (students are required to demonstrate this skill in this unit)
6. Evaluated (students are evaluated on this skill in this unit) (p. 333)

TABLE 4.2
Developmental Curriculum Map Matrix

	Program Outcome 1	Program Outcome 2	Program Outcome 3
Course 1	I		D
Course 2	D	I	
Course 3	M	D	M

Mapping, however, has often been a solitary exercise undertaken by program, department, or assessment chairs. Via e-mail, department chairs receive an Excel spreadsheet in which they either place ticks in the matrix for the program or which they forward to individual faculty to put ticks in for their specific courses. Little thought, less conversation, and minimal effort are generally involved. The maps are then typically submitted to assessment offices for the purposes of producing records of assessment activities in advance of accreditation reports or to indicate alignment and coverage of learning outcomes. The reasons for this approach are understandable. Assessment has been a source of irritation, because its value has been unclear and processes have tended to be seen as additional work or add-ons that have little bearing on the actual practice of educators responsible for more than just teaching. When conducted in this manner, curriculum mapping yields very little because it is individually done, externally facing, and administratively driven. When we ask in presentations how many people have undertaken curriculum mapping, many hands are raised. When we ask if they thought it was useful, fewer are raised, and when we ask if they have done anything with the map following its creation, even fewer raised hands appear. Finally, we ask if individual faculty members each mapped the curriculum, would the map look the same? The answer is a resounding no. Further, would a map of the curriculum done by learners look the same as a curriculum map developed by faculty? Again, the answer is a resounding no. This means that the solitary approach to indicating curriculum alignment on paper is not overly reliable and won't foster the sort of collective, supportive work needed within a learning system.

Others have considered issues with the somewhat simplistic ways in which curriculum mapping has been presented or undertaken, pointing instead to the importance of collegial dialogue in the process. Sumsion and Goodfellow (2004) share their experience in undertaking curriculum mapping and note that maps have not been reliable when completed by a single faculty member in isolation. They note differences in interpretations of outcomes, variations in the meanings assigned to addressing outcomes, and differing assumptions behind the process itself. They argue that instead, curriculum mapping should be a "collaborative meaning-making [process] about what we want our teaching to achieve" (Sumsion & Goodfellow, 2004, p. 343). Without discussion, there is no way by which shared understanding can be reached on what it means to indicate on a map that a learning outcome is being addressed.

When curriculum maps become the centerpiece of collective reflection about the learning students are building and where they build it, mapping becomes a potentially transformative exercise. When faculty (and staff) examine their shared curriculum together, they confront their individual assumptions. They learn that what they thought was happening in one part of the curriculum may not be so, or that colleagues assumed someone else was concentrating on one outcome area rather than another. The fact is, whether we realize it or not, teaching is collaborative. Learners encounter each member of a program's faculty and move through different faculty members' classes at different times. We share our learners from one class to another, but conversations about how our curriculum, pedagogies, and assignment designs intentionally leverage this fact rarely occur. When undertaken collectively or reviewed as part of a collaborative discussion about where learning happens or how it happens in different parts of the program, suddenly the discussion changes. Rather than assuming that curricula are aligned, faculty often find that their assumptions need to be revisited altogether. Distinctions in how each member understands outcomes or in how members attempt to facilitate student learning emerge. More than a gap analysis is needed; instead, faculty find that they need to revisit intentional curricular design.

These distinctions in how different faculty understand outcomes are not always bad. Learners need not encounter the same pedagogical strategies in every class they take. Were programs to prescribe particular approaches to teaching, they would not only strip away the areas of strength for individual faculty members but also reduce students' opportunities to transfer their learning from one experience to another. Being aware of one another's approaches, however, positions us to help students make connections across learning experiences. Additionally, disciplines are defined as much by their focus of inquiry as they are by the debates about types of questions, methods, and theoretical frames within them. Gerald Graff (1993), in *Beyond the Culture Wars: How Teaching the Conflicts Can Revitalize American Education*, suggests that educators would serve their students better by introducing them to those points of contention. Doing so, he argues, would help students see how knowledge is produced. We needn't, therefore, eliminate disagreement about what outcomes mean or about how we teach our students. Consensus should not be confused with complete agreement. Rather, the goal is to become familiar enough with the range of experiences learners will have among colleagues that we can help them to see where they are encountering similar ideas or modes of working and where they are encountering new perspectives or approaches that can expand their own learning.

Curriculum maps can also create an isolated, linear notion of student learning that excludes a host of other possible ways of looking at learning environments. Curriculum maps are lenses. They enable us to see some parts of our learning environment better, but they exclude other elements of our learning environments, because they are designed to focus our attention on an individual program's curricular structures. Curriculum mapping can be far more productive if we broaden our scope and recognize the potential for creating other maps that focus our attention on other relationships. For example, maps might be developed that correlate general education outcomes with cocurricular experiences, as Elon University's Visual Experiential Transcript has done (Elon University, n.d.). Alternatively, maps might help faculty examine the relationships between general education outcomes and courses within a particular major. We might also map the learning we facilitate in a program to workforce expectations or particular career fields. Mapping in these different ways turns our attention to more than the linear, vertical pipelines of learning that we might see by limiting our investigations to our own programs. Mapping in layers, as it might be considered, produces a richer understanding of what and where our students are learning—or not—and equips us with insights about potential trouble spots that need to be addressed or potential points of synergy that we have overlooked. So if mapping is a way of seeing relationships among specific elements, what all can we map and why should we take the time to do it?

There are various reasons to undertake mapping. For example, curriculum maps help to reveal whether and where the planned curriculum addresses desired outcomes (Lancaster, 2015), leading to gap analysis that identifies where particular areas of learning may not be addressed. Is each outcome being addressed in the curriculum and where? Some have done curriculum mapping to explore the degree of coherence among learning outcomes at different levels, including course, program, and institution. Is learning associated with outcomes being reinforced and developed across learning experiences? Others have explored scaffolding of learning and levels of achievement in an effort to make the curricula not only a collection of courses students take but also a portrayal of a developmental journey (Bortman, 2013). Do students have multiple opportunities to develop learning associated with a particular outcome over the course of their experiences? Curriculum maps can provide a means to see connections and make them more transparent to students and faculty. Mapping allows visualization of how students develop knowledge and skills over time by moving from lower-level courses to upper-level courses and can also indicate points of "over teaching" or gaps in addressing outcomes (Liu, 2015, p. 24). Different approaches to mapping need to be thought of as different lenses. In the previous questions, each map constructed to learn about specific aspects of alignment or relationships between two different parts of the curriculum provides a distinct perspective on the curriculum.

The benefit of using multiple lenses to examine how we've built our learning environments is that our attention becomes focused on discrete parts. That focus allows us to make meaningful, targeted changes to our learning environments, because we have a clearer understanding of where problems are. For example, Ozdemir and Stebbins (2015) mapped university-wide learning outcomes to program competencies, course objectives, and learning assessments. The lens they constructed focused attention on the ways assignments in courses align to and support the larger learning goals of the institution. The reflective process of exploring alignment facilitated significant changes in courses and competencies as well as the structure of course objectives and assessments. This is just one example. There are many ways to look at mapping a curriculum. To take up another example, in a guide to curriculum review by the University of Western Ontario Teaching Support Center, McNay (2009) provides a resource that explores the difference between the hidden curriculum and written curriculum in terms of how learners actually experience that which faculty write down. McNay's materials encourage faculty to examine curricula in terms of that which is written, that which is actually taught, that which is learned by students, and that which is assessed. When approached in this way, faculty and staff create opportunities to identify the extent to which there is alignment among what outcomes imply about what learning is valued, what we actually do with students, what students seem to think they are supposed to learn, and what we are actually attempting to document. In some cases, mapping with this mind-set reveals a mismatch between an explicit curriculum and a hidden curriculum that emerges less in our documents and more in our practice. This is another distinct lens.

Maps, as the previous examples suggest, need not employ the traditional two-axis matrix of courses and outcomes, even if it is the most common form. In the University of Wisconsin–Waukesha and University of Wisconsin–Parkside work as part of the AAC&U Quality Collaboratives project, faculty participants used a process of color-coding learning outcomes for the bachelor of applied arts and sciences (BAAS) courses according to Bloom's taxonomy and AAC&U's VALUE rubrics, which were being used as assessment tools (Foy et al., 2014). The result enabled a visual mapping of courses that helped identify student skill gaps and progression difficulties, equipping students and advisers to scaffold student learning. They also made "spidergraphs" based on the DQP from the alignment maps, developing an overlay of the learning outcomes associated with the DQP, BAAS degree, and University of Wisconsin Shared Learning objectives. These visuals illustrated the unique and shared nature of the BAAS. The lesson to be drawn here is that maps can take a variety of forms, and the best form is the one that helps a particular group of faculty discern the potential strengths and weaknesses of the learning environment in which they work based on their own reflective questions on shared practice.

The traditional matrix, however, can also be manipulated and deployed to train a different type of lens on particular pieces of the learning environment. Table 4.3 presents a sample curriculum map that examines which learning outcomes are assessed, and how, in specific courses. In this map, the courses and learning outcomes are flipped, with courses on the horizontal axis and outcomes on the vertical axis, to allow for visualization of two important aspects, the development of knowledge and skills over time and the diversity of assessment approaches, which together culminate in a capstone project and reflective paper. Mapping to an assignment and specific assessment level is useful because faculty are then better able to identify areas where students struggle, which enables faculty to reassess their own approach to the teaching of the material (Skinner & Prager, 2015). Such work can easily be done in partnership with centers for teaching and learning. Yet courses rarely address every outcome in meaningful ways, and there is no course in which students move from being introduced to a learning outcome to mastering it. Further, Lancaster (2015) found that faculty are inclined to overstate their courses' connections to learning outcomes. As a result, faculty tend to indicate on maps that their courses address more learning outcomes than they actually do. Instead, as the NCA (2015) argues, curriculum mapping should focus on the courses in which learning is actually assessed through some sort of assignment.

This means our maps need multiple layers that reveal not just where outcomes are addressed, but how, how often, and in what ways students

TABLE 4.3
Curriculum Map of Assessments

	Course 1	**Course 2**	**Course 3**
Learning Outcome 1	Exam	Lab paper	Capstone project
Learning Outcome 2	Essay	Exam	Reflective paper
Learning Outcome 3	Oral presentation	Group assignment	Capstone project

demonstrate their learning. An example of a layered approach to viewing curriculum emerges in a series of case studies of outcomes-based education implementation in Canada. Liu (2015) share a process of curriculum mapping that involved a series of steps in which instructors indicated which outcomes were addressed in their courses in relation to provincial program standards. The instructors then analyzed course learning outcomes semantically to see if the expected level of performance was occurring based on verbs used in the outcome statements. This information was placed into a course outcome chart that was color coded to indicate which outcomes were assessed and where scaffolding occurred. Finally, to have a map of alignment to the provincial standards, the highest level of performance for each outcome was transferred to a separate chart to see a matrix of all the courses in a program. The net result was a complete picture of how courses scaffolded learning across the curriculum to enable students to reach the learning goals represented by the outcomes based upon verb analysis, thereby meeting the standard set out in the provincial document.

All this information about the extent to which learning environments are aligned as documented in maps represents little more than potential. What to do with the maps remains an issue. All too often they sit, inertly, in data management systems, receiving no attention and being of little ongoing practical use. A survey of the Association for Assessment of Learning in Higher Education (AALHE) Assess listserv members on curriculum mapping revealed that how to update or maintain the maps was an issue, as was the perceived cost or benefit of taking the time to make them (Miknavich, 2016). In Liu's (2015) case studies, exploring how a course or assessment actually met a specific learning outcome in the mapping process led to changes in learning outcomes and assessment plans, but knowing what the map would be used for before beginning the process was important. This lesson brings us back to the perfunctory completion of maps in solitary spaces. That isolated approach derives from the perceived absence of purpose, at least an absence of purpose outside of accreditation. Without purpose, mapping seems like just another bureaucratic add-on. When we provide a clear purpose for applying different lenses to our curricula, meaningful engagement can happen, just as the previous examples indicate.

Yet in each of these instances, the focus was on mapping the curriculum. As we noted previously, the lenses we choose enable us to see some pieces of the learning environment more clearly, because they screen out other pieces. This fact necessarily means that we don't see other learning spaces, such as the cocurricular. Thus, we need to remain aware of curriculum mapping as a way of seeing certain elements, mainly the curricula (hence the term *curriculum mapping*) without seeing others. Mapping a particular part of the learning experience puts a lens on what should be addressed if learning is not occurring at the level we desire, but addressing that problem may not be a matter of curricular revision or reform. Often, because the curriculum was mapped, the curriculum is what is changed. But what if other elements of the learning environment can help us to address the problems we see? In a learning systems paradigm, we need to be aware of all the spaces in which our students learn and explore the relationships among various elements, not just the curriculum within a specific program. So what happens to curriculum mapping if we add the elements of the learning systems paradigm as a framework to help us make sense of our work?

Curriculum Mapping in the Learning Systems Paradigm

Although we present each of the four elements of the learning systems paradigm in the following sections in a specific order, it is important to note that this does not imply a linear or step-like means to mapping. In practice, there will be significant overlap in the consensus-based and alignment processes, as well as consideration of the learner in terms of learner-centeredness. Although in some ways communication does come at the end, it should also be considered when thinking about who should be involved in reaching consensus of what is to be communicated along the way. Thus, as in most things, the reality of the work is much messier and more muddled than presented here, but there is value to explore what happens to curriculum mapping when we consider the practice in relation to each of the elements of the paradigm.

Consensus Based

As we argued in chapter 2, consensus-based approaches involve faculty-led conversations, reflections, and explorations with other campus divisions, employers, alumni, and others to develop a shared understanding and consensus on outcomes and the learning they represent. This shared understanding serves as the foundation on which outcomes can be revised for enhanced clarity and on which educational experiences can be designed. This means that we need to explore if there is agreement on what the learning outcomes on our maps mean, or if agreement exists about what we are even mapping. Through conversations, we can develop a shared understanding of what the outcomes mean for us, making mapping reflective regarding how courses address outcomes within a shared picture of the whole. We also need to decide what it means to say an outcome is addressed in a course—meaning is it one assignment? Is it a demonstration? Of what type? Is a single paper enough? What does it mean, in other words, to say that in this specific course students demonstrate their knowledge and skill regarding a particular learning outcome?

In the NCA LOC project, the learning outcomes were viewed as tools for "reflecting on the curriculum and pedagogies used by groups of faculty in their own departments" with "collective and collaborative reflection" as the core task (Marshall, 2015, p. 19). Such collective reflection requires exploring not just whether a program is constructed in ways to support student attainment of learning outcomes, but how. It is from these conversations about reaching shared meaning that Liu (2015) argues the conversations are more valuable than the mapping document produced. Yet, as K. Brown and Malenfant (2015) have made clear, there is much to gain from adding various partners to the conversation, especially librarians. Although faculty within a specific program may reach consensus on the intended educational design of their program, involving a variety of stakeholders can be very useful, as Kim (1993) argues, to help "make explicit the underlying dynamic structure" (p. 48) of the variety of elements and learning spaces within an institution. Broadening involvement in mapping improves alignment because it helps us see the connections and relationships among the various elements of the educational system.

Mapping can go even further than drawing together academic programs and librarians, and it needs to, if we recognize that students have opportunities to learn outside our courses. Student affairs, therefore, can be a powerful ally and valuable partner in mapping for a more complete picture of how and where our students learn. Involvement of student affairs in mapping is important because in many instances academic affairs and student affairs have created their own learning outcomes, in isolation, and may not have explored connections between the two. Without reaching a collective consensus across the institution's organizational groups, a view of the institution as a whole becomes difficult for faculty and staff, not to mention the learners who are left to navigate the space (LePeau, 2015). When student affairs participates in conversations, they can help determine sources of curricular and cocurricular support for learning and develop an understanding for how each unit within an institution contributes to student learning. Beyond student affairs, Studley (2016) argues it is also important to consider the world of work. Mapping how career development fits with other curricular experiences is important, as demonstrated by examples including the work of Hampden-Sydney College on engaged reflection and coordination of career pathways, the SUNY Works system-wide initiative integrating classroom and job experiences, or LaGuardia Community College's use of digital badges for career competencies (Studley, 2016). Thinking about curriculum mapping as consensus based within learning systems means that we need to think broadly about who should be involved in developing a collective understanding of how different parts of the system can support learning that is in line with the outcomes to which we are collectively striving.

Such cross-institution conversations take time. Taking the time to build consensus in the curriculum mapping process has yielded important benefits, as shown in the experience of Norfolk State University, where time helped create a "climate of collegiality, autonomy, flexibility, and transparency in order to successfully implement the complex processes of curriculum mapping" (Cuevas, Matveev, & Miller, 2010, p. 15). Working across divisions as Norfolk State University did makes great sense if we consider the very existence of institutional learning outcomes. If institutions designate outcomes that all graduates should demonstrate, the implication is that everybody in the institution (at least those having direct connections with students) plays a role in developing that learning. How often, though, do faculty sit down with librarians, student affairs staff, and community engagement professionals to think about how they, together, can provide students learning experiences to reach those outcomes in ways that scaffold and support them? Broad involvement is important because we have collective responsibility for degree-level learning outcomes (Studley, 2016). In a consensus-based approach to curriculum mapping, therefore, before mapping begins, reflective conversations need to take place to address the following questions:

- Purpose: What are we mapping and why?
- Scope: What parts of the learning system are included or left out by this approach?
- Participation: Who should be involved in the conversations?
- Form: How many layers do our maps need to address educational complexity?
- Limitations: What ways of seeing are we excluding in our maps?

Answering these questions together establishes a common frame of reference for discussion, which, in turn, promotes collective engagement in the mapping process. Broadening participation through intentionally collaborative approaches opens up possibilities for reconceiving the complementary roles played by curricula and cocurricula within the learning environment. In other words, it enables us to understand how each piece of the institution carries part of the load, but not all of it.

Aligned

It is not surprising that students claim they experience an incoherent education. We don't see the connections ourselves and most are only loosely formed. Many of those connections need to be tightened up. Birnbaum (1988) argues that under conditions of loose coupling, considerable time and effort is devoted to developing a shared construction of social reality through conversation and dialogue. For our purposes, that means a process is required in which those who work within the learning environment collaborate toward a common understanding of how their different roles and responsibilities add up to a complete experience for learners. It also signals that if the greatest benefit of DQP and Tuning has been the conversations of faculty exploring shared construction of learning, then the relationships prior to the discussions were loosely coupled. In our discussion of alignment in chapter 3, we connected alignment as an exploration of relationships to Weick's (1976) distinction between tightly and loosely coupled elements. Mapping promotes conversations that identify where parts of the learning environment are connected and enables faculty and staff to be more intentional in determining the degree of alignment. In some cases, alignment needs to be tight. In others, it can be loose. If we want to maximize the potential for student learning within the institution, we need to choose the degree to which different parts are aligned tightly and loosely and decide on the criteria determining a tight or loose alignment. Mapping is a tool that develops our awareness of where connections are so that we can decide which need to be tightly aligned and which can be loosely aligned. The learning systems paradigm, as we have said, encourages an approach to alignment that reflects collaboratively about the relationships among parts of our learning environments. Consensus makes that reflection collaborative. Once consensus is reached around purpose, scope, participation, form, and limitations of a mapping process, those involved can turn to addressing issues of tight and loose alignment.

Alignment involves curriculum mapping within a program but also considers issues of scaffolding, assignment design, mapping of career pathways, and cocurricular engagement. In curriculum mapping, faculty and staff align educational experiences throughout the institution for intentional integration, coherence, and fostering of multiple pathways. It means asking questions about connections between learning experiences akin to those outlined by Norm Jones and Daniel McInerney (2016) in relation to the role of a course within the major, general education program, and students' larger educational experience. It helps to make tighter connections for better alignment across our educational system. As Thomas Reeves (2006) suggests, eight factors need to be connected for a successful learning environment: goals, content, instructional design, learner tasks, instructor roles, student roles, technological affordances, and assessment. Reeves goes on to state that assessment is generally the most misaligned factor, a point we will turn to in the next chapter when addressing assignment design. The larger point made by Reeves is that there should be alignment not just within an assessment but between assessments and the other factors of the learning environment. We rarely have tight alignment, however, between the various elements and parts. Exploring alignment allows us to see the degree to which various parts of the learning system work together to achieve our shared goals.

Remember that, even if all mapping processes try to define relationships, mapping can take multiple forms. At Norfolk State University, curriculum maps explored alignment among five components—learning outcomes, courses, syllabi, instructional activities, and assessments of learning—to see whether students were provided with sufficient opportunities to develop each of the intended outcomes (Cuevas, Matveev, & Miller, 2010). Within work on pathways at community colleges, Brau and colleagues (2013) argue that for students to be successful and have a clear roadmap to learning and success, curricular, cocurricular, and student support services must all be aligned. Anderson (2002) argues that considerations of curricular alignment should include looking at relationships among learning outcomes, instructional activities, and assessments to examine interrelationships based on verbs and nouns. Looking at the verbs and nouns in learning outcomes in relation to descriptions of activities provides a means to look at what is stated versus what is actually done. To not only visualize but also hear alignment, Samuel Merritt University developed musical maps, providing an example of a way to hear and see the alignment of assignments, courses, and program- and institution-wide learning outcomes through the sonification of color-coded maps of learning. Tones were mapped to each outcome so an "in tune" curriculum represented alignment whereas an atonal one represented misalignment (Samuel Merritt University, n.d.). In another example of work with community colleges and student programs, the Office of Community College Research and Leadership developed a nine-step curriculum alignment module for exploring when, where, and how extensively workforce standards and curricular content associated with a program of study were aligned (Mordica & Nicholson-Tosh, 2013).

Discussions around curricular alignment encourage faculty recognition of the inherent collaborative nature of teaching and help develop awareness of how their courses participate in overall curricular goals. They also allow for developing shared understanding about how the various elements of an educational experience fit together, or may instead be misaligned. Questions regarding alignment may include the following:

- What are the various pieces of the educational system that need to come into alignment?
- How do courses build toward mastery and increasing expectations for particular outcomes?
- How do assignments and activities elicit student demonstrations of a specific learning outcome?
- How do different educational experiences contribute to the collective work of meeting learning outcomes?
- How do individual faculty contribute to this collective work in individual courses?
- How do various units within institutions contribute to student learning?
- Where is there a need for tight alignment among different elements of the learning experience?

Answering these questions allows for exploration of what it means to say that one part of an educational experience is aligned with or connected to another. It provides a means by which we can unpack what it means to scaffold, define how much support is needed, determine where and how often learning is reinforced, and even develop a shared picture of what it means to say that learning has been demonstrated. But it is all for naught if we have explored and/or built the educational experience without learners in mind.

Learner Centered

We can take the time to develop consensus, discuss relationships, and map them, but if we don't consider the learner experience of the curriculum, the impact may be minimal. Without an understanding of students' lived experience, our maps risk being idealistic representations of the learning environment that don't actually resemble students' experience of them. There are many institutions that outline an intentional, integrated, scaffolded learning experience without exploring how learners actually move through it. The two do not always correlate, which is why it is important to consider how learners move in and out of educational experiences and how what is mapped may hinder or support such movement. One way to explore misalignment between design and experience is to explore the actual course-taking patterns of students to see what paths through the curriculum they have already identified and shared with each other. Examining student course-taking patterns is important, as Paul Gaston (2015) points out, because most students do not move in a clearly identified path, but wind around and shift direction. A means to understand learner movement through an institution beyond examining course-taking patterns can be found in studying the work of Heileman, Babbit, and Abdallah (2015) on visualizing student flows through majors, through the entire institution, and where points of entry and exit may be seen. Communicating and sharing the maps with students and advisers can help students select courses not based on graduation needs or the timing of a course, but rather through scaffolding connections based on learning development (Cutrufello, 2013).

The learning systems paradigm encourages consideration of how the educational system reorganizes educational experiences around *all* students and their learning. Taking a learner view includes consideration of issues of equity, learning-focused transfer, alternative delivery models, flexibility in offerings, integration of prior learning assessment, provision for stackable credentials, and building multiple pathways. Instead of focusing on a single academic program and the structure of academic programs alone, we can also explore how students experience the curriculum, where else outside of the program's curriculum students learn, what in students' experience we might leverage for the program, and how we are ensuring equity. To what extent do students see connections between the program and other areas of learning? Focusing on the learners who move through the educational environment allows us to make realistic maps that can be useful to the students we serve. We can do that by making visible connections between student learning and other areas of experience. Learners need to see that their involvement in various activities is part of a cohesive program (Cuevas, Matveev, & Miller, 2010). Communicating to students is also important because the majority of learning outcomes are taught indirectly rather than explicitly, and what faculty thought they were doing and what students perceived to be the focus do not always add up (Sumsion & Goodfellow, 2004). Potentially more importantly, we need to involve students in the process because they informally advise each other and have already found ways through or to make connections.

Involving learners in discussions of mapping is also helpful to ensure that the maps are student friendly. At University College Dublin, students were involved in reform processes from the beginning via liaison positions and representation on committees as well as specially convened focus groups (McMahon & O'Riordan, 2006). This approach led to the students being highly supportive of the change process and approving of the new approach. Further, their involvement in the process also included "structured scrutiny of proposed curriculum documents" (McMahon & O'Riordan, 2006, p. 15). From that work, a more coherent picture of the learning experience emerged, allowing for integration and purpose in approach and structure (Gaston, 2015). The net results of engaging students in mapping like this are increased student understanding of why they follow a particular curriculum and how cocurricular experiences can support their learning; on a practical level, it leads to enhanced advising materials that help to communicate all this to students.

At the University of Birmingham, England, students did not see the connections between assessments in their programs and the larger program goals. Anke Buttner (2015) shares the experience of developing assessment maps to illustrate the relationships among assignments in a student-friendly context. Through student interviews and student focus group data, students described where they found information on assessment, what worked well, and what they needed to be more informed. In the focus groups, students also shared the information that would be useful to them on an assessment map, including items such as deadlines, assessment type, timing of feedback, expectations, and exemplars. Through conversations with students it was uncovered that without a view of timing of assessments, students had periods where they were flooded with assignment demands and times when nothing was expected of them, leading to a coordinated effort to spread out assessments, deadlines, and expectations more effectively across the program (Buttner, 2015). From learning about the student experience, faculty were able to ensure students received feedback in time to apply lessons learned to assignments in other courses that were connected or related, the visualization of which helped students see the interconnections between their work in one course and application of it in another. The University of Greenwich in London, England, provides another interesting example of keeping consideration of the student experience in mind. The tool "Map My Programme" utilizes Google motion charts to visually show the dates when assessments are set and handed in to help spread out and manage student workload. It even shows, in real time, the impact of any changes made to the timing of assessments (University of Greenwich, n.d.). The project included working across five institutions to develop a means to visualize assessment and feedback to inform program design. The value of the tool is that it serves as a catalyst for discussions in terms of planning and timing of assessment. Further, student feedback on the tool has led to valuable information on how best to time feedback in ways that it can usefully inform future work (Kerrigan, Headington, & Walker, 2011).

Maps are always particular to specific unique combinations of contextual factors. Each institution has its own learners who come from distinct communities with their own challenges. That means a map from one institution will never work for another, even if their curricula are identical. The distinct learner population will always dictate how an institution is designed. Maps of a community college experience may need to include accommodations for students to step in and step out in ways that a research institution of "traditional" students would not. Further, although some institutions are able to implement a lock-step, student cohort approach to curriculum, dictating when students take specific courses and in what order, others are not. Some institutions may have students that step in and step out, have the freedom to select any course of their choosing to take at any time, and may listen to fellow students to make course-taking order decisions. Although it is important to communicate with advisers, it is equally important to ensure that learners are aware of the information and that in the curriculum mapping process, learners are either involved or considerations of actual student experience are routinely raised in the mapping process. Questions to consider related to learner-centered mapping include the following:

- In what ways have learners been involved or consulted in the mapping process?
- What assumptions are there about how learners experience the curriculum, and how do we know if they are correct?
- What paths and patterns already exist in terms of learner movement through the curriculum?
- Where do learners think they have acquired the learning outcomes of interest? And was the experience within a course or somewhere else?
- Are learners aware of the connections among their learning experiences? In what ways?
- Is the map representative of our learners' lived experiences?

Taking the time to consider learners and their experience of the learning environment in the curriculum mapping process can help identify where there may be tight alignment we are not aware of and where there is loose alignment in places that we may have assumed were more tightly aligned. Involving learners in the mapping process also serves as a means to broaden the consensus on learning outcomes and provides discussion points around unpacking implicit design of educational environments. Considering learners also ensures that the maps made are not idealistic representations of curriculum. Learner involvement also speaks to the need to ensure broad communication regarding the understandings developed—and intentionality documented—from the mapping process.

Communicated

Communication and collaboration with learners and other audiences through transparent discussions around outcomes and the overall educational system work to make the implicit explicit. Communication involves exploration and integration with advising, alternative transcripts, admissions, and employers. Instead of creating maps that stay within assessment management systems, are used for reporting, are never updated, and eventually disappear, ask what happens to the map. How are we sharing the information? Are learners aware of the map and do they recognize the links among outcomes, courses, and assignments? Do learners understand the rationale for program structures, prerequisites, and assignment sequences? Can students make connections between their learning elsewhere and the learning within the program—and vice versa?

Once maps are developed, they need to be shared widely and often. Without such communication, we are not likely to see any impact from the process of putting lenses to our learning environments. McMahon and O'Riordan (2006) found that in an aligned curriculum structure, students were able to make better informed curriculum choices, and they reported that knowing the intended outcomes for each course enabled better choices to be made between optional elements of the curriculum. Beyond the potential communication advantages for students, maps allow institutions a mechanism by which to communicate their educational intentions and design (Lancaster, 2015). They can provide an overview of the structure of the learning environment and help those working within it to see how they contribute to the shared learning outcomes of the degree. It allows a means to communicate the connections among various elements and address why learners should be engaging in the various activities as well as how each supports their learning. Curriculum maps can serve as advising tools that provide learners with an overview of the role of each course in the curriculum and why some experiences need to occur in a particular order.

Finally, from the shared consensus developed in the mapping process and collective understanding of the various parts of the learning environment, their relationships, and how learners experience the education they foster, faculty also have a means to communicate with each other. In orientation of new faculty for instance, the maps can be used to express the roles of specific courses within a larger structure. Further, as Liu (2015) indicates, the maps help instructors diversify their assessment approaches, create opportunities for integrated evaluation where two instructors collaborate and use a common assignment to evaluate learning, and help students see the connections between the two courses. In the case of Kansas City Kansas Community College, determining the linkages between assignments in specific courses and the learning outcomes of the college allowed for the creation of competency maps permitting faculty, students, and advisers to make course selections based on areas of strength and weakness for specific students in relation to the learning outcomes of interest (Hutchings, 2014).

Questions to consider related to communication include the following:

- Where are curriculum maps located and how are they shared?
- Are the maps easily accessible for multiple audiences?
- In what ways might the maps be used and how might possible uses require involvement of different participants in the process of mapping?
- What is the plan for communicating the curriculum maps to different groups?
- When feedback is received on the maps, what is the process of revision or updating?

Exploring the various uses of curriculum maps can help to determine potential audiences such as academic advising, career services, student affairs, librarians, students, related programs, general education committees, and others with whom we need to share the maps. Building into the process an active dialogue of multiple audiences can help to move the maps from being static documents to living points of discussion, ones that can actively inform and shape practice.

Broadening Beyond the Curriculum

In this chapter we have provided a description of ways in which curriculum mapping has been undertaken in beneficial and in not so beneficial ways. We have applied the four elements of the learning systems paradigm to curriculum mapping and offered examples of the possibilities that can occur from such an approach along with questions to help guide practice, but we have remained within a view of mapping the *curriculum*. In a learning system we necessarily must take a broader view. We need to think about mapping in general and consider what happens when we map within a learning *system*. What happens when we begin to make connections and map across the curriculum, cocurriculum, and other activities?

Cross-Walk Development

In work with DQP and Tuning, faculty and staff make a distinction between cross-walking and mapping that is important for us to consider within a broader view of the educational environment. Whereas mapping provides a means to indicate visual relationships between two or more elements in a progression of development, cross-walking provides a means to outline how one thing is like another. For instance, which of an institution's specific learning outcomes are the same as those in the DQP and which are not? Which specific program learning outcomes for history are the same as those outlined by the AHA disciplinary document and which are different? A cross-walk allows a means to indicate how certain frameworks are the same as or different from another, whether the frameworks are those from AAC&U's ELOs, the DQP, certification standards, credential requirements, accreditation requirements, employability skills frameworks, specific occupational skill standards, or the Common Core. The point being that a cross-walk allows institutions to indicate how their work, which may be documented in a map, is related to the broader learning frameworks and requirements in the field. A case study of McKendree University in Lebanon, Illinois by Emily Teitelbaum and Kathryn Schultz (2016) provides an illustrative example.

McKendree University participated in a DQP project through the Council of Independent Colleges consortium on DQP work. In their DQP project, there were various frameworks with which their institutional efforts needed to align, including their own institution-wide student learning outcomes, the proficiency statements of the DQP, AAC&U's ELOs, and the National Collegiate Athletic Association's Life in the Balance Key Attributes. Each of the different frameworks was related to a project or initiative occurring on the campus and a cross-walk was needed for how they addressed or were related to each other. The cross-walk was constructed to "explore the relationship between the learning proficiencies of each initiative they were involved in against McKendree's SLOs [student learning outcomes]" and to "align the outcomes of the various initiatives in order to further refine the institutional SLOs" to help identify a unifying language between the initiatives (Teitelbaum & Schultz, 2016, p. 5). The DQP served as an external point of validation for McKendree's learning outcomes and helped to identify areas of strength and uniqueness for the institution. In part it is through cross-walks that the DQP provides a point of connection for integrating initiatives across an institution. Considerations of cross-walking are also extremely important for community colleges that sit at the intersection of many sometimes competing points of connection. Maps created by community colleges may include consideration of work-based learning and cross-walks to certifications, employability skills

TABLE 4.4
Cross-Walk Template

Institution-Specific Learning Outcomes	DQP	AAC&U ELOs	Programmatic Accreditation Requirements	Employability Skills Frameworks	Certification Requirements
Learning Outcome 1					
Learning Outcome 2					
Learning Outcome 3					

frameworks, and occupational standards in addition to transfer partner learning outcomes. Table 4.4 presents a template for cross-walking a few of the many possible points of connection.

Cross-walking can provide a mechanism for indicating how various ongoing and current activities meet the needs of different structures, such as state requirements, accreditation boards, or external standards. It can also provide a means for those within institutions to see how their work intersects and connects (or in some cases doesn't) to various external frameworks.

Mapping

Once we move past considering mapping as bound to exploring the curricula, we can begin to examine what we can map within a learning environment. The easiest point of entry is to map the cocurricula, but Table 4.5 provides an outline of possible other elements to consider as well. In Table 4.5, there are elements such as prior learning, required courses, recommended or elective courses, activities and experiences that support learning outcomes, work-based learning experiences, certifications or licensures that connect with the learning outcomes, possible career paths, and learner-identified experiences that connect with learning outcomes. Such an approach allows for a wider lens to how various pieces fit together and can support specific learning outcomes and/or the integration of learning throughout the educational journey.

Another way to conceive of mapping that grew out of work with DQP and Tuning is to consider the entirety of a degree. For instance, how does general education connect with and support major courses and how does

TABLE 4.5

Learning Environment Mapping Matrix

Learning Outcomes	Prior Learning	Required Courses	Other Required Courses, Recommended Electives	Activities and Experiences That Support Learning Outcomes	Work-Based Learning Experiences	Certifications and Licensures	Possible Career Paths	Learner-Identified Experiences
Learning Outcome 1	Prior learning that is accepted in relation to specific outcomes	Courses that address specific outcomes	Other courses that support and reinforce specific outcomes	Cocurricular elements that support specific outcomes	Employment and other experiences that reinforce specific outcomes	Possible certifications connected to the outcomes	Possible career paths related to the map	Elements identified by learners as supporting learning outcomes
Learning Outcome 2								

the cocurriculum support both general education and the major? In addition, what sorts of career paths are available from such connections? Utah State University provides an example of how such integration is possible. In a case study of Utah State University's (USU's) work with both DQP and Tuning, Natasha Jankowski and Norm Jones (2016) explored the integration that occurs when a focus is on degrees as a whole instead of the parts. USU examined the entire curriculum and how the university collectively supported students. Changes were made throughout the institution to better align efforts in support of student learning from initial student entry in orientation, to advising and first-year experiences, through general education, the major, and to completion. The maps created through the conversations were utilized as advising tools, and involvement of librarians aided support for exploring the relationship between information literacy efforts on the part of the library in relation to course-based experiences. Further, the map development included student input and a study of the student experience at USU to find points of perceived disconnect. In addition, mapping at USU allowed for intentional integration of HIPs, involvement in the Multi-State Collaborative, use of AAC&U's VALUE rubrics, and other related initiatives to form a comprehensive view for the entire institution and its students on what it means for USU to foster Citizen Scholars (Jankowski & Jones, 2016). Table 4.6 provides an example of the elements that could be considered in such degree-level conversations.

Another example of mapping at a degree-level comes from Salt Lake Community College. Adam Dastrup (2015), a faculty member in the Geosciences Department, used the DQP to map associate degree–level learning outcomes to the Geography for Life Standards outlined by the National

TABLE 4.6
Degree-Level Mapping Matrix

Learning Outcomes	General Education	Major Courses	Activities and Experiences That Provide Support	Possible Career Paths
Learning Outcome 1	General education courses that support the learning outcomes	Courses that address specific outcomes	Cocurricular elements that support specific outcomes	Possible career paths related to the map
Learning Outcome 2				

Council for Geographic Education and the National Geographic Society, as well as the Department of Labor's geospatial technology competency model, statewide articulation agreements, and program learning outcomes. Dastrup (2015) writes, "The result of the DQP audit and degree mapping was a restructuring of the Geography AS [associate of science] degree that provided students a strong academic foundation grounded in core principles of geography and geospatial technology that aligned with national standards and competencies" (para. 11). Through the mapping process, several new courses on geospatial technology were added, and courses that did not provide pathways to either completion or transfer were removed. The resulting curriculum develops student learning strategically and explicitly. Within the revised curriculum, assignments were modified and a new capstone was created to help students demonstrate their body of knowledge and associated skill sets. Along the way to program completion, Dastrup (2015) built in a certificate to assist students with marketability and examined the mapping matrix to determine program strengths for recruiting.

An additional example worth exploring of the potential to move an institution from being composed of various units to becoming an integrated learning system is that of the University of Central Oklahoma (UCO). Beginning in 2007, UCO set out to develop a structure to capture student learning as students moved through the institution (Hynes, Pope, Loughlin, & Watkins, 2015). A model was created for curricular, cocurricular, and extracurricular activities, with a focus on developing the entire student within a transformative educational experience. A framework was developed to move the entire campus toward being a learning community around a shared conception of transformative education. The tool that resulted is the Student Transformative Learning Record (STLR), which is designed to capture, assess, and document student learning in ways that allow students to then present their strengths in a reflective e-portfolio. The process begins with the creation of an assignment or cocurricular activity that is tagged to one or more of six central tenets of transformative learning; students then complete the assignment, event, or project, and related student materials are assessed by faculty and staff using a common rubric. Student engagement is indicated as exposure, integration, or transformation. Students are then able to view the assessments and activities in a student dashboard and can select examples of their work across all experiences to develop and maintain an e-portfolio. Students curate their work and can also provide supplemental documentation in the form of multimedia images of artwork, research posters, sound bites, music, videos, writing, reflections, or any other assessed evidence of their knowledge and skills (Hynes et al., 2015).

Concluding Thoughts

DQP and Tuning provide reference points, not prescriptive mandates, and as reference points, they provide a point of alignment for learning. The process of responding to the DQP and frameworks generated through Tuning encourages shared understandings of what and how a given learning environment facilitates student learning. As the NCA (2015) states of its own discipline-specific work, "Activities prove to be most productive when undertaken as collective reflection regarding not just *whether* but *how* a program is or is not constructed to support student attainment of learning in communication" (p. 3). Working with them establishes a common vision of the different structures institutions have installed, the nature of their contribution to student learning, and the ways in which productive synergies can emerge across those structures. It is important to know that, although the DQP and Tuning provide tools for starting these conversations, the VALUE rubrics have also proved a useful resource to explore connections through shared language (Association of American Colleges & Universities, 2017; Jardeleza et al., 2013). In each case, the role of these tools has been to provide a common reference point around which conversations about how we organize and integrate our learning environments can develop.

Using the learning systems paradigm to examine curriculum mapping as well as expand the view to mapping more broadly helps to move the process to conversations of shared meaning-making and away from more administrative concerns. It stimulates a strategy for creating integrated, coherent learning environments. Moreover, it prompts exploration of the relationships among various elements of the learning system in ways that break down isolated, disconnected silos. What has been needed to explore the connections through mapping is a "whole new outlook on the nature, structures and even purpose of curriculum documents—in essence, a paradigm shift" (McMahon & O'Riordan, 2006, p. 14). We cannot simply send our learners to another course, expert, or learning experience to gain skills and expect them on their own to integrate and find coherence in what they have learned in different places (Newman et al., 2014). The myth that students will create coherence for themselves derives from fundamental assumptions about both the ease of transferring knowledge and the specialized roles each faculty member, staff person, and student plays. As we have said throughout this book, transfer of knowledge, an ability essential to finding coherence across disparate learning experiences, has been the greatest challenge for learners. Our assumptions about specialization within the system typically hinder our abilities to see how our roles complement one another in the student experience. We should not ask our students to do what we are not willing to do ourselves or make connections we do not see. That is why it is necessary to explore hidden assumptions and ensure that the maps are not static documents for reporting. Rather, they need to be strategies for cutting through those assumptions so that our institutions convey coherence instead of assuming it.

Located in Orlando, Florida, Valencia College's experience exemplifies this idea. For Valencia College, mapping helped to uncover assumptions held about how students learn and what they are capable of learning (Educational Policy Improvement Center, 2011). Their process revealed that there is not a single strategy that leads to student success; instead, it is the collaborative work of the college as a whole working to align content, assessment, developmental education, and the cocurriculum into a meaningful learning experience for students that yields the positive results for which we hope. Maps are living documents and are more than administrative processes. A process like Valencia College's demonstrates the potential for mapping to achieve "a higher level of curriculum understanding. The process should not be viewed as a desk review but as a sharing exercise and a collaborative tool" (Liu, 2015, p. 26). Undertaken with that attitude, it can be a transformative area of work.

Maps, however, pose a danger. Let's return to our journey metaphor. When we travel from one place to another frequently, we can stop looking at our map and become reliant on knowing a particular and favorite way of making the trip. We can become so accustomed to our route that we forget there are other possible ways of getting to our destination. That is precisely what happened to a group of faculty we met at a conference. They had mapped their program and discovered that a senior-level class posed perpetual problems. The students were confused as to how it fit with the rest of their classes and did not understand how it meant to contribute to their learning. The faculty seemed uncertain about its role and struggled to make sense of it. But they kept trying. They made changes to the class repeatedly, only to end up with the same result. On a train from Philadelphia, the chair realized that dropping the class was an option. Just because the map said that the course was part of the curriculum did not mean they had to keep it.

In this case, the faculty had allowed the familiar route indicated on the map to blind them to the other possible routes they might take. The actual learner experience of the curriculum was pointing them to a problem with that course, but the map had become overdetermined. Looking at the map, the faculty saw only the old route, so the map became a blinder that caused them to wear deep grooves into the road from which they had struggled to divert onto new roads. Whether they examine the alignment of curricula, the synergies between academic and nonacademic programs, the patterns of students through their learning experiences, or the degree to which a program prepares students for employment, maps in the learning systems paradigm are stimulants to thought and reflection. Maps help us to discover new roads and byways that can enhance and strengthen learning environments for our students.

5

APPLYING THE PARADIGM
TO ASSIGNMENT DESIGN

s we discussed in the previous chapter, mapping includes the role of assignments in eliciting student demonstrations of the learning outcomes of interest. But assignments are not often shared or discussed, let alone examined for their relationship to learning outcomes. As Black and William (1998) argue, faculty rarely review the assessments they use, nor do they discuss them critically with peers, leading to little reflection on what is actually being assessed. Although there has been some movement and growing interest in sharing assignments and activities from experienced teachers in K–12 (Singer, 2015), collaborative discussions of assignments in higher education are rarer. In Tagg's (2003) work on the learning paradigm, he argues that students should be engaged in completing meaningful and visible tasks that involve authentic performances that are connected over time—in other words, scaffolded, authentic assignments. Assignment work in an authentic learning environment requires "observations of student engagement and analysis of artifacts produced in the process of completing the tasks" (Reeves, 2006, p. 304), meaning the assignments students undertake in their learning journey are ways of helping students work through the substance of what we ask them to learn. Assignments, in short, enable not only us but also our students to see student learning. Assignments are a means of assigning a grade, as faculty are well aware, and not all assignments are assessments, nor should they be. But they can also be constructed as powerful tools for meaningfully engaging students in active learning (Bain, 2004) and providing evidence of student demonstration of learning. However, as argued in the work by the NCA (2015), if assignments are not aligned to learning outcomes, then students are not given opportunities to demonstrate expected learning and we end up developing a separate structure in order to assess student learning, potentially divorced from the teaching and learning process occurring in a variety of learning spaces. As Adelman (2015) argues, and as evidenced in the DQP, learning outcomes should include operational verbs from which assignments can be designed, making connections intentional and coherent. However, tying assignments to learning outcomes persists as a challenge in creating tightly aligned learning experiences for students.

Working through that challenge brings clear benefits. In a study of the DQP's impact on the field, we found that faculty became enthusiastic about assessment from conversations regarding assignment design (Jankowski & Giffin, 2016a). Although work with the DQP brought increased clarity around learning outcomes and the ways different groups contribute to their attainment, it also supported a shift in the field to a greater focus on assignments as the basis of assessment. In a survey of provosts, almost 70% of institutions reported the use of classroom-based performance assessments as a means to address institution-level learning outcomes (Kuh, Jankowski, Ikenberry, & Kinzie, 2014). When asked which approaches to assessment were most meaningful, provosts indicated classroom-based assessment (Kuh et al., 2014). The shift to focusing on assignments also appeared in a more recent survey, with 96% of respondents reporting that use of the DQP stimulated faculty work on design or refinement of assignments (National Institute for Learning Outcomes Assessment, 2016a). Reports indicated that student performance on assignments increased, too, as have the connections between the assignment and the end goal of learning (Jankowski & Giffin, 2016b). In a survey of assignment design workshop participants, or charrettes as NILOA calls such workshops, 80% of faculty participants stated that the assignment workshop (which we will discuss later) helped them see their assignments through the eyes of their students more clearly, 78% revised additional assignments, and 59% claimed they were more aware of aligning their assignments with desired institutional outcomes (Jankowski & Giffin, 2016a). These findings are reinforced by the work of McCullough and Jones (2014), who conducted a qualitative investigation of faculty satisfaction with assessment through three institutional case studies composed of interviews with 43 faculty members. They found that satisfaction varied across programs but that faculty across the institutions reported that multiple challenging assessments throughout and across courses, as well as in the senior project or capstone experience, were strengths of effective assessment practices. A point of commonality in all of the work is that focusing on assignments provided a mechanism to actively and meaningfully engage faculty in assessment in ways that they found valuable and exciting. Further, the work of the Multi-State Collaborative to Advance Quality Student Learning is built from in-class assignments which are then evaluated by trained faculty (Crosson & Orcutt, 2014). In a report on the work of VALUE built from the Multi-State Collaborative, AAC&U (2017) state that "the work of VALUE . . . contributed to a significant shift in faculty mindset about assessment by centering the assessment conversation in faculty member's most important work—in courses, in their own assignments, and in direct relationship with teaching and learning" (p. 31). How do we get there? In this chapter we explore the work of NILOA in relation to assignments and apply the learning systems paradigm's four elements to assignment design. We begin with providing an overview of the work NILOA has done with DQP and Tuning as it relates to assignments.

In our work with DQP and Tuning within the AHA and NCA, faculty were interested in thinking intentionally about what the learning outcomes look like on the ground, in their classes. NILOA developed a model assignment design workshop called a charrette to support this growing interest as an outgrowth of its work with the DQP (National Institute for Learning Outcomes Assessment, 2016b). The strategy emerged in response to requests by faculty for help in actualizing their work with DQP and Tuning. As faculty reviewed the proficiencies in the DQP and those that emerged through Tuning processes, the question routinely came—what does this look like in a class, in the form of an assignment? How do we create an assignment that is designed to intentionally elicit student learning of the outlined proficiencies? How do we modify our existing assignments to better align to the DQP- or Tuning-developed outcomes? Instead of attempting to design assignments to meet the proficiencies from scratch, NILOA brought faculty together from across the United States in assignment charrettes to modify their existing assignments so that they aligned more tightly with DQP and learning outcomes developed through Tuning. The term *charrette* derives from a practice in nineteenth-century architecture education in which designs were gathered on a deadline, with teams furiously adding finishing touches to models as their models were wheeled away—the work was collaborative, peers learned from and supported each other, and teams had to complete work in a limited amount of time. The use of the term in the context of assignment design speaks to the brief but intense work of collaborating with faculty peers on the refinement and alignment of assignments to learning outcomes. In the NILOA assignment charrettes, faculty collectively discuss how assignments reflect the array of proficiencies that constitute a degree in an intentional learning environment (Ewell, 2013; Johnson & Schuck, 2014). The charrettes result in revised assignments that are designed to provide opportunities for students to demonstrate learning aligned directly to outcomes of interest.

NILOA has been working with groups of faculty, staff, and students from over 400 campuses to revise and strengthen assignment alignment and make available an online library of high-quality, peer-reviewed assignments linked to DQP outcomes. The assignments and accompanying reflective memos are shared by faculty from a wide range of fields and institutional types, all of which are committed to advancing and documenting student learning (www .assignmentlibrary.org). The interactive library, which carries a Creative Commons license and invites users into dialogue with faculty, builds on and further stimulates ongoing institutional efforts, engaging faculty and staff at the grassroots level in ways that make a difference in the classroom (National Institute for Learning Outcomes Assessment, 2014). The online library provides a mechanism to highlight these efforts and elevate the scholarly nature of the work with assignments in the library including a scholarly citation and faculty receiving a letter for inclusion in their promotion and tenure review process. The assignments range from introductory courses to capstone projects; from general education to discipline-specific courses; and from different modalities, including online.

The materials in the assignment library go through a three-stage review process involving the NILOA project team and three to six faculty peers from various fields. Whether through the in-person assignment charrettes or through the online review process, faculty receive a variety of feedback on their assignment regarding how to better align their assignment to learning outcomes of interest. After reviewing the feedback and making revisions, faculty field test the assignments in their classes, gather student feedback on the assignment, revise again, and resubmit their materials to NILOA where they undergo a final review to make sure all required elements are included. However, assignment design is an iterative process, and many of the materials continue to go through revision and refinement with updates provided along the way. Authors are encouraged to submit updated versions of their materials and to continue reporting how the assignment is being used in their classrooms, and viewers are encouraged to comment on how the assignments have been adapted within their own practice or may have informed their own assignment design. This is important to note, because the assignments in the library are not meant to be downloaded and implemented without change, but instead are meant to provide ideas and invite dialogue and conversation on assignment design.

An additional feature of the assignment library is the inclusion of a series of featured assignments that include video clips, student work samples, and reflective commentary from colleagues and employers. We plan to continue featuring assignments, add additional tags to the library to enable users to better search by project including alignment with VALUE rubrics, and secure employer endorsement for various assignments, as well as include employer-developed assignments in the library in the form of employer chal-lenges. In addition, toolkits are available that pull from the collective knowl-edge developed from NILOA's assignment work that outlines how to engage in assignment charrettes through a facilitated approach (National Institute for Learning Outcomes Assessment, 2016b). Unfacilitated charrettes (National Institute for Learning Outcomes Assessment, 2016d) are also available, including language and examples of how to invite faculty to participate; information on how to advertise and structure the event; and agendas, forms, and additional resources, along with examples from various institutions.

While the assignments in the library were aligned to the DQP, any learning framework serves the same function. As noted previously, both AHA and NCA have utilized the charrette approach to provide support for faculty engaged with their discipline-specific outcomes, with some members carrying their work forward to submit assignments to the library. As such, any set of learning outcomes can serve in the same way; they needn't be over-arching frameworks offered up as tools for larger national conversations. The outcomes produced by a single institution for a general education program is a learning framework for that institution, just as the outcomes developed by an institution's sociology or marketing program provide frameworks for those majors or minors. What that means is the charrette model for stimu-lating reflection offers a valuable tool for institutions and their programs to promote similar conversations internally.

Complicating Alignment

Biggs (1996) wrote of the need for constructive alignment between learning activities or the things that faculty do through pedagogy and course design to support student attainment of outcomes, assessments, and intended learning outcomes more than 20 years ago. At this point, his idea is well embedded in the scholarship of teaching learning and drives many faculty members' activi-ties. More recently, Biggs and Tang (2011) have provided a more recursive look at the relationship among the three elements, and others have added the importance of exploring the relationship among assessment, learning outcomes, and criteria used to evaluate student learning. In most instances, the relationship between various elements has been presented as depicted in Figure 5.1. In NILOA's work with faculty from institutions participating in the Multi-State Collaborative to Advance Quality Student Learning, the ele-ments of interest include the assignment and its relationship to the VALUE rubrics used to evaluate student demonstrations of learning. In this instance, the focus is on the relationships among the evaluative criteria, supportive

Figure 5.1. Common depiction of learning outcomes and assessment relationships.

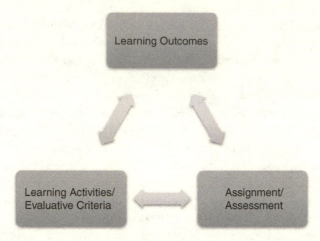

activities and assessments, and learning outcomes. In principle, this relational arrangement of the elements of assignment design are sound, ensuring that assignments are actually eliciting the learning that our outcomes intend for students and that the criteria by which the demonstrations are evaluated are intentionally connected to the learning outcomes and assignment design. The problem is that, in practice, the means by which the three elements are brought into constructive alignment are rarely as neat as the now common triangle illustration might suggest.

For example, Hill (2009) shares an experience of using Biggs's (1996) constructive alignment approach in a case study of the process to constructively align a business course. Hill argues that alignment among the three pieces of the triangle depicted in Figure 5.1 is based on the premise that students will be more engaged if they understand what the intended learning outcomes are (his theory of change), raising issues related to the element of communication within the learning systems paradigm. Alignment is actualized, as a result, by coupling clear communication with the associated learning activities. The initial step in the process was to identify employment characteristics of IT business analysts by engaging in discussions with employers. What they learned was that the program did not include opportunities for students to practice their skills in a variety of circumstances. That input prompted faculty to review the learning outcome statements, consider issues of pedagogy, and revise assignments. Hill (2009) claims that faculty unexpectedly found presenting the previous information to students not only helped raise student awareness of the relevance of the assignments, but also led to faculty realizing they needed further clarification of the learning outcomes. Thus, a shift in one area of the relationship triangle led to changes in the others. And yet a problem emerged; although the three parts of Biggs's model were more clearly aligned, students still found their experiences were fragmented, and they struggled to grasp the entire programmatic picture. The faculty concluded that student awareness of the curriculum in a holistic sense and connections between the assignments within the program were needed. They determined that the focus on constructive alignment within an individual course had still resulted in a sense of disconnected experiences, because the alignment had not been undertaken in relation to the whole of the experience. Hill (2009) claims that constructive alignment has potential, but significant benefits will not be seen until the whole curriculum approaches alignment. Enter the DQP and its focus on degree-level learning.

DQP proficiency statements are written to elicit demonstrations of learning through assignments embedded in learning experiences across the entirety of a degree. In the documented processes of reviewing the DQP, faculty engage in conversations about "curricular revisions, distinctions between degree levels, the relationship between general education and the major, redesign of program review, design and alignment of assignments, and considerations of alternative documentation of learning" (Jankowski & Giffin, 2016b, p. 5). In other words, faculty who have been involved with the DQP have examined assignment design within the larger context of student learning as a whole rather than isolating it in the confines of individual courses. In his look at assessment within the DQP, Peter Ewell (2013) writes that the use of action verbs in the DQP statements provides initial guidance to faculty in constructing both assignments and questions to elicit student demonstration of mastery through an entire degree. Instead of being an add-on, Ewell (2013) argues that assessment becomes embedded throughout the curricular and cocurricular experience; it is integrated into practice and throughout the learning environment. Faculty have responded favorably to these ways of thinking about the functional role of assignments within curricula. We have seen increasing interest in faculty-led peer review sessions where assignments are not reviewed only in relation to their alignment with learning outcomes but also in relation to the role of a single assignment within the larger frame of the degree (Hutchings, Jankowski, & Ewell, 2014), exploring how assignments scaffold over time and how introductory assignments lead to capstone experiences.

Pat Hutchings (2016), one of the developers of the charrette model, provides examples of curriculum mapping and alignment from a faculty-eye view, making the argument that "one thing we have learned thus far is that for many faculty the value of alignment . . . comes most powerfully into view when they begin sharing assignments with one another and talking about what they see" (p. 8). When NILOA has gathered faculty together, it has done so across disciplines and institutions, and when assignment conversations are conducted at a single institution, they occur across multiple departments. In part, cross-campus conversations are beneficial for seeing the connections between courses, foregrounding the learning outcomes in the design process, and revealing areas of shared concern where learners struggle across the learning environment. Foregrounding the learning outcomes is important, because in the design of assignments, other concerns, such as whether the assignment is interesting or innovative, may have been the focus of design, not that the assignment is well aligned with learning outcomes. Hutchings (2016) further argues that alignment is multidirectional, requiring many views, making the process of alignment not a task to be completed but an ongoing process of negotiation. Figure 5.2 provides an image of the negotiation among the assignment, the learning outcomes, and the evaluative criteria, through a process that is cognitive, collective, and ongoing.

The process of negotiation that we have seen with assignment conversations has been one that is iterative and recursive. Instead of beginning with learning outcomes, the process begins with the assignment. In a collaborative group, faculty review an assignment and its relationship to learning outcomes,

Figure 5.2. Assignment design relationships.

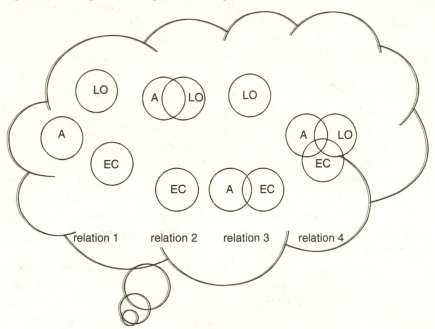

Note. Terms are *alignment* (A), *learning outcomes* (LO), and *evaluative criteria* (EC).

in our case those of the DQP, but remember that any well-conceived learning framework would work, such as that developed by AHA or NCA from their Tuning projects or locally crafted outcomes documents. Conversations about what students will actually do to demonstrate their learning spark insights into refinement and clarification of the learning outcomes. Discussions move from relation 1 in Figure 5.2 to relation 2. In the process of revising the learning outcome, faculty become aware of the need to revise the instructions of the assignment so that tighter relationships are created between the assignment and the learning outcomes. Then the conversations move into discussions of how the assignment is evaluated—what are the criteria by which this assignment will be judged? In those conversations, relation 3 in Figure 5.2, faculty discover the need to revise the assignment, and, through conversations about what is being evaluated, the learning outcome again needs to be revised. The process is one of bringing each of the pieces more closely together and navigating the changing relationships among the three. As two of the three pieces are aligned, it can create misalignment with the third—hence the messy process of repeatedly revising and checking what we have described. Further, once the assignment is shared with students and feedback on their perceptions of the criteria obtained, additional revision of instructions, learning outcomes, and evaluative criteria occur in an iterative process. In the case of the Multi-State Collaborative to Advance Quality Student Learning work, the process begins with considering the assignment in relation to a shared rubric as opposed to a learning outcomes framework, but the discussions and negotiations among the elements remain the same.

The net result of such persistence is that faculty discussions end up with an assignment, learning outcome, and evaluative criteria that looks much more like relation 4 in Figure 5.2. Their conversations revolve around a series of questions addressing an essential issue: how we know that an assignment is designed to elicit student demonstration of the learning outcome. The process is more complicated because the conversation takes place relative to the degree, so what is the role of this assignment in relation to the degree? How is it connected with other assignments so that they scaffold over time? What learning is it building on from general education? What other learning experiences are assumed in its design? What other learning outcomes does it require students to utilize, ones that they may need to use but not be evaluated on? How much support is needed for them to complete the assignment so that it is an accurate demonstration of their knowledge and skills? Such a process is muddied and negotiated in ways that the opening triangle of relations conceals.

Some institutions are not able to begin conversations with assignments in hand, sometimes due to political or cultural considerations. In the case of

a community college working with the DQP, general education conversations were difficult to begin. The assumption, as reported in institutional
activity reports for the DQP data-collection process, was that students would
pick up the skills in each of the general education areas through required
courses somewhere along their progression through a degree. Acquisition was
then assessed with standardized tests at graduation. Movement had occurred
toward embedding assessment in the classroom with assignments, but faculty
involvement in general education assessment had been minimal. To engage
faculty in the assessment process by building on what was naturally occurring
in the classroom, the community college began with reviewing rubrics and
asking faculty which general education competencies the rubric addressed.
Then they asked if any faculty had general education course assignments that
addressed the rubrics. The process was one of mapping the rubrics to general
education competencies and DQP proficiencies, thereby creating a lens to
explore assignments. Few faculty had felt ownership of general education,
and so the DQP provided a framework that was not connected to general
education directly. The DQP, in other words, became a bridge for faculty
into general education by positioning them to ask and answer what students
can do that crosses disciplines.

Applying the Learning Systems Paradigm

You may have noticed that the discussions in our examples are collaborative and involve thorough considerations of alignment. The examples also
highlight the power of communicating alignment to students. But within
the learning system, we also need to consider the learner view. In NILOA's
work on the assignment charrettes, faculty take the feedback received from
their peers and return to their institution, revise their assignment, and subsequently use it in a course. We also ask that faculty engage with students about
their own understanding of the assignment, either through providing feedback or through engaging in a think-aloud with the faculty member in which
the students talk through what they believe the assignment is asking. After
using the revised assignment and gaining student feedback, the assignment is
revised again and submitted for final review and then placed into the online
assignment library. In essence, the process is one of extended peer review
that touches on each of the four elements of the learning systems paradigm.
While the assignment library and original charrette process focus on the
DQP, assignments provide a way into various other points of conversation
and convergence within a learning system, providing points of commonality. In the following section, we apply the learning systems paradigm's four
elements to assignment design.

Consensus Based

Assignment conversations are inherently consensus based. By working in teams with fellow faculty, discussions create a shared understanding of the collective outcomes toward which we strive and ways to help students attain them via assignments. In cross-disciplinary groups, ideas are shared and faculty reach awareness about the collective nature of where and how students struggle. The focus on the degree, regardless of discipline, in the DQP allows for conversations that cross boundaries. In a charrette that brought collaborative teams together, librarians were important allies, as were centers for teaching and learning and student affairs staff. Conversations at the College of the Marshall Islands used the DQP as a means to talk about learning that occurs across the entire degree program of study (Accrediting Commission for Community and Junior Colleges, 2015). The approach of embedding assignments across the curriculum to evaluate student attainment of general education not only allowed variation within disciplines and programs but also created points of consensus and shared vision as a whole for the institution and those within.

But the conversations and consensus are possible without use of the DQP. At the University of Pittsburgh, faculty discussed student works and debated what students should learn, how it should be measured, and how programs were supporting or struggling to meet stated goals (Kurzweil, 2015). In short, they engaged in scholarly discussions around issues of learning. Their discussions led to the realization that the assignments were not aligned to the learning outcomes, and more importantly, that there was no shared understanding of what the outcomes even meant. In such a situation, even if assignments are constructively aligned within courses, students will likely have the kind of fragmented learning experience described by Hill previously. We have all heard students remark about our colleagues, "I just haven't figured out what she is looking for" as they complain about assignments. That statement is symptomatic of precisely the kind of disparate understandings of outcomes that faculty at Pittsburgh encountered. As we explained in chapter 4, consensus does not require absolute agreement, but where there are differences, students will benefit if those differences are explicated. Doing so enables students to navigate assignments in different classes with an awareness of how different approaches can speak to the same areas of learning.

In the assignment conversations of faculty charrette participants, there was also consensus on the areas where students were struggling, such as with finding relevant resources, knowing when to apply different approaches, and seeing how the assignment connected with real-world experiences. For instance, in a charrette conversation of cross-disciplinary faculty looking at an assignment in a public relations course, the faculty were discussing how to make the assignment reflective of the need to quickly change directions due to unplanned events. The faculty members in the group came up with the idea that when students were presenting their public relations approach for specific events, such as bringing displaced youth to a doggy day care for interaction with the dogs, the faculty member leading the class would insert a crisis. In the case of the dog interactions, a dog bites one of the children. What does the student do? The students would have to react and come up with a way to communicate and address the crisis as part of their group presentation, in real time. Other faculty in the charrette discussion group decided that adding an element of uncertainty to their assignments would also be beneficial, and the group discussed ways to incorporate the consensus on relevancy into their individual assignments.

Assignment conversations have also been a mechanism to allow different voices to participate in conversations on alignment and assignment design. In our work at NILOA, we have brought together adjunct faculty, faculty from minority-serving institutions, faculty working to make connections between 100/200 level courses and the capstone experience, student affairs staff, students, and employers. Focusing on assignments provided a means to move around language barriers by focusing on "doing" such that participants could reach consensus across multiple audience groups on what it meant for students to demonstrate mastery of specific learning outcomes or how different groups asked students to demonstrate their learning. In the work of VALUE, AAC&U (2017) notes that focusing on assignments "challenges faculty to interrogate their own teaching practices and assumptions about how their students in particular come to master important knowledge, skills, and abilities within the context of their classes" (p. 49). Within the area of consensus, the following questions to reflect on assignment practices arise:

- Do we have a shared understanding of what the learning outcomes mean and represent in terms of student demonstration?
- Should the conversations take place within a specific discipline or department, or should there be cross-disciplinary discussions?
- Who should be involved in conversations around assignment design? How are librarians, student affairs, students, centers for teaching and learning, and faculty involved?
- In this assignment, are we excluding demonstrations of learning that may occur in other areas of the learning environment?
- Is there agreement on what it takes to demonstrate the learning outcomes in the form of an assignment?

Aligned

Given that assignment design, as we have discussed it, is inherently about alignment, we have already addressed several of the issues about assignments and alignment in this chapter. It is worth noting, however, that working with the DQP has served to coalesce various points of conversation. For example, to move from students experiencing a disconnected curriculum, faculty have been working to combine depth and breadth through general education and the major (Hutchings & Jankowski, 2015). DQP and Tuning provide a sense of connection, where carefully designed assignments become a vehicle for documenting institutional outcomes while also addressing discipline-specific learning. The importance of alignment is the basis for the next principle included in NILOA's (2016c) policy statement: Connect learning goals with actual student assignments and work. Working with DQP and Tuning has also led, in fact, to different types of gatherings around assignments, including the charrette model and the rubric-focused approach of the Multi-State Collaborative to Advance Quality Student Learning where faculty come together from across a state to explore how their assignments connect with and align to the VALUE rubrics in question. Making tighter relationships between the assignment and the evaluative criteria ensures that when we look at how students are performing, we are getting more reliable data on what they can do, because the assignment has clearly asked them to demonstrate their learning on the criteria outlined in the rubrics. Individual campuses have taken up their own approaches to the alignment of outcomes, learning, and assignments, particularly in relation to integration of learning experiences, scaffolding, and capstone experiences. Alignment considerations are key in part because of the validity concerns raised when assignments are not aligned to learning outcomes or the evaluative criteria (Jordan-Fleming, 2015).

Issues of validity arise in relation to assignment alignment on questions such as "How do we know that this assignment actually elicits students' demonstrations of the learning outcomes in question and not something else?" Basically, does it ask students to demonstrate what we want them to demonstrate? In more technical language, does it measure what we intend it to measure? As faculty, we need to be able to clearly state why we think a specific assignment measures the learning outcome that we claim it does. If we are unable to explain the connections, then we are in some ways building a house of cards. As the focus of assessment has become more embedded in the classroom to report on and link with institution-wide learning outcomes assessment, general education learning outcomes, and/or program-level learning outcomes, if we are not clear about how the course-specific assignment is connected to and elicits the learning in an institution-wide learning outcome, then none of the relationships hold.

Further, if we are making claims about our students' learning based on shared rubrics, as in the work of the Multi-State Collaborative, without tight alignment we may not be able to make valid inferences of student learning demonstration. As a result, we may end up making changes to the curriculum or course design when it is actually the assignment that needs to be altered. Thus, for assignment design to operate in a way that allows looking at the relationships between course-level through to the institution-level, we need to be able to articulately argue for how we think the relationships hold between and among the levels. We need to be clear about how the assignment is aligned with and elicits demonstration of degree-level learning or serves to operate as a means to scaffold student development toward the learning outcomes of interest.

Simply put, without clear alignment, if students are struggling on specific learning outcomes, it is not clear what to change to improve learning, or we may end up making changes based on inaccurate data. For example, a campus that had recently implemented changes to assignment design and placement of assignments around issues of student writing found that student writing scores went down after the first semester of implementation. Faculty and support staff were puzzled, because writing intensive courses had been added along with student support via a writing center. On closer inspection, it was found that the student writing samples that had been reviewed were all submitted in the same week and that many students had more than one paper due during the same week. In essence, the gathered assignments were not good instances of student writing; instead, they were examples of student first draft writing skills. By not exploring the assignments in question in relation to the whole or considering the wider lens of a multi-layered map, faculty may have made changes to the curriculum itself when what was needed was different timing of the assignments to allow students opportunities to be successful. When assignments were evenly spaced across a semester, writing improved.

The most common opportunity for misalignment is that the action verb in the learning outcome statement does not connect with what students are actually asked to do within the assignment. Cliff Adelman (2015) offers a focused look at the various verbs used in learning outcomes and how they do or do not relate to the demonstrations of learning we are interested in students demonstrating. But positioning assignments as a point of entry allows for exploration of multiple areas of connection. For example, what is the role of a specific assignment within a course, within a program, in connection to general education, or to institutional learning outcomes? How can exploring the role of assignment design with graduate student teaching assistants provide meaningful future faculty development on issues of assessment but also provide more connected learning experiences for students in their courses? How can we use the assignments and their connection to larger program goals as mechanisms to share with adjunct faculty why they are engaging students in the types of learning that they are, as well as how students will build on their demonstration on a specific assignment in later courses? Norman Jones and Daniel McInerney (2016) provide examples of the different types of questions that can be asked about not only the role of courses but also the role of assignments in relation to a specific course, major, general education profile, and degree. Starting with a view of a singular assignment can provide a lens to relationships beyond those found within a specific course. Focusing on how students demonstrate their learning also provides a means to connect with student affairs, explore the assignments given in on-campus work, and provide a means to work around language barriers with employer groups by focusing on what we each ask students to actually do to demonstrate their knowledge, skills, and abilities. Thinking about alignment as it relates to assignments raises questions such as the following:

- How do our assignments and activities elicit student demonstrations of a specific learning outcome? In your own assignment what are you asking students to actually *do* or *demonstrate*?
- How does the assignment align with learning outcomes? Evaluative criteria? Learning activities?
- What areas of learning need to come into alignment to support student demonstration of learning?
- How do individual faculty contribute to this collective work in their individual course assignments? How do course assignments connect? Where are other places of possible demonstration?
- How do we know that we have mapped our assignment to rubric criteria? How have we mapped our assignment approaches across our curriculum?

Learner Centered

Considering learners in relation to assignment conversations is vital because, as Norton (2004) argues, "The most powerful roles that assessment can have . . . [are] its effect not only on what students learn but *how* they learn" (p. 687). Black and William (1998) found that challenging assignments and extensive feedback led to greater student engagement and attainment. They explain that students need to be active in their own assessment. Students can be design partners and help create assignments (Cook-Sather, Bovill, & Felten, 2014). Learning becomes more meaningful and students are more likely to engage when they construct their own projects (Land, Hannafin, & Oliver, 2012). Student-led approaches also foster self-directed learning "by enabling students to productively engage complex, open-ended problems that are aligned authentically with the practices, culture, or processes of a domain" (Land et al., 2012, p. 3). Norton (2004) argues that students learn through doing the task if it is constructed in a way to encourage deep learning. Yet too often assignments require students to "describe" or "compare and contrast," leading to minimal engagement on the part of the student (Adelman, 2015). The verbs of the DQP focus on active tasks directly related to learning processes, meeting Norton's (2004) call for assessment tasks that are performances of students' learning. For example, learning can be strengthened by engaging students in processes by which they create their own assignments, including the evaluative criteria, and complete them.

Further, we know that for feedback to be meaningful to students, they need to have opportunities to *do* something with it (Black & William, 1998; Kluger & DeNisi, 1996). If we have not considered feedback in assignment design conversations, we have missed an opportunity for not only our students' but also our own learning. In addition, if we are going to claim that our assignments actually do elicit student demonstrations of learning in courses, demonstrations that can be used to look at institution-level learning, then assignments need to offer a solid demonstration of students' knowledge and skills. Timing of the assignment in relation to other experiences becomes important—and something to map, as discussed in chapter 4—to help ensure a meaningful demonstration of proficiency.

For an example of active student involvement in deep learning experiences, Kenneth Albone (2015) shares the group communication course at Rowan University in Glassboro, New Jersey. Students are assigned to small groups to identify and attempt to resolve a problem on campus that affects the students. Through the course of a semester, the teams work on the project and provide a possible solution that is then shared with the office on campus best situated to address the issue. Faculty then gather student feedback on the assignment, leading to changes by the instructor for enhanced clarity (Albone, 2015). Another assignment is offered by Steiner (2016) on regulating learning. Students need help in determining both how to regulate their own learning and which strategies or techniques will help them reach their goals (Dunlosky, Rawson, Marsh, Nathan, & Willingham, 2013).

Highlighting, flash cards, or storyboarding, for example, may not be productive for all students, who need to be able to identify the best strategies for developing their own learning. To address student management of their own learning, something that is rarely explicitly taught, Steiner (2016) devised an assignment that asks students to practice various self-regulated learning strategies of their choosing that are associated with success in college. They try out different approaches and learn what works for them. Students learn study strategies by selecting a test they are worried about in a current class. They submit test-preparation materials and a reflection at the end. The idea is that students need to know the strategies and options available to them as well as determine when to use them (Steiner, 2016). Thus, while our assignments may at times align with learning outcomes, our assignments for students can also be focused on fostering learning in general.

In an assignment design charrette that brought students together to discuss what assignments they thought might address specific learning outcomes, what students developed were multidimensional, time intensive, and more challenging than most assignments they had encountered. Are we hindering our students' learning by not connecting assignments across courses so that they have opportunities to engage in larger issues, define the problem, and determine solutions beyond the normal time allotted in a semester or quarter? Such an approach reinforces the inherently collaborative nature of teaching and helps to further connect learning across and throughout the curriculum and cocurriculum. Peggy Maki (2017) writes that what our students need is *real-time assessment*, assessment that provides meaningful feedback and is actionable mid-stream to enhance and support their learning. Bringing a learner-centered view to assignment conversations involves exploring the function of assignments within a supportive, formative assessment environment. It raises questions around when students receive feedback on assignments in terms of if they have time to actually engage with the feedback and make changes for the learning potential to be realized (Jankowski, 2017). It also explores the different places that students learn and the potential for making connections between learning in a classroom and the various experiences and learning that occur outside of a traditionally structured learning environment. Moreover, it directs attention to the need for students to develop a portfolio of their work in ways that they understand and see the connections, so that they are able to speak actively about their learning and provide demonstrations of what they know and can do. Further, there are clear implications for equity as it relates to issues of assignment design (Montenegro & Jankowski, 2017). Is there one specific means by which learners need to demonstrate their knowledge and skills, or are we designing assignments that privilege a specific way of demonstrating over others? Questions that a learner-centered lens brings to assignment conversations include the following:

- In what ways have learners been involved or consulted in the assignment process? How are they seeing the assignment differently?
- Is it one assignment for all students, or are there multiple paths to demonstrate learning in ways that are culturally responsive and mindful of our learners?
- In assignment conversations, is there consideration of student movement through different scaffolded educational experiences in terms of assignment placement? Where do points of transfer and convergence occur in relation to assignments in different spaces of the learning environment?
- What assumptions do we have regarding our students as learners that are implemented in our assignments? Are they accurate?
- Where do learners think they have demonstrated attainment of learning outcomes, and do they connect with our own perceptions?

Communicated

Throughout this chapter we have discussed the importance of communicating connections and considering the learner in relation to assignment instructions. Transparency in assignment design matters for underserved student populations; more transparent assignments provide underserved students with a better opportunity to demonstrate their knowledge and skills (Winkelmes et al., 2016). N. Jones (2012) argues that Tuned disciplines regard students as partners. Part of the process for doing so is to make the learning outcomes clear to students so that they develop a vocabulary to talk about their learning. The conversations among faculty members in the charrettes surfaced implicit assumptions that needed to be explicit for students, often through realizations that the instructions did not clearly communicate the purpose of the assignment in relation to the whole (Hutchings, 2016). Even if assignments are tightly aligned with learning outcomes, evaluative criteria, and each assignment's place within the curricular path, students still need an explicit mapping of the justification for the scaffolded nature of assessment tasks (Evans, 2013). Otherwise, the connections that we, as faculty, build into the learning environment will be left implicit, forcing learners to do additional work to figure out how they are supposed to make those connections. Not all learners are equally equipped to navigate various learning experiences, thus clear communication on the purpose, role, and end result of the assignment help to not advantage certain learners over others.

Although communicating relationships to students is key, students' meaningful feedback to instructors is also important. At the University of California, Merced, the Center for Research on Teaching Excellence sponsors Students Assessing Teaching and Learning (SATAL) (Signorini, 2014). Undergraduate students are trained in research design, data gathering, and effective reporting and provide support to faculty in their assessment efforts. One project undertaken by SATAL students was focused on helping students provide effective feedback to instructors on course evaluation forms (Signorini, 2014). Communication, thus, will bear the strongest benefits if it works in multiple directions: faculty to faculty, faculty to students, and students to faculty. Consider the possibilities if we do not: Faculty may devise assignments that, even if perceived as complementary, work at cross purposes; faculty may give assignments to students who perceive the intended learning in ways outside our desired ends, resulting in learning not being demonstrated in the ways we anticipate and giving us incorrect understandings of the degree to which they are learning; or students may become frustrated with working hard in what they believe to be the right areas of learning but actually are not.

An example that came from the faculty discussions of the charrettes was that of an assignment for nursing students on clearly communicating medical terminology to audiences not familiar with the language. The assignment required students to create a pamphlet addressing a single topic, with the idea that the pamphlet would help signal to students the need to address an audience not familiar with the intricacies of medical terminology. However, students kept getting caught up on the pamphlet design. Some made beautiful pamphlets and took the opportunity to stretch their design skills; others struggled with how to present information in a pamphlet form. However, the learning outcome of interest was not whether students could create a pamphlet. The pamphlet was the means to demonstrate their ability to clearly communicate medical terms, but the pamphlet was getting in the way. The assignment was revised to clearly communicate to students that translation skill, not pamphlet design, was being evaluated. The faculty member provided a pamphlet template that could be used for those not interested in engaging in design. The option still existed for students to explore design and create their own pamphlet if they so chose, but the focus on the learning outcome of interest was clearly communicated to students in ways that had only been implicit previously. In the work of Transparency in Learning and Teaching, Mary Ann Winkelmes underscores the importance of clearly communicating to students the purpose of an assignment, the task, and the criteria by which they will be evaluated along with annotated samples of successful student work.

(Visit www.unlv.edu/provost/teachingandlearning for more information on the project.) In essence, communication is about making clear the relationships explored in alignment and the understandings developed through consensus processes. It also elevates the importance of assignment writing as a genre of its own that faculty and staff need to learn.

In a piece exploring the importance of instructional clarity, Blaich, Wise, Pascarella, and Roksa (2016) argue that "instructional clarity and organization plays a powerful role in promoting student growth on important liberal education outcomes" but they continue to state that "many college students do not experience high levels of this important good practice in their classes" and that "faculty often discount the value of enhancing clarity and organization of their courses because they either do not wish to 'spoon-feed' students or because they do not understand how students experience their classes and assignments" (p. 7). However, clear instruction is connected with student retention, graduation, and learning (Jankowski, 2017; Blaich et al., 2016), and sharing our design does not change the criteria by which we evaluate if students are successful in meeting them. Focusing on communication also leads to benefits beyond assignment performance. Blaich and colleagues (2016) state, "Students talked about benefiting from hearing about the purpose of pedagogies, exercises, and assignments. These explanations helped them frame and make sense of what was going on and showed that faculty were putting care and effort into their teaching" (p. 10) which leads to increased motivation to complete the assignment in meaningful and intentional ways. Questions that arise around communication within a learning systems paradigm include the following:

- How are we communicating the value, purpose, and intent of our assignments to various stakeholders, including students?
- With whom do we share information on the design of our learning environments and assignments as being supportive of and fostering attainment of the learning outcomes of interest?
- How are we engaging with our learners in dialogue around their understanding of the role of assignments?
- How clear are the assignment instructions and evaluative criteria to learners at different levels of expertise with the content in question?

Concluding Thoughts

A focus on assignments squarely removes assessment from being an add-on to being embedded in our daily work and practice. Alignment is important because no assignment should be an island (Hutchings et al., 2014), mean-ing that in a learning system we need to look at not only individual assign-ments but also "the arc of assignments over time and . . . the ways that faculty can work together on their design and use" (p. 6). Assignments can be meaningful sources of evidence regarding student learning as well as powerful pedagogically by signaling to students what is expected of them and what faculty value. Yet assignment work has been mostly invisible and insufficiently supported. NILOA's efforts to work with faculty became important faculty development opportunities, uncovering the messy and inherently scholarly nature of the work (Hutchings, Jankowski, & Schultz, 2016). Our efforts led to strategies for getting started (Hutchings et al., 2014) and toolkits for conducting assignment work (Ford, 2016; National Instititue for Learning Outcomes Assessment, 2016b, 2016d).

Assignments also provided inroads for collaboration with others. In the case of Illinois College's work with the DQP and civic learning, it was found that class activities were not meeting all of the civic learning objectives (Dean & Dagan, 2011). The DQP provided a means for working with a wider range of disciplines and discipline-specific assignments connected to civic engagement. Students benefited from engaging in activities that asked them to reflect on community engagement that was directly or indirectly tied to coursework or cocurricular experiences, bringing student and aca-demic affairs together around a shared institutional mission (Dean & Dagan, 2011). In another example of student affairs involvement, Horst, Ghant, and Whetstone (2015) asked students to describe their experiences and learning related to cocurricular experiences with community service using a model of critical reflection. And others, such as WiGrow in Wisconsin, have used the idea of Iowa Grow and the relationship between on-campus employ-ment and student learning to reinforce learning outcomes (University of Wisconsin–Madison, n.d.). Partnering with centers for teaching and learn-ing can be a vehicle to help grow conversations (Skinner & Prager, 2015), but a single faculty member participating in a meaningful assignment design conversation can also lead to institutional initiatives focused on assignments, as was the case with Daemen College and the DQP (Giffin, 2016).

Terry Rhodes (2015) argues that the future of assessment is realized through project-based assignments that are used formatively to advance student learning as well as summatively to document institutional per-formance. The work of assignment design squarely places assessment in the hands of faculty and staff, building on authentic work from students. Rhodes (2015) argues that "rather than passive recipients of knowledge, students are becoming active participants in their own educations while developing their abilities to assess their own learning process as they acquire knowledge" (p. 112). The mindful scaffolding and sequencing of assignments that emerges from such efforts is built from collaborative assignment design (Rhodes et al., 2016).

Another avenue that is opened through assignment conversations is the possibility for altering relationships with employers. By using assignments as the point of conversation with employers instead of looking at outcome statements alone, faculty can engage in conversations regarding the *doing* of learning outcomes. What do employers really mean by saying they need "team players"? What is it that they actually do and what does it look like? Such action-based conversations provide mechanisms by which shared understandings can be developed among faculty, staff, and employers. Students can then benefit from assignments that are examples of their knowledge and skills in ways that are shared with and understood by employers. In work with DQP and Tuning, Marshall University met with dozens of local employers and discussed the most important skills for entry-level positions. They communicated with students about how their coursework would make them valued employees by helping them build strategies for conveying that information in résumés, cover letters, and interviews. The conversations also helped to clarify the skills that would allow someone in an entry-level position to advance. The conversations helped close a gap between what employers needed and the capacity of Marshall graduates to talk about their demonstration of those skills. Students were not including mentions of projects, internships, or work from their portfolios on résumés, because they did not see the connections between their assignments and work. In short, they were unable to translate their knowledge and skills in interviews. The work of Marshall University with employers led to better communication with students about the connections between coursework and related experiences, as well as the skills that would get them jobs—making explicit the connections between assignments and employment in ways that did not vocationalize programs. The process was one of making and communicating connections, not overhauling programs to become job-training centers.

As Jordan-Fleming (2015) argues, assignment writing is a processional skill. It is a skill that needs to be protected from assumptions that lead to disconnects between what faculty thought they were asking of students in assignments and what they actually asked students to do. The work done around assignments has made minor modifications to what faculty were already doing, such as adding an audience to a writing assignment so that the students were not writing papers for a specific faculty member, allowing students to choose the topic or issue instead of defining it for them, or adding reflection questions to group work such as "How did you hinder the ability of the group to move forward?" (assuming that, at some point in time, each student did). Further, faculty added an additional column to rubrics asking students to evaluate themselves. The evaluation was not simply to say where they thought they were but what they needed to do to improve. The minor changes led to large benefits for the students and provided more meaningful, connected information for institutions to report. The conversations energized faculty to continue working collectively and share their work. As mentioned earlier, the NILOA assignment library provides citations for each assignment, available under a Creative Commons license. This is intentional. The work is of the faculty, based in scholarship, and begins conversations that move into dialogue about system interactions.

6

PERCEIVED BARRIERS
IN THE LEARNING
SYSTEMS PARADIGM

Throughout this book, we have made a philosophical argument for a framework that can structure and guide the work of educators in building learning environments and experiences that better foster student learning by recognizing that learning happens both inside and outside classrooms or their virtual equivalents. We followed that argument with a practical definition of *alignment* that takes the learning system as its scope and offered discussions of how this framework can drive collaborative approaches to alignment through mapping and assignment design. Choosing to work within the learning systems paradigm entails adopting a new perspective, one that may challenge faculty, staff, and administrators to rethink their basic assumptions about the structure of institutions, the modes of working within them, and our roles in educating learners. That choice is to undertake a journey—one hopes not to Mordor, but barriers, nonetheless, can crop up along the way.

Organizations and institutions that have taken up projects involving DQP and Tuning, or other related initiatives or learning frameworks, have encountered a variety of barriers. They tend to revolve around the scope of work, challenges of particular institutional contexts, establishment of collaborative spaces, distrust of the goals of such projects, and issues directly related to personnel. Although we'll work through discussions of different kinds of challenges that emerge, it is important to keep in mind that context matters. Different institutional types will encounter different types of hurdles. Community colleges, for example, wrestle with issues related to open admissions and missions divided between transfer to four-year institutions and career technical education and nondegree or certificate-seeking learners. Universities encounter challenges having to do with the devaluing of teaching in relation to research that tends to prevail, particularly in highly intensive research universities. Online or competency-based institutions may wrestle with issues relating to nontraditional learners and staffing models. The framework provided by the learning systems paradigm, however, is flexible and can be utilized in the different contexts. Maneuvering through challenges depends on institutionally defined reasons for working within the paradigm. But it also requires a recognition of the conflicts and confusion that can arise when working within or across two different paradigms.

Knowing Where to Start

We have described a large educational landscape as the subject of the paradigm. We have discussed aligning assignments and course outcomes. We have talked about bridging one part of the curriculum to another, either making connections within programs or finding synergy across programs, whether in other disciplines or general education. We looked at creating collaborative work environments that can draw together faculty responsible for curricula and staff responsible for cocurricula. We have mentioned reaching out to the larger community of partner institutions, civic groups, and employers. That is, admittedly, an enormous range of levels at which to work, so where do you start? If you want to dive in, where do you begin? The answer to that question depends in part on what is already underway but also on what priorities need to be addressed.

In other words, each institution needs to determine its own entry point. Many of the institutions taking up DQP to address large-scale campus reforms often scaled back their aspirations after discovering that working institution-wide can be overwhelming. Their initial goals of comprehensive reform had to be refocused once they discovered that key pieces of the paradigm we have set forth needed to be established first. For example, in AAC&U's Quality Collaboratives, the dyads of two- and four-year institutions found that establishing consensus required more time and energy than expected (Jankowski, 2015). To do justice to the aims of the project, developing shared understandings and building the relationships they depend on became a priority, they needed to spend time building consensus. To generalize from these examples, institutions might begin by choosing one of the four elements of the paradigm as a starting point. If a lack of consensus troubles your work, then beginning with strategies to encourage consensus-building may make the most sense. If misalignment seems to interfere with the efficacy of teaching and learning, then investigations of alignment might provide an entry. If activities around the institution seem focused on compliance to accreditors or to what Tagg (2003) terms the *teaching paradigm*, then exploring learner-centered approaches may serve your institution best. And if your institution struggles to communicate what it does and why, then perhaps that needs to be your starting point. What does your campus need? That can be the best determiner for where to begin. An additional area to examine is what activities are currently underway. Is curriculum mapping occurring within the institution? If yes, then how can the elements discussed in applying the paradigm to curriculum mapping be included in the process underway?

Similarly, there may be programs best positioned to try out aspects of the paradigm. For example, in the DQP pilots of the Accrediting Commission for Community and Junior Colleges (2015), community colleges in California moved from thinking in terms of comprehensive revisions to locating work within a couple of discipline-specific programs. Those strategic shifts in scope enabled institutions to "try out" work within the paradigm on a limited scale before expanding efforts more broadly across the institution. This was the approach of West Hills College Coalinga, which selected two disciplines, agriculture and business, to engage in a process of alignment with DQP. Faculty in the two programs cross-walked their outcomes to DQP proficiencies, reflected on discipline-specific variations of the proficiencies, developed strategies for embedding them in curricula, and designed assignments. Based on their positive results, the campus decided to extend the work. A year later, David Marshall visited the campus to assist in drawing a larger group of programs into similar work. Institutions might consider an approach like West Hills College Coalinga by piloting projects in programs that seem most ready to undertake this kind of work before rolling it out more broadly. A benefit to this approach is that those faculty and staff who work on the smaller-scale pilots are able to serve as homegrown facilitators for colleagues and peers who join the work later. Further, beginning with a specific program, project, or coupling the work to an existing initiative did not end up narrowing engagement in the larger learning system. In the impact study, we found that the longer faculty and staff within institutions worked with the DQP, the more people were involved and the wider the lens of the work (Jankowski & Giffin, 2016a).

Another way to engage strategically is to tie new work within the paradigm to existing projects within the institution. In the DQP pilots around the country, work seemed to catch on most quickly when institutions incorporated DQP and Tuning into problems already being addressed. Applicants to the Council of Independent Colleges DQP consortium project had to indicate with which ongoing initiative the work would connect, whether it was program development or review, general education revision, or examining the relationship between the curricular and the cocurricular (Jankowski & Giffin, 2016b). Such a strategy creates a productive synergy in which these tools or others like them can help to energize the efforts already being undertaken by faculty and staff.

We cannot offer a series of steps that anyone can follow. The idiosyncrasies that make institutions of higher education wonderfully unique mean that homogenizing approaches will likely not be as effective as locating the pressure points or areas of interest and concern within our institutions. Solutions need to be homegrown and distinct to the needs of our institutions, because our contexts, demographics, and missions are all distinct. Situating our work in our unique circumstances and moving forward with the learning systems paradigm in mind offer the best means of devising strategies and creating learning environments that have the greatest possible impact for our institutions' particular students. Is there space to bring questions about assumptions at play in the learning environment to an existing department meeting? Is there a cross-campus committee that can support a wider view of discussions on alignment? Is there a means to widen participation in reviewing materials to involve multiple audiences? Asking and answering such questions can help in the work of examining and fostering a holistic learning environment.

Faculty Concerns Around Participation

When we travel to assessment conferences and planning meetings for initiatives such as those involving DQP and Tuning, one question pops up like a clockwork cuckoo: How do we engage faculty in this work? The alternative version of this question uses phrases like "buy-in" or "invest themselves." Let's be clear: Faculty are engaged in the work of fostering student learning. Framing the invitation to participate in consensus-building around alignment and learner-centeredness as this question does assumes faculty are disengaged. Although different institution types have differing degrees of engagement due to differences in teaching responsibilities, faculty have "bought in" to the responsibility of supporting learners in their educational experiences in whatever shape that takes. However, not all faculty are equally engaged in the different elements of the paradigm, since individual faculty members bear other responsibilities to varying degrees. Multiple hats will mean that not all faculty will have equal interest or involvement in each of these areas.

To some extent, lack of interest in developing a strong, coherent learning environment may be related to how little preparation faculty have as professional educators or how poorly we have communicated the value and purpose for undertaking the work. Particularly at four-year colleges and universities, most faculty lack any training in teaching and assessment, with their graduate experiences being almost entirely focused on developing research within their discipline. Faculty, thus, may not have been acculturated to thinking about what it means to foster learning within a specific discipline, let alone across disciplines to encompass a degree, and we view the process within the delivery model that Tagg (2003) describes. This is, after all, how most of us were taught. Faculty reluctance, where it exists, may have more to do with working within a different paradigm of education, which creates a blind spot in relation to this emergent, collaborative approach to higher education. Maneuvering through may require explicit explanation and discussion that differentiates the learning systems paradigm from both Tagg's learning paradigm (2003) and the teaching paradigm to which he contrasted it (see chapter 2). It also requires a recognition of the variety of backgrounds among faculty, such as those coming from business and industry or those who have not been acculturated to research activities but do have their master's degree, heightening the need to develop consensus through conversations on developing shared meaning. Understanding who our learners are and how to communicate work within the learning systems paradigm to them is important, but understanding our faculty and their values, and actively listening to them without reducing their concerns to distrust and complaints will also serve to move the work along. In the work of the AAC&U Quality Collaboratives with university and community colleges, faculty from each institution uncovered misplaced assumptions about their colleagues (Jankowski, 2015), an activity that enabled differences to emerge along with common ground.

Just as we must discuss the assumptions we hold about our students that may be false, we need to examine the assumptions we bring about faculty, staff, and other partners in order to meet people where they are and not where we perceive them to be coming from. For example, faculty are often tagged as being full of resistance and complaints about changes or issues associated with assessment, but those "complaints" may be a means of defining the problem and raising concerns or observing conflicts around such issues. Reflecting on AHA's Tuning initiative, Daniel McInerney (2017) observes,

> Rather than viewing debate and controversy as forces of dysfunction and disorder in a collective group, the *disciplinary* society viewed its vigorous internal discussions on Tuning as healthy signs of individual engagement and organizational openness. Rather than stifling, marginalizing, or ignoring opposition, AHA acknowledged criticism, provided a forum for debate, and responded to the concerns some members expressed. (para. 10)

Concerns and conflict are not inherently bad or disruptive; they can actually be productive. In departmental work, McInerney recounts that complaints and concerns gave way to problem-solving and solutions. He explains,

Our department had stumbled unknowingly on the strategy of "backward design," starting with the final requirement of a program and tracing back the steps students needed to succeed in that task. The discussion showed me that intelligent thoughtful faculty members probably have many complaints to voice, but eventually, they also start to come up with answers to the problems they observe. (para. 11)

Complaints are statements of perceived problems, and, while they may be voiced with some consternation, the identification of problems leads to the identification of solutions. If, however, we allow our assumptions about a complaining faculty hinder our perception of the problems complaints reveal, we remain unable to solve those problems.

Shifting these conceptions may also benefit from highlighting the degree to which the ways of working we have described live in a world of research. As our core chapters demonstrate, questions drive the work, just as questions drive the inquiry of research. When conceived as research, working in this paradigm can leverage faculty's strengths toward a common end and create synergies across the campus, not only among faculty but also drawing in offices of institutional research, among other constituencies, to locate data. Ohlemacher (2015) describes the dialogical modes of strengthening student learning using the foundation of appreciative inquiry, in which participants "uncover what gives life to the organization . . . , envision what might be possible . . . , translate the ideal into action . . . , and actualize their plans and determine how to sustain their success" (p. 5). The approach is built around constructivist inquiry, a form of research that, in this case, attempts to analyze the existing learning environment by asking questions that direct paths forward. It does so by asking faculty to recount stories of their experiences as educators as a means of addressing conceptual understandings, sentiments, and meanings associated with those experiences. Appreciative inquiry works collaboratively and in ways that anticipate a shared vision of the future. Using a mode of inquiry like this facilitates movement forward because it is driven by questions that emerge organically through lived experience, which mitigates the lack of formal training in curriculum, pedagogy, and assessment.

Using such strategies melds working within the learning systems paradigm with professional development. As faculty, we become sensitized to the ways in which students learn, how our actions and understandings of students contribute to their learning, and means by which we can strengthen their success collaboratively. We have argued in numerous presentations that using learning outcomes as we have described is as much about faculty learning as it is about student learning. We learn not only how our students are doing but also what kinds of strategies seem to help them construct knowledge and the means we can use to encourage that. Involving centers for teaching and learning in conversations about our learning environments, therefore, can be extremely helpful. Karen Ford (2016), for example, walks faculty through hands-on exercises that gradually build appreciation for and understanding of assignment design and rubric use. Her strategies operate from a perspective of discovery through experience, akin to Ohlemacher's use of appreciative inquiry, that develops not just deeper awareness of the practical benefits of such tools but also the value of consensus-building and working collaboratively. The ways of engaging in assessment that these examples illustrate return to faculty approaches to reflection about teaching and learning that compliance mentalities have put at a distance. Assessment, in this frame, reauthorizes faculty to employ embedded and constructive modes of engagement.

Consensus-building does not require the creation of engagement. It requires a new form of engagement, but teaching responsibilities, research expectations, and service obligations are all activities that require time, and juggling various demands can create a sense that there is little room for anything else. As we have noted, working in the ways that the learning systems paradigm encourages requires time-intensive work in conversations. Scheduling that time is a challenge in itself, but making time and space is another. As Levin and Hernandez (2014) observe, forging campus cohesion is challenging, because nobody is looking for one more thing to do. Generating interest and willingness to participate in these kinds of conversations requires political calls for involvement (which can be a delicate process) as well as an openness to a variety of professional perspectives. Moreover, mechanisms need to be in place to conduct work like this. When working within programs, existing structures can be leveraged to reduce additional commitments. For example, department and committee meetings can be dedicated to conversations that build consensus and develop means of working through issues of alignment that are learner-centered and explicit. Working across programs and divisions often requires administrative support, but even here efficiency can be established by identifying those well positioned to do the work. Assessment offices, centers for teaching and learning, and offices of institutional research, all of which are frequently well networked across campuses, are in positions to establish lines of communication and to help coordinate activities.

Making use of well-positioned offices and individuals does not address all the time concerns. Making faculty available to participate and providing them with support to do so remains a key component for advancing meaningful work within the paradigm. Funds to reassign faculty time to active roles in collaborative efforts are often necessary, as is helping faculty to see themselves as important to the process. The first is a problem of administrative priorities, whereas the second is one of faculty understanding. Both can, to some extent, be addressed by explicating the value of prioritizing the work. At the risk of working in generalizations, administrators and faculty want to know that there is value to the kinds of initiatives in which they are being invited to participate. DQP and Tuning have demonstrated tremendous potential, as we have described, as tools for working within the learning systems paradigm, but assuming the value of such efforts is obvious and apparent is naïve. Administrators have their own perceived areas of priority—a topic we will address later. Many faculty, especially those with lengthy careers, have seen special projects and new initiatives come and go, leaving little meaningful impact on their institutions. That experience breeds skepticism. Reframing work around the value propositions behind it and around the ways in which collaboration and consensus-building create stronger results in student learning may prove a more successful strategy for both administrators and faculty than assuring those in the institution that initiatives are important.

We should acknowledge, too, that processes for promotion and tenure can be a disincentive for faculty who might participate in institutional initiatives. Admittedly, this area of concern is one that may be specific to research and comprehensive institutions, though liberal arts colleges will likely see similar issues. Institutions indicate, at least on paper, that faculty are evaluated around a balance of research, teaching, and service; however, most institutional cultures tend to prioritize these as being of descending importance. Comprehensive universities may strike a closer balance between research and teaching, but service tends to be regarded as less impactful on decisions for promotion and tenure, with assessment of student learning falling most often into the category of service. Participating in initiatives such as those we have described throughout this book can, as a result, seem counterproductive to securing promotion and tenure.

As we have demonstrated, these initiatives and those related to them are shifting the national discourse around student learning and the ways we foster it. On an individual level, faculty involved in DQP and Tuning have addressed this problem by situating their activities within the context of these national conversations about teaching and learning. At a department level, programs can choose to formally prioritize participation in such work through promotion and tenure guidelines. Documents supporting promotion and tenure can describe the way. California State University, Stanislaus's Department of Social Work did just this by requiring faculty to provide evidence of student engagement in learning with course assignments and activities that correspond to learning objectives. Similarly, the Department of Liberal Studies describes proficiency in internal communications as including "course assessment and rubrics." Such strategies foreground that activities associated with teaching and learning are important components of faculty's professional experience and legitimize the effort and research required to do it well. *Research* may seem an odd term to use in this context, but the work of identifying productive pedagogies and designing assignments and curricular approaches requires research, reflection, and application, just as the academic research on which faculty at many institutions are tenured and promoted. This is one reason that NILOA's assignment library vets assignments through a peer review process, requires them to be field-tested, and provides citations for them. Engagement in matters of teaching and learning is scholarly work, and this is recognized in the kinds of efforts made by institutions such as California State University, Stanislaus.

One final faculty concern around participation has to do with the involvement of adjunct members of the teaching community. Adjunct faculty comprise an increasing percentage of the teachers in higher education, which means that a larger percentage of students are learning with them. Levin and Hernandez (2014) speak to these issues directly. If we do not ensure some means of incorporating our part-time faculty into these areas, the impact will be minimal. There are obvious challenges to their inclusion. Paid on a class-by-class basis, they are typically not compensated for their participation. Compensation speaks to disincentives for involvement, but there can be other benefits. Anecdotally, some adjunct faculty who have participated in the NILOA assignment design workshops were able to obtain full-time positions, because they could speak knowledgeably and from experience about the ways in which they had engaged in meaningful work around curriculum, pedagogy, and assessment. Angela Félix (2017) provides an example of the work of Rio Salado College in making adjunct faculty an integral part of assessment of student learning and fostering institutional success. Adjunct faculty are actively involved in curriculum development conversations, have access to professional development courses where they can earn badges in different areas of learning outcomes, and are recognized for their efforts in an Outstanding Adjunct Faculty reception. While not every institution may be in a position to provide the comprehensive support offered by Rio Salado, their example offers a variety of possible avenues into the work.

Another deterrent can be the implicit or perceived class structure among faculty. As we have said, however, adjunct faculty are an integral piece of our learning environments, and their roles actually bring benefits to work within the learning systems paradigm. Often, adjunct faculty teach at multiple institutions, which gives them a more complete picture of where and how students learn, particularly when they teach at both community colleges and universities. That insight can advance thinking about alignment between institution types or about developing strategies for smoother transitions in transfer. Additionally, adjunct faculty's assignments often travel among institutions, which can provide information regarding how students interpret tasks in different parts of the learning system. At the very least, involvement of our adjunct faculty needs to happen at the level of orientation. If our program works within the framework of the learning system and is attentive to the relationships among parts and the role each part plays in fostering student learning, then adjunct faculty need to be incorporated into that vision. Orientations for adjunct faculty in the learning systems paradigm, therefore, take up that work by introducing them to the program's understandings of outcomes and the rubrics that facilitate communication around how students demonstrate their learning (N. Jones, 2012).

Faculty Suspicion

Faculty may also be suspicious of such initiatives. Some early responses to the DQP and the frameworks deriving from Tuning revolved around concerns that these two tools attempted to impose external standards on higher education in the way that K–12 systems have been working under standards. The anxiety is that adopting a national framework will homogenize our institutions, stripping away the specific missions, organizations, and approaches that make U.S. higher education so powerful. That diversity of institution types and the diversity that exists within types would be lost, creating a cookie-cutter higher education system. That view, however, actually runs in contrast to what tools like DQP, Tuning, and related initiatives endeavor to do.

Frameworks, as we have said, function as reference points, not mandates. But what does that mean? Perhaps the best way to explain it is by metaphor: Frameworks like the DQP and those produced in Tuning are armatures. In sculpture, an armature is typically a metal wire support that is positioned in the pose desired for a human sculpture. A dozen artists might all start with armatures in the same pose. The underlying structure, in other words, may be approximately the same. What the sculptors form around the armature, however, can be astoundingly varied. Human forms take all manner of shapes. Artistic styles are myriad. Particular features are distinct. Degree profiles serve in the same way. Cross-walking between frameworks and institutional documents recognizes the common armature beneath the various parts that make up a distinctive whole. The ways in which individual institutions choose to address and support the learning expressed in outcomes need to be unique to institutions. Each has its own mission, local contexts, particular student demographics, program strengths, resources, and a host of other factors whose combination in individual institutions can result only in uniqueness.

The politics of the anxiety have to do with concerns about standardization. McInerney (2017) recounts such suspicions, among others, regarding the AHA Tuning initiative, observing, "News of the first U.S. meetings on Tuning may have evoked a stream of protests, warnings, and even conspiratorial theories from educators concerning the straitjacket of standardization under which academe would soon operate in both teaching and testing" (para. 8). Being attentive to the standards to which we hold students, however, does not equal standardization. Standardization would create homogenous institutions, but DQP and Tuning encourage faculty and staff to reflect on how they, in their unique context, can strive to help students construct their own learning. A review of institutional and general education outcomes reveal fundamental commonalities in what learning is determined to be essential to degrees in the United States. Although different institution types might have different approaches, with community colleges taking a necessarily different approach from comprehensive universities, for example, the vast majority of postsecondary institutions foreground intellectual skills such as those identified in the DQP. Most institutions have some sense of community engagement or civic responsibility. And just as many encourage students to develop learning in a particular area and be capable of applying their learning in different contexts. We have a common essence, but not a common shape.

Suspicions have arisen, too, around the broad-based consultation and collaboration work within learning systems. When David Marshall first attended meetings about undertaking facilitation of Tuning initiatives, his initial response to the idea of consulting with employers was one of alarm. His concerns immediately jumped to a perceived vocationalizing of higher education, in which learning for civic engagement and personal development were minimized as having no value at all. Similar concerns have arisen for others who first encounter DQP and Tuning, concerns around becoming accountable to outside entities for the particular shapes of their curricula or about a slide toward the imposition of accreditation-like requirements for disciplines. Each of these suspicions shares an anxiety about giving control over what and how we teach to outside entities. As Nancy Kidd (2015) explains of the NCA's LOC initiative,

> The LOCs do not exist to assuage employability or other concerns of prospective majors or their parents, but they do make the relevance of the discipline explicit. The LOCs can be used to advocate for disciplinary support from legislators and accreditors, for the hiring of our students by employers, and for students to become Communication majors. (p. 7)

Kidd's argument is a good one. She argues that working in directions such as this gives faculty opportunities to advocate for their disciplines and express how their own particular programs foster learning. Further, conversations with employers from institutions using the DQP shifted in ways allowed through shared language around learning and demonstration of learning. Focusing on assignments, or what learners *do* with what they know became a point of meaningful engagement between faculty and employers beyond agreeing that a common list of outcomes was valued without a shared understanding of what the learning outcomes mean or represent in terms of actual student learning.

Concerns Around Administration

Every institution undergoes changes in leadership. Presidents retire and provosts move on, and as they do, entire administrative cultures can shift dramatically. Some institutions have to cope with such changes more frequently than others, and the impact on how faculty and staff work—and on what they work—can be great. Sometimes, new administrative visions complement initiatives, but often they can seem to conflict, and momentum can be hindered. Few administrators want to interrupt valuable efforts, but as new ideas are introduced from offices higher up the chain, disruptions can result. The problems that can arise from changes in administration or administrative instability may fall in any number of categories, but most prominent are the uncertainty around how to integrate new ideas with existing administrative priorities and the clash of cultures in instances of competing models of organizational functioning. Both can be mitigated to varying degrees by collaborative campus cultures that employ processes of collective reflection and action.

New ideas can potentially energize work already happening on a campus, even if they can feel threatening to the effort and progress already made—recall McInerney's (2017) description of the AHA's embracing of conflict as a sign of engagement and productive discussion. The challenge before faculty and staff in this situation is not to choose between their own ongoing initiatives or the new ideas. That mode of thinking sets up a false dichotomy that may hinder progress more than it helps. Defensively digging in heels and refusing to budge sets up a confrontational atmosphere that few people enjoy. The challenge, rather, is to think through the ways in which the new injection of ideas can be incorporated into the existing efforts in the institution. Working within the learning systems paradigm involves thinking, as we have said, about the relationships among different parts of the learning environment in a collaborative way that brings together faculty and staff from across the institution, with each recognizing the distinct roles played within the learning environment. Incorporating new ideas becomes a matter of understanding which parts of the learning environment the ideas connect with in order to synthesize administrative priorities within existing efforts.

The clash of cultures draws on similar thinking. The mode of working in the learning systems paradigm that we have advocated works in accord with Birnbaum's (1988) collegial model, in which decision-making occurs through consensus that respects the viewpoints of multiple parties. Birnbaum's other models may be more descriptive of some administrators or administrative systems. An administrative culture that promotes the bureaucratic model might assign clear tasks to different parts of the institution that discourage cross-divisional collaboration and turn away from consensus-building. One that works within the political model may foster an atmosphere in which different parts of the institution compete with one another for resources, which might be assigned based on the relationships the leader has with different divisional heads. Establishing a collaborative environment, however, can help to preserve the consensus-driven ways of building the learning environment we have advocated. When individuals are responsible for conducting initiatives in the institution, changes in leadership can stymie progress, because the individual can end up siloed by policy and practice. When broad-based coalitions share responsibility, the shared investment and responsibility reduce the likelihood of that isolation occurring. Having broad involvement of institutional constituents throughout an institutional learning system ensures that at least one group that may be of interest to current administrative projects can make connections between the new efforts and how they fit with and support existing work. In essence, multiple advocates are available throughout the campus community to justify the value and purpose of the work—a broad base of involvement allows multiple ways in. One last point from the work of Birnbaum (1988) is salient. We need to remember that authority is not always defined by the position of the person providing a direction but by the willingness of the people doing the work to accept it. There is much agency throughout institutions of higher education, a point that is sometimes forgotten.

Each of these strategies depends, too, on making explicit the value propositions that underlie the initiatives being undertaken. The difficulty of prioritizing ideas arises when they are asserted as being obviously important, as if their value is apparent on the surface. That is another assumption that needs to be broken down. Why is the idea important? What value does the initiative carry? To whom? What problems does it address? How does it address them? Why does it matter to me? What is my role within it? These kinds of questions turn a potential conflict of thought about what the institution prioritizes into a conversation of potential impact. When coupled with efforts to incorporate new ideas into work within the learning systems paradigm, as discussed previously, these questions also offer a way of finding the possible synergies between them.

Working in Compliance-Driven Environments

The learning systems paradigm's emphasis on student learning experiences and the assignments by which students demonstrate their learning necessarily brings us into the orbit of assessment. The general perception of accreditation "forcing" institutions to do assessment has created a compliance-driven approach to how we assess student learning and report our activities, a topic we will address further in the conclusion and which Kuh and colleagues' (2015) book, *Using Evidence of Student Learning to Improve Higher Education,* addressed at length. That perception causes a sense that learning outcomes are a means of driving assessments, but outcomes are intended to drive teaching and learning. Assignments and other forms of assessment are a means of determining the degree to which students are successfully constructing the learning we set for them and foster in our courses. Where the compliance-driven perspective on assessment deviates dramatically from the paradigm is in the relative solitude in which assessment activities are completed by faculty. Chacon (2014) notes in her study of assessment practices that "faculty were largely working on their assessment in isolation, which was also creating a great deal of confusion" (p. 6).

Laboring under the weight of compliance ultimately derives from a different paradigm, one that emphasizes accountability as the end of accreditation rather than the creation of a mindful approach to building learning experiences. This older paradigm documents, often in superficial ways, processes that describe individual programs in circumscribed terms. An approach to working through this challenge is to reframe the perceived purpose around the relationships among the different parts of the learning environment so that student learning is reinforced and integrated. Confronting that paradigm in direct opposition will likely be counterproductive. Rather, listen to the complaints that faculty bring to the discussion (Chacon, 2014). Those complaints reveal valid concerns about workload, inefficient systems, and disconnected processes, among other things. Addressing the concerns validates the frustrations inherent in the counterproductive paradigm, provides insight into the disdain for assessment, and lays a foundation for intervening with the principles of the learning systems paradigm.

In the work of DQP and Tuning, an unexpected impact was how the work engaged faculty in meaningful assessment of student learning through a process of critical reflection. As quoted in the study on the impact of DQP, a faculty member remarked,

> I didn't realize when we started this project that I would be saying now—this work has shifted our faculty culture! All from conversations around the meaning of the degree. Those conversations enriched dialog with faculty across disciplines, encouraged more attention to applied learning, and made us enthusiastic about discussing pedagogy and assignment design. (Jankowski & Giffin, 2016a, p. 12)

Further, a faculty member in a Tuning survey stated,

> These are the kinds of conversations about the discipline that we should've been having from the start. I didn't know how much I longed for these conversations until they began—it has brought us together as a department in ways I had not thought possible and refreshed a sense of collegiality and togetherness we all long for.

A related concern revolves around the adoption of data management systems as a silver bullet for assessment efforts. At their most basic level, data management systems are virtual filing cabinets or archives, repositories for the information gathered throughout assessment processes and, within the learning systems paradigm, produced through processes of consensus-building and alignment. But think about a filing cabinet; it doesn't do anything with its contents but hold them. Data management systems are not designed to process and make meaning from outcomes, maps, and particular assignment designs. Expecting them to do so is unrealistic. Before engaging with data management systems, thought needs to be given to the role of the management system in assessment processes—its use and possible misuse. Operationally, there need to be strategies in place for gathering information everywhere learning happens and for using the information once gathered. Workload has to be a part of that thinking. One of the persistent complaints about assessment is that collection and presentation of data is inefficient. Reporting data in manageable ways poses a variety of challenges. How can information gathering be integrated into existing practice? How can information be organized for use? How and where can information be presented to foster reflection and discussion? Again, listening to complaints provides one avenue through these challenges; in most cases the complaints are very specific and relate to things that can be changed. Faculty may complain about existing systems but, in doing so, often imply alternatives. Careful listening can tease these alternatives out and launch new approaches that are more friendly to both the concerns raised and the modes of working encouraged by the learning systems paradigm. Forms, for example, may not be built in ways that capture what faculty are actually doing. Let faculty design the forms. Doing so becomes another opportunity for building consensus.

Concluding Thoughts

Each of these potential barriers relates to one persistent topic: redefining notions of collaboration. Briggs (2007) observes, "Efforts to improve the undergraduate core and major and to ensure that students graduate with a minimum set of competencies have challenged faculty members to coordinate courses and programs to an extent unprecedented on many campuses" (p. 676). New ways of working bring with them learning curves and questions: How do we identify with whom we should collaborate? How do we create spaces in which to collaborate? How do we collaborate around teaching and learning? How do we collaborate across divisions and with administrative personnel? How do we collaborate around assessment and with assessment personnel?

Our institutions are rarely networked in ways that make these questions easy to answer, and few offices interact broadly with all divisions across an institution. Offices of institutional research and/or assessment may be a place to turn. In keeping with its *Statement of Aspirational Practice,* the Association of Institutional Research (IR) is emerging as a resource for facilitating the kinds of cross-institution collaboration encouraged by the learning systems paradigm, because institutional research tends to look broadly across the learning environment (Jankowski & Kinzie, 2015; Jankowski & Marshall, 2015a). Work with DQP and Tuning has demonstrated the efficacy of institutional research in facilitating collaborative interactions, but success depends on a broadened role for institutional research. Faculty and staff do not always know what they need to ask institutional researchers, and so IR staff have to be attentive to the kinds of questions faculty are asking and the kinds of information they are seeking. Assessment professionals provide another mechanism of support for the learning system. In a paper exploring various roles of assessment practitioners, Natasha Jankowski and Ruth Slotnick (2015) outline five interrelated roles that can help foster connections across the learning environment including serving as a narrator/translator, facilitator/guide, and political navigator. As argued in the paper, "the outlined five essential roles squarely position the assessment practitioner as critical to developing a culture of improvement embedded within teaching and learning as opposed to creating a separate reporting structure divorced from students and their learning" (p. 95).

Finding individuals well positioned to network an institution, however, is only part of the solution. Understanding what collaboration looks like is another. Briggs (2007) set out "to explore how a group of exemplary academic departments organize and talk about their efforts to keep the curriculum effective and up-to-date" (p. 680) and found the "prominence of any one form of curriculum collaboration appears to be less critical to continuous program planning than engaging in a variety of forms of curriculum collaboration" (pp. 684–685). She continues, explaining that "an examination of the curriculum collaboration examples reveals an emphasis on (a) working together on tasks that result in tangible products (e.g., programs, clusters, courses, instructional materials), (b) monitoring the curriculum, and (c) learning together" (p. 685). Briggs differentiates academic collaboration around curriculum from teamwork, because teamwork assigns individual roles, whereas curricular collaboration is undertaken as a shared activity in which each faculty member engages in the same type of work. The model Briggs presents holds a great deal in common with Wenger's (1998) idea of communities of practice, in which individuals with common interests create a group intentionally organized to share knowledge in a mutually beneficial exchange that improves practice.

These models redefine collaboration in the direction of learning. Although collaboration around the various elements of the learning systems paradigm aims to accomplish something—improved student learning in an integrated, coherent learning environment—that approach to collaboration is driven by efforts to learn. Faculty and staff learn from one another's ideas about what learning is essential and what it looks like; they learn where learning happens across the institution and outside of it; they learn how students perceive their learning experiences; they learn how outside stakeholders conceive of essential learning. Collaboration within the paradigm draws disparate participants in a learning environment together for the purpose of learning about where and how students learn so that productive synergies supporting student success can be developed.

7

REFRAMING ACADEMIC
QUALITY

We end where we began. We started this book with a context-setting introduction that situated our argument for the learning systems paradigm and its actualization on a local level within a question about the purpose of higher education—on degrees that matter. As we noted there, stakeholders in and out of higher education have made arguments for workforce development, civic engagement, and personal development. In each case, the purpose has been tied to concerns about the "use" of degrees. Inherent in concerns about utility are questions about quality. How do we determine if institutions of higher education are producing graduates qualified (note the shared etymological origin with *quality*) to use their degrees in the world? Stakeholders have tried to establish multiple frames for defining *quality* in postsecondary education. They have tied quality to levels of gainful employment or income levels. Others have tied quality to comparative measures of the impact of receiving an education within a given community, measures that calculate and contrast income ratios for those graduating and those not attending an institution. An industry of rankings publications have developed their own complex formulas for determining quality institutions, formulas that include alumni giving, research funds, physical resources, faculty publications, grant acquisition, and a host of other factors (Bowman & Bastedo, 2009). Learning is rarely a component, and when it is, proxies such as student-faculty ratio serve as indicators.

Nationally, quality is affirmed through processes of accreditation by both regional and specialized accreditors. For both, learning outcomes assessment stands as a major determining factor. As a result, accreditation has become the major driver for outcomes assessment on campuses (Kuh et al., 2014). Figure 7.1 represents the typical assessment cycle. The production of learning outcome statements stands as a starting point, in which the desired learning within a program is described by those responsible for the program. Means

Figure 7.1. The typical assessment cycle.

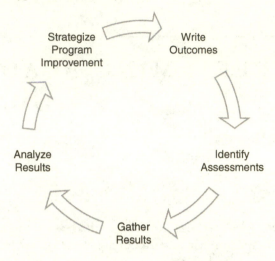

of assessment are then identified to measure student learning in relation to those outcomes, including direct and indirect means or external measures, such as the National Council Licensure Examination (NCLEX) exam in nursing. Once students complete these assessments, those responsible for the program gather data; analyze them; and, based on that analysis, strategize ways of improving results by adjusting elements of the program.

According to both of NILOA's institution-level surveys of assessment activities, in 2009 and 2013, expectations of regional and specialized accrediting agencies have remained the primary motivator for assessment of student learning (Kuh & Ikenberry, 2009; Kuh et al., 2014). That's a sad statement, if we take it to mean concern for whether we're actually succeeding in helping students learn is not our main motivator. Anyone working in higher education, however, knows this to be untrue. To be fair, program improvement was a close second in the provost surveys, so national perspectives on assessment are not wholly divorced from concerns for the quality of student learning. The fact is, *assessment* has become a word associated with meaningless, bureaucratic, add-on activities that do not match what we actually do in our classrooms and programs. As a result, a culture of compliance has grown in which institutions see accreditation as an end in itself, an attempt to "figure out" what accreditors want, and worry about whether or not the information they have matches accreditors' expectations (Ewell & Jankowski, 2015; Kuh et al., 2015). Figure 7.2 represents the impact this has on the assessment cycle. The general perception is that assessment is done to meet external expectations. To do so, perfunctory assessment procedures are undertaken,

Figure 7.2. A compliance-driven view of the assessment cycle.

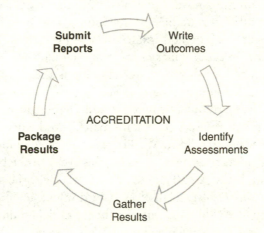

results are gathered, and reports submitted to assessment offices in an almost entirely externally facing process. As Lee Atwater is reported to have said, "Perception is reality." Unfortunately, this perception leaves students and their learning on the margins of what ideally focuses our reflection on how we can better facilitate student learning. We instead have created a process which ends with submitting reports, one that is divorced from teaching and learning and viewed as burdensome for faculty and staff.

Ultimately, we have a mismatched union between higher education institutions and accrediting agencies. The irony is that institutions are, themselves, the accreditors. Accrediting associations are member organizations and responsive to institutional needs. Their focus, they explain, is on mission-driven approaches to achieving student learning. In a NILOA (2016c) policy statement, the argument is made that institutions should "focus on improvement and compliance will take care of itself," a point reinforced by the president of the WASC Senior College and University Commission in her response of "Amen!" (p. 6). Institutions, however, tend to want accreditors to tell them what to do to meet reaccreditation or affirmation expectations, an impossibility since the agencies seek mission-driven approaches. Further, campus leadership has not been particularly helpful in framing the self-study process as one of reflection and exploration (Ewell & Jankowski, 2015). As a result, institutions often produce self-study reports that list processes and disconnected activities they anticipate accreditors are looking for, but in doing so exclude contextual information specific to the institution. They leave out what they were attempting to understand about student learning on their campuses and why. Peer reviewers are then left to comment on these reports without the contextual information they need to determine whether institutions are self-examining in ways congruent to their missions or to determine the degree to which they are helping students attain the learning they have identified as essential. The end result: 80% of institutions are required to undertake follow-up action on assessment in their reports (Provezis, 2010).

The consequence of this mismatched union is a sense of lost agency for institutions of higher education and a vicious cycle of frustration and anxiety. We might, furthermore, attribute the add-on, bureaucratic feel of many assessment programs to precisely this mismatch and the perception of secret expectations that lies behind it. Working within the learning systems paradigm, however, offers a means of breaking this cycle. In the NILOA (2016c) policy statement, NILOA staff and senior scholars make the point that issues of compliance will resolve themselves if institutions maintain a focus on quality, however individual institutions choose to define quality in student learning. Four other principles enable institutions to get to that point:

1. Develop specific, actionable learning outcomes statements.
2. Connect learning goals with actual student assignments and work.
3. Collaborate with relevant stakeholders, beginning with faculty.
4. Design assessment approaches that generate actionable evidence about student learning that key stakeholders can understand and use to improve student and institutional performance.

These principles shift the typical assessment cycle radically away from angst-riddled, decontextualized procedures that seem to dominate higher education in the United States toward processes that keep learners firmly located in the center of our work. Differing from a culture of compliance, the learning systems paradigm encourages faculty and staff to seek out information that indicates how well students are learning and/or how well various areas of the institution are supporting the learner experience. Figure 7.3 depicts this shift. Rather than trying to figure out what accreditors want to see, institutions working within this paradigm reflect on what faculty and staff teach or do and how they teach or do it. That derives from an acceptance of the responsibility we bear as educators to facilitate our students' learning and acknowledges our concern over whether or not our students are being successful. But accepting this responsibility and striving to be effective educators also means we experiment with new strategies. Adrianna Kezar (2015) observes that many people hold implicit beliefs that any change is a move away from or compromise to educational quality, rather than an enhancement. Whereas experimentation can produce, at times, mixed results, the intentional strategies to strengthen students' learning that have emerged from work within the learning systems

Figure 7.3. A learner-centered view of the assessment cycle.

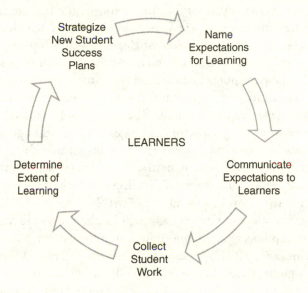

paradigm have more often than not produced excellent results. Working within the learning systems paradigm would be one such experiment for campuses not already engaged in it.

Communicating Quality

Given the pervasive desire of faculty and staff to support student learning, these issues point to problems of communication at a variety of levels. Compliance-driven assessment often yields grumbles and complaints about additional work disconnected from what actually goes on in classrooms and at kitchen tables stacked with assignments needing to be graded. Those stacks point to the ways that meaningful assessment of learning can be happening. Faculty, in most cases, are engaged in evaluation of learning through activities, assignments, and tests. Although grades, which aggregate the different areas of learning we hope to foster, may not be the best means of determining learning in those different areas, grading *can* be a process by which we do that. And many faculty already are. What we tend to lack are clear ways to communicate findings—sometimes because we have only aggregated information, but other times because we lack the systems to facilitate that communication or our systems have been collecting the wrong sorts of information (Kinzie & Jankowski, 2015).

Distrust exists regarding communication of student quality. We have already discussed the distrust inherent in the cultural discourses around whether higher education is adequately developing student learning. But distrust—or at least the perception of distrust—exists up and down the system. One might argue that compliance-driven outcomes assessment is motivated by the perception that external constituencies do not trust in the work done by faculty and staff within institutions or doubt the efficacy of what we do to foster student learning. Distrust certainly marks many faculty and staff perceptions of the assessment process. A path through perceptions of distrust may be a particular approach to communication: argumentation. We do not use the terms *argument* or *argumentation* in their popular association as ranting and blind assertions of being right while another is wrong. Rather, we use the terms in ways akin to E.M. Nussbaum's (2012) explanation of argumentation as a means by which implicit ideas are made explicit and prior conceptions and misconceptions are revealed.

E.M. Nussbaum (2012) notes that, in a learner-centered learning environment, "argumentation can result in students considering a richer array of facets and variables in their thinking, can expose faults in students' own conceptions and can increase student understanding and commitment to alternative ideas" (p. 114). These potential benefits are all things we desire for learners, but they can also be means for us to develop richer understandings of why we approach educating students as we do—not just for ourselves, but for those with whom we communicate. Doing so will require us to explicate the warrants by which we support the claims we often make implicitly about how students learn. *Warrants,* in the sense used by McNeill, Lizotte, Krajcik, and Marx (2006), are theoretical principles that explain why a piece of evidence supports or disconfirms a particular claim. In the case of fostering learning, our warrants would entail the assumptions we bring to the construction of our curricula, pedagogies, assignments, and cocurricula, as well as our assessment of them. As Toulmin (2003) observes, in ordinary discourse warrants are typically left implicit unless there is a need to explain them. We have need, but we have been uncertain as to how to explain our warrants. Our struggles to unpack our own assumptions around learning are understandable, given the fact that most faculty are not trained in pedagogy or assessment. As Professor Farnsworth exclaims on the satirical cartoon *Futurama* (Burns & Haaland, 1999), "Please, Fry, I don't know how to teach; I'm a professor!" Our training exists within disciplinary research methodologies and the subject matter to which we apply them. Argumentation, therefore, offers us a means of self-understanding as we help others, including accreditors, understand why we do what we do. Assessment is a place in which we can explicate the ideas about student learning on which we have founded our praxis, first to and for ourselves, and then toward others. The development of the Excellence in Assessment (EIA) designation was done in part to address the need for effectively communicating our stories of learning to a variety of audiences. The EIA is jointly sponsored by the Voluntary System of Accountability, AAC&U, and NILOA and serves as the first national designation to recognize colleges and universities that integrate assessment practices through internal alignment (Kinzie, Hinds, Jankowski, & Rhodes, 2017). Building from NILOA's Transparency Framework (2011), the application process invites institutions to reflect on their assessment processes, focusing on intentional integration, meaningful alignment, and faculty-led assessment, including intentional involvement of student affairs, students, and external stakeholders. The end result is a coherent narrative about institutional assessment (Kinzie et al., 2017).

Communication at the program-level, then, may need to improve around assessment. In the preceding chapters, we have offered a variety of starting points for how those conversations might begin, but, as we have said, where a given faculty begins will depend on the particular program and context. Internal to programs, conversations around assessment may require unpacking the implicit warrants that drive the shape of our curriculum, the particular pedagogies we employ, and the strategies we use to elicit demonstrations of learning by our students. Why, in other words, do we do things the way we do? This question, ultimately, is the basis of assessment. Ultimately, assessment is a research project, and every faculty member is, in some way, trained in research. Academic faculty are associated with research, but career technical educators are, too. For example, diesel mechanics instructors are trained in the careful observation of complex mechanical systems, the identification of suboptimal functions in the system, and the development of solutions to return those functions to an optimal state. And research is a process of discovery driven by good questions. Internal communication among faculty within assessment processes is important. In some cases this may require, as Kezar (2015) notes, a "move from the mindset of faculty as independent contractor to being a member of collective, institutional action" (p. 17). When reviewing student learning, collective action is essential. Different faculty may be seeing different patterns and anomalies, and exploring these together, including where we see those patterns and why they might be emerging, begins to move us closer to understanding our own warrants and becoming more intentional about the approaches we undertake as a result of them.

Programs also need to communicate outside of themselves, often to offices of assessment or to assessment coordinators. In this relationship we risk the same mismatches that exist between accreditors and institutions, with program faculty wanting to know what the assessment team requires, and assessment teams needing a contextualized explanation of processes and current learning from faculty. Note that we are not using the word *results.* Assessment "results" imply an end, whereas meaningful assessment is an ongoing process of curiosity and question-asking about learning. Assessment teams need more than results. Communicating how the program assesses and why provides context that can frame discipline-specific strategies. Explaining what program faculty are learning through their assessment processes about how students are learning will develop a richer understanding than the all-too-typical "are our students successfully meeting the outcomes" approach. In other words, unpacking our warrants and engaging in good argumentation will equip assessment personnel with the understanding they require to situate our learning about our students' learning within the larger space of the institution. Doing so may derive other benefits, too. Communicating assessment activities and the lessons drawn from them in contextualized ways can open opportunities for working more synergistically across campus divisions, particularly when assessment personnel and committees are looking for points of potential contact across them. Work with DQP and Tuning tends to generate the potential, as Dannels (2015) indicates, because they are intended to foster reflective, sustained interactions among students, faculty, and administrators while strengthening the quality of teaching and learning at various levels. Faculty do not always understand the institution as a complex system and they may need help seeing it as such (Kezar, 2015); assessment practices that work in this way can help to build such understanding.

Institutions, however, work within larger complex systems, involving partner institutions in local regions, civic organizations, K–12 schools, and employers. We tend not to think about outside stakeholders as a group with whom we might share our conversations regarding assessment practices, but there can be benefits here, too. For example, historians participating in the AHA's Tuning initiative consulted with local employers about what students in history graduate knowing and being able to do, based on the outcomes developed in the project. In some cases, those conversations led to partnerships in the form of internships. Had program faculty not communicated with these stakeholders, those opportunities may not have emerged for students. Talking to outside stakeholders enables them to better understand what students learn. If we accept that, for example, a community college and its primary destination partners collaborate by sharing learners at different times, then the benefits of this kind of stakeholder communication should become clear. Four-year institutions can be better prepared to leverage learner strengths and struggles by being aware of the students coming to them. By sharing what we know about our students' learning with stakeholder groups outside the institution, we prepare them to receive our learners as they move into new phases of their educations or into the workforce.

Audience matters in such dialogue. Different audiences hold different concerns, different levels of awareness, and different ways of speaking. The NCA (2015), as we might expect, was acutely aware of this fact as they considered how to share their work with various groups of stakeholders. They produced multiple documents to convey the purpose, goals, and substance of their learning outcomes initiative, including a one-sheet explanation of what students in communication learn to better inform employers, with other versions of the document clarifying degrees in communication and the learning they represent geared toward faculty nationwide, students and parents, advising personnel, career services, and other groups. That kind of initiative draws larger stakeholder populations into our scope and helps to open communication in ways that can foster the collaborative processes we have described throughout this book.

For each audience, two common questions undergird what we might communicate. Why do we do what we do to foster and evaluate student learning? How does what we do benefit our students? Answering these questions is a process of unpacking the warrants behind our actions, explanations of why and how we work that rarely get discussed. Communicating this kind of information to different audiences puts student learning back at the center of our work and integrates assessment into much of what we already do. Sharing with others the rationales behind our curricula, pedagogies, and assignments enables our audiences to capitalize on the work we do with our students to prepare them for future challenges. In terms of assessment, explicating our rationales communicates what we take quality to mean within our own programmatic, institutional, and local contexts. Obviously, different types of institutions serve different types of learners. Around particular institutions within those types, missions may focus on serving particular community needs. Learners attending institutions in impoverished communities may struggle with being underprepared in ways that learners attending large, private research institutions may not. That context has a very real impact on how we work to develop student learning. When we center the quality debate around our students in our contexts, we make their learning the measure of quality. Given the fact that assessment occurs within very specific institutional contexts, and given the fact that accreditors look for alignment between our individual missions and how we, as members of a specific institution, facilitate and improve learning, *quality* becomes a locally defined term. We serve our learners, our stakeholders, and ourselves better if the ways we communicate reflect that.

An additional audience to which we must communicate assessment information is learners. Students stand to benefit a great deal when we communicate the rationales for how we structure learning experiences to them. Doing so requires making outcomes explicit, as well as explaining how our curricula are structured to foster learning and how our assignments challenge students to develop their learning in relation to outcomes. When learners have this context, they are better able to direct their energies toward the learning we aspire for them to have. With reflective or metacognitive assignments, they become not only more aware of their learning but also of how the ways we ask them to work equip them to use their learning elsewhere (Jankowski, 2017). However, they won't know if we don't share them.

Another way to communicate more clearly beyond the campus may be institutional efforts to revise transcripting practices. Transcripts largely communicate how much time students spend in classes and the grades they receive. That information reveals relatively little about the learning students attain while sitting in those classes. Transcript models built around students' work in relation to outcomes may provide a better picture of how students are prepared for further education or the workforce. Transcript supplements and cocurricular transcripts and the work on comprehensive student records offer other strategies for better documenting the learning students have constructed on their educational journeys, but, as we have said, these kinds of changes require larger institutional work on how the institution as a whole reports, views, and validates student learning.

NILOA's (2011) Transparency Framework grows from these principles and provides a heuristic for determining ways of communicating what we are learning about how we and our students are doing. Essential to each aspect of the framework is clarity of both language and location. Every field uses its own technical language to describe what it does, and education is no different, but our audiences may take that language as jargon that interferes with their understanding. Clearly worded explanations are, therefore, essential. Moreover, assessment processes and results tend to be buried on institutional websites or not exist in forms accessible to those who may be interested. Clarity about where those who are curious can find such information facilitates the kinds of conversation this information can generate. To that end, the framework also encourages means of accepting feedback. That element may raise concerns, but if we are to be responsive to our contexts, feedback systems are essential—or we risk closing down valuable information that may (or may not) help us to address student learning better.

Concluding Thoughts

Each institution has a unique story to tell. We have not been accustomed to telling those stories. New pressures on higher education are beginning to necessitate that we do. As we noted at the outset of this book, a variety of factors have shifted perceptions of higher education. Increased cost for degrees, concerns about preparedness of our students, and skepticism about the value of degrees have contributed to an erosion of confidence in American higher education. A recent poll by Public Agenda indicates that most Americans feel a college degree is not the only way to get ahead, with 58% stating that college is unnecessary (Schleifer & Silliman, 2016). This runs counter, perhaps, to a Gallup (2014) poll, in which 37%, up from 30% in 2011, believed that U.S. institutions offer high-quality degrees, but together they suggest American confidence in higher education is rather low. Telling our stories is one way to intervene in this trend.

So let's return to Natasha Jankowski's airplane conversations, which we mentioned in our introduction. When she tells seatmates that she works for a national research institute that tries to figure out how we know if students learn in college, the typical reply is something to the effect of "I didn't learn anything in college." When Natasha presses them, they can rattle off a host of things they believe they have learned, but in spite of what we do, not because of it. They report being unaware of how their learning experiences have equipped them to be civically engaged and personally fulfilled employees. They attribute learning to processes of personal development without the support and challenges we put before them. They suggest that they have learned on the job what it takes to be successful.

What this indicates, if we rely on the anecdotal evidence, is that our students fail to see why and how we have fostered their learning, not just in content areas, but in the areas reductively referred to as "soft skills." If the purpose of college is multifaceted, consisting of developing fulfilled, civically engaged members of the workforce, then our students may not be connecting what they do with us in any of those three areas of their lives. And yet our students populate the country, having completed degrees and gone on to one career or another. They make up the very civic organizations and employer groups that lament the quality and relevance of higher education, a fact that might explain the apparently low levels of confidence in what we do. All those seatmates are potential advocates for higher education who are unable to advocate because their experience of higher education has not been transparent. We never told them what we were striving for.

American higher education has tremendous untapped potential to change this situation. We have simply lacked a strong paradigm for leveraging it. Kuhn (1996), in his explanation of scientific paradigms, argues that fields undergo changes and confront new challenges over time that require the emergence of paradigms capable of working through them. The new context in which U.S. higher education operates has necessitated a new paradigm, one that can address the questions that external pressures have generated for us. To date, the paradigms we have worked within have addressed pieces of institutional experience, but not the whole. Consider the different discourses operating within a single institution: administration holds concerns over, among other things, budgetary implications of the various components of the institution; academic affairs holds concerns over teaching students and, in some institution types, conducting research; and student affairs holds concerns over providing complete educational experiences that address students' personal development. In each of these three areas, journals and books address these concerns. The result may well be a fractured conceptual frame for reading and working within higher education, with the different areas speaking conversantly within themselves in theories, practices, and jargon particular to them, but not across these divisions.

One might argue that higher education has existed in what Kuhn (1996) calls a pre-paradigmatic state, lacking conceptual structures that bring order to how we understand the field. Although each of the subareas of institutions have, perhaps, worked within their own paradigms, higher education, as a field, has lacked a paradigm for fully comprehending itself. The learning systems paradigm attempts to remedy that lack. By understanding that institutions are complex systems, as Kezar (2015) notes, we who work within them—and within the larger field of higher education—can become more intentional and more strategic about how we work together to foster student learning. By doing so, we can address the questions that all those external pressures are raising and, in the process, create more coherent and explicit learning experiences for students, the best advocates we have for what we do.

NILOA National Advisory Panel

James Anderson
Interim Dean
Edward William and Jane Marr Gutgsell Professor
University of Illinois Urbana-Champaign

Wallace Boston
CEO
American Public University System

Molly Corbett Broad
President
American Council on Education

Judith Eaton
President
Council for Higher Education Accreditation

Richard Ekman
President
Council of Independent Colleges

Keston Fulcher
Director of the Center for Assessment and Research Studies
Associate Professor, Graduate Psychology
James Madison University

Mildred Garcia
President
California State University, Fullerton

Paul Gaston III
Trustees Professor
Kent State University

Susan Johnston
Executive Vice President
Association of Governing Boards

Norman Jones
Professor
Utah State University

Peggy Maki
Higher Education Consultant

George Mehaffy
Vice President for Academic Leadership and Change
American Association of State Colleges and Universities

Lynn Pasquerella
President
Association of American Colleges & Universities

George Pernsteiner
President
State Higher Education Executive Officers Association

Mary Ellen Petrisko
President
WASC Senior College and University Commission

Kent Phillippe
Associate Vice President, Research and Student Success
American Association of Community Colleges

Robert Sheets
Research Professor
The George Washington University

Ralph Wolff
Founder and President
The Quality Assurance Commons for Higher and Postsecondary Education

Ex-Officio Members

Peter Ewell
President Emeritus
National Center for Higher Education Management Systems

Stanley Ikenberry
President Emeritus and Regent Professor
University of Illinois

Natasha Jankowski
Director, NILOA
Research Assistant Professor, University of Illinois
Urbana-Champaign

George Kuh
Founding Director, NILOA
Adjunct Research Professor, University of Illinois Urbana-Champaign
Chancellor's Professor Emeritus, Indiana University

Paul Lingenfelter
President Emeritus
State Higher Education Executive Officers Association

Past NILOA National Advisory Board Members (Titles at Time of Service on Board)

Joseph Alutto
Distinguished Professor of Organizational Behavior
Fisher College of Business
The Ohio State University

Trudy W. Banta
Professor of Higher Education
Indiana University–Purdue University Indianapolis

Douglas C. Bennett
President
Earlham College

Robert M. Berdahl
President
Association of American Universities

Jodi Finney
Practice Professor
University of Pennsylvania
Vice President
National Center for Public Policy and Higher Education

Stephen Jordan
President
Metropolitan State University–Denver

Mary Kalantzis
Dean, College of Education
University of Illinois Urbana-Champaign

Margaret Miller
Professor
University of Virginia
Editor, Change Magazine

Charlene Nunley
Doctoral Program Director, Professor Doctor of Management in
Community College Policy and Administration
University of Maryland University College

Carol Schneider
President Emerita
Association of American Colleges & Universities

David Schulenburger
Senior Fellow
Association of Public and Land-Grant Universities

Randy Swing
Executive Director
Association for Institutional Research

Michael Tanner
Chief Academic Officer/Vice President
Association of Public and Land-Grant Universities

Belle Wheelan
President
Southern Association of Colleges and Schools Commission on Colleges

George Wright
President
Prairie View A&M University

NILOA Staff 2008 to 2017

NILOA Senior Staff

Gianina Baker
Assistant Director

Timothy Reese Cain
Senior Scholar
Associate Professor, Institute of Higher Education at
the University of Georgia

Peter Ewell
Senior Scholar
President Emeritus, National Center for Higher Education
Management Systems

Pat Hutchings
Senior Scholar
Carnegie Foundation for the Advancement of Teaching

Stanley Ikenberry
Co-Principal Investigator
Emeritus Regent Professor and President Emeritus, University of Illinois

Natasha Jankowski
Director, NILOA
Research Assistant Professor, Department of Education Policy,
Organization, and Leadership
University of Illinois Urbana-Champaign

Jillian Kinzie
Senior Scholar
Associate Director, Indiana University Center for
Postsecondary Research & NSSE Institute

George Kuh
Founding Director, Co-Principal Investigator and Senior Scholar
Chancellor's Professor Emeritus of Higher Education, Indiana University

Paul Lingenfelter
Senior Scholar
President Emeritus, State Higher Education Executive Officers Association

David Marshall
Senior Scholar
Professor and Director of the University Honors Program, California State University San Bernardino

Filip Przybysz
Communications Coordinator

Kathryn Schultz
Project Manager

NILOA Staff, 2008 to 2017

Staci Provezis, Project Manager
Carrie Allen, Research Analyst
Sharanya Bathey, Research Analyst
T. Jameson Brewer, Research Analyst
Karie Brown-Tess, Research Analyst
Robert Dumas, Research Analyst
Nora Gannon-Slater, Research Analyst
Laura Giffin, Research Analyst
Jason Goldfarb, Research Analyst
Julia Panke Makela, Research Analyst
Nishanth Mandaara, Research Analyst
Balaji Manoharan, Research Analyst
Erick Montenegro, Research Analyst
Suhas Hoskote Muralidhar, Research Analyst
P. S. Myers, Research Analyst
Verna F. Orr, Research Analyst
Jelena Pokimica, Research Analyst
Richa Sehgal, Research Analyst
Gloria Shenoy, Research Analyst
Anthony B. Sullers Jr., Research Analyst
Emily Teitelbaum, Research Analyst
Jennifer Timmers, Research Analyst
Terry Vaughan III, Research Analyst

NILOA Degree Qualifications Profile/Tuning Coaches

To advance and accelerate campus initiatives to enhance student learning, the National Institute for Learning Outcomes Assessment (NILOA) is pleased to offer a practical, useful resource to improve student learning at institutions—the Degree Qualifications Profile (DQP)/Tuning Coaches. DQP/Tuning Coaches are available to help colleges and universities with their improvement efforts. Drawn from different types of institutions around the country, the coaches are experienced faculty, administrators, and staff who know firsthand about the utility and value of the DQP and Tuning and can assist with local-level implementation opportunities and challenges. Because they are knowledgeable about the DQP, Tuning, assignment design, assessment, and strategies for institutional change, the coaches can encourage and support institutions at various stages of DQP/Tuning work. DQP/Tuning coaches are available for a one-day campus visit at no cost to the host institution. A coach will be paired with the requesting institution based on a match of interests, intended outcomes, and expertise.

Sandra Bailey is the director of assessment at Oregon Tech, a position she has held since 2010. In this role she has guided institutional and program assessment efforts, communicated results to constituents, and documented a growing culture of continuous improvement. Bailey now leads a task force engaged in a comprehensive general education review using assessment results to guide the redesign of general education at Oregon Tech. She is a member of the Faculty Engagement group of the Multi-State Collaborative to Advance Learning Outcomes and Assessment and has been an invited presenter for various national assessment conferences.

Ellen Baker Derwin is the associate dean of curriculum and assurance of learning and associate professor of communication for the School of Arts and Sciences at Brandman University. She oversees continuous improvement, new program and course development, and assessment. Derwin chairs an interdisciplinary faculty team to redesign general education using the DQP framework. She also chairs the general education curriculum team for competency-based education (CBE) and created several modules for

Brandman's inaugural CBE program. She holds a doctorate in psychology from Fielding Graduate University.

Laurie G. Dodge is the vice chancellor of institutional assessment and planning and vice provost at Brandman University. She oversees program assessment and program review, new and revised curriculum, and state authorization. She also helped lead the creation of the institutional learning outcomes using the DQP framework. Dodge is serving as chair of the Competency-Based Education Network (C-BEN); has served on congressional briefings on competency-based education; sits on the University Professional & Continuing Education Association (UPCEA) Advisory Board & Presidential Task Force; and conducts national workshops on design, assessment, and teaching and learning for competency-based education.

Tami Eggleston is professor of psychology and associate dean for institutional effectiveness at McKendree University in Lebanon, Illinois. She is the coordinator of the Teaching for Excellence (T4E) faculty-development program and is a Higher Learning Commission (HLC) peer reviewer. Eggleston regularly presents at conferences and campuses on a variety of topics, including student learning outcomes, assessment tools and best practices, rubrics, data use, assessment plan design, strategic planning, engaged teaching, technology use, online and blended learning, and team building.

Tyrone Freeman serves as the director of undergraduate programs and visiting lecturer in philanthropic studies for the Indiana University (IU) Lilly Family School of Philanthropy in Indianapolis. In this role, Freeman is growing the first BA program in philanthropic studies. He leads the ePortfolio and assessment efforts of the school and teaches in the undergraduate and graduate programs in philanthropic studies. Prior to joining the faculty, Freeman served as associate director of The Fund Raising School and as director of development at the IU School of Education at Indiana University–Purdue University Indianapolis.

Laura M. Gambino is the associate dean for assessment and technology and professor of information technology at Guttman Community College (CUNY). In her role as associate dean, Gambino oversees assessment of Guttman's institutional student learning outcomes, periodic program reviews, and assessment of programs such as Summer Bridge, global learning, and academic support. Gambino, a leading ePortfolio practitioner and researcher, oversees the college's institution-wide ePortfolio program, leads the Integrated Planning and Advising for Student Success (iPASS) project, has presented nationally and internationally, and regularly serves as a consultant to higher education institutions.

Elise Martin is the dean of assessment at Middlesex Community College. She oversees learning outcomes assessment at multiple levels and provides administrative support for curricular and pedagogical initiatives leading to student achievement of institutional and programmatic learning outcomes. She is involved in the Vision Project to advance learning outcomes assessment in Massachusetts. Martin is also a member of the New England Educational Assessment Network, has served on the board of directors for the New England Faculty Development Consortium, and has done consulting for several community colleges in Massachusetts.

Daniel McInerney is professor of history and associate head of the Department of History at Utah State University. He has been part of statewide Tuning projects in Utah, holds a membership on the Tuning USA Advisory Board, and serves as senior adviser on the American Historical Association Tuning Project. He has given dozens of presentations on the Tuning process to audiences in Utah as well as introducing the work to institutions in Kentucky, Idaho, Texas, Montana, and the Midwestern Higher Education Compact. He holds a doctorate in American studies-history from Purdue University.

Brad Mello is associate professor and chair of the communication department and a member of the university-wide general education committee at Saint Xavier University in Chicago, Illinois. He is a team leader and the grant author for the National Communication Association's student learning outcomes DQP/Tuning project. He received his BA and MA in speech communication from Penn State University and his PhD in communication from the University of Oklahoma.

Stephanie Poczos is an assistant professor and the director of the New Undergraduate Initiatives and Harrison Professional Pathways programs at National Louis University (NLU). She was one of the principle designers of the Pathways program, which is an affordable and adaptive undergraduate program that provides comprehensive, personalized support for students of any socioeconomic status. The Pathways program utilizes the DQP in three tracks of study with 35 customized competencies built and aligned inside of problem-based assessments in the courses. Stephanie has worked in many areas of NLU, most notably designing and implementing the BA in the applied communications program. She has taught and developed courses at a variety of universities, including Charter Oak State College, which was one of the first colleges to utilize a competency-based learning model. Stephanie holds an EdS in educational leadership and an MA in teaching from NLU and a BA in communications from the University of Iowa.

Nancy Quam-Wickham is the chairperson of the Department of History at California State University–Long Beach, a position she has held since 2005. Prior to this, she was the editor of the *History Teacher Journal.* She is a participant in AHA's Tuning project and has presented her work on Tuning in history at a number of professional meetings. She holds a bachelor's degree from San Francisco State University and a doctorate in history from the University of California–Berkeley.

Ruth C. Slotnick is the director of assessment at Bridgewater State University. Slotnick oversees all institutional academic assessment activities and assists programs and departments with assessment planning and continuous improvement goals. At the national level, she was a recipient of and coinvestigator on an AAC&U Quality Collaborative grant, a three-year project supported by the Lumina Foundation to examine the alignment of student learning outcomes at two- and four-year institutions using the DQP and the AAC&U LEAP VALUE rubrics. At the state level, Ruth serves as a member of the Advancing Massachusetts Culture of Assessment team and the New England Educational Assessment Network. She holds a PhD in higher education research from the University of South Florida and an MEd in art education from Pennsylvania State University.

Sharon A. Valente is associate provost for educational effectiveness at Marymount California University (MCU). She has been involved with MCU's work with the Council for Independent Colleges and NILOA on the use of the DQP. Her prior experience includes service as director of institutional assessment and effectiveness at the University of St. Thomas in Houston, Texas, and as director of evaluation and policy studies at the Savannah College of Art and Design. She also served as university coordinator of assessment at Ashland University in Ohio.

Ereka R. Williams is an associate professor in the Department of Curriculum and Instruction at North Carolina Agricultural and Technical State University, where she has been on the faculty since 2003. Williams has served in a host of national, regional, and on-campus roles, including cochairing the university's DQP Pilot Project. She holds a doctorate in curriculum and instruction-teacher education from the University of North Carolina at Greensboro.

Additional Resources on Degree Qualifications Profile and Tuning

Assignments

Eubanks, D., & Gliem, D. (2015, May). *Improving teaching, learning, and assessment by making evidence of achievement transparent.* (Occasional Paper No. 25). Urbana, IL: University of Illinois and Indiana University, National Institute for Learning Outcomes Assessment.

National Institute for Learning Outcomes Assessment. (n.d.). *DQP assignment library* [Assignment Library Initiative]. Retrieved from http://assignmentlibrary.org

National Institute for Learning Outcomes Assessment. (n.d.). *DQP assignment library: Course-embedded assessment resource list.* Retrieved from http://degreeprofile .org/resource-kit/course-embedded-assignments/

National Institute for Learning Outcomes Assessment. (n.d.). *DQP assignment library: Rubrics* [Rubric Resources]. Retrieved from http://degreeprofile.org/ resource-kit/rubrics/

National Institute for Learning Outcomes Assessment. (n.d.). *Resources for developing effective assignments* [List of Additional Resources for Assignments]. http:// assignmentlibrary.org/uploaded/files/Assignment_Resources.pdf

Switzer, D., Coots, A., Mulrooney, J., & Rhodes, T. (2016). *Faculty perspectives: Selecting assignments to assess learning outcomes using authentic student work* [Webinar on the Multi-State Collaborative to Advance Learning Outcomes Assessment (MSC)/VALUE Initiative]. Retrieved from https://www1.taskstream .com/resource/assignments-artifacts-mscwebinar3/

Degree Qualifications Profile

Berg, L., Grimm, L. M., Wigmore, D., Cratsley, C. K., Slotnick, R. C., & Taylor, S. (2014). Quality collaborative to assess quantitative reasoning: Adapting the LEAP VALUE rubric and the DQP. *Peer Review, 16*(3), 17–21.

Hutchings, P. (2014). *DQP case study: Point Loma Nazarene University, San Diego, California.* Urbana, IL: University of Illinois and Indiana University, National Institute for Learning Outcomes Assessment (NILOA).

Kinzie, J. (2014). *DQP case study: University system of Georgia—Georgia State University and Georgia Perimeter College.* Urbana, IL: University of Illinois and Indiana University, National Institute for Learning Outcomes Assessment (NILOA).

Kinzie, J. (2015). *DQP case study: American Public University System.* Urbana, IL: University of Illinois and Indiana University, National Institute for Learning Outcomes Assessment (NILOA).

Lumina Foundation. (n.d.). *Degree Qualifications Profile: Examples of use at institutions* [Examples of Use at DQP Institutions: 25 Ranging from Accreditation Education to Entire Institutional Redesign]. Retrieved from http://degreeprofile.org/examples-of-use/

Lumina Foundation. (n.d.). *Degree Qualifications Profile: Student affairs and cocurriculum* [Student Affairs and Cocurricular Resource List]. Retrieved from http://degreeprofile.org/resource-kit/student-affairs-and-co-curriculum/

Lumina Foundation. (n.d.). *Degree Qualifications Profile: Transfer/Articulation* [Transfer and Articulation Resources]. Retrieved from http://degreeprofile.org/resource-kit/transferarticulation/

National Institute for Learning Outcomes Assessment. (n.d.). *DQP: Webinars and videos* [Project-Specific Webinars]. Retrieved from http://degreeprofile.org/webinars-videos/

National Institute for Learning Outcomes Assessment. (2016). *Alignment with external expectations.* Urbana, IL: University of Illinois and Indiana University, National Institute for Learning Outcomes Assessment (NILOA).

National Institute for Learning Outcomes Assessment. (2016). *The birth and growth of the Degree Qualifications Profile.* Urbana, IL: University of Illinois and Indiana University, National Institute for Learning Outcomes Assessment (NILOA).

National Institute for Learning Outcomes Assessment. (2016). *General education and/or program development and review.* Urbana, IL: University of Illinois and Indiana University, National Institute for Learning Outcomes Assessment (NILOA).

National Institute for Learning Outcomes Assessment. (2016). *Improving student transfer.* Urbana, IL: University of Illinois and Indiana University, National Institute for Learning Outcomes Assessment (NILOA).

National Institute for Learning Outcomes Assessment. (2016). *Revision and alignment of learning outcomes.* Urbana, IL: University of Illinois and Indiana University, National Institute for Learning Outcomes Assessment (NILOA).

Transcript Related Work

American Association of Collegiate Registrars and Admissions Officers and NASPA. (2015). *A framework for extending the transcript.* Retrieved from http://www.aacrao.org/docs/default-source/PDF-Files/extending-the-transcript-framework-final-draft-.pdf?sfvrsn=2

National Institute for Learning Outcomes Assessment. (2016). *Resources on badges.* Urbana, IL: University of Illinois and Indiana University, National Institute for Learning Outcomes Assessment (NILOA).

Parnell, A., & Green, T. (2016). Linking learning inside and outside the classroom: Cocurricular experiences add value. *Leadership Exchange, 13*, 4.

Tuning USA

American Historical Association. (n.d.). *Tuning the History Discipline in the United States.* Retrieved from https://www.historians.org/teaching-and-learning/tuning-the-history-discipline

Developing and implementing learning outcomes in communication. (2015). *Spectra, 51*(4). Retrieved from https://www.natcom.org/spectra/

Institute for Evidence Based Change. (2012). *Tuning American higher education: The process.* Encinitas, CA: Author.

Journal of American History. (2016, March). *Special issue on Tuning.*

Lumina Foundation. (n.d.). *Document archive* [Tuning Document Archive]. Retrieved from http://degreeprofile.org/document-archive/

National Communication Association. (n.d.). *Learning outcomes in communication.* Retrieved from https://www.natcom.org/LOC/

Additional Learning Frameworks

AAC&U Essential Learning Outcomes. Retrieved from https://www.aacu.org/leap/essential-learning-outcomes

AAC&U Essential Learning Outcomes VALUE Rubrics. Retrieved from https://www.aacu.org/value/rubrics

A Beta Credentials Framework. Retrieved from http://connectingcredentials.org/framework/

Beta Credentials Framework Guidebook. Retrieved from http://connectingcredentials.org/wp-content/uploads/2016/02/CC_User-Guide_v6.pdf

Credential Transparency Initiative. (n.d.). *From chaos to clarity: A vision for the U.S. credentialing marketplace.* Retrieved from http://www.credentialtransparencyinitiative.org/

Employability Skills Framework. Retrieved from http://cte.ed.gov/employabilityskills/

Interstate Passport Initiative—Framework. Retrieved from http://www.wiche.edu/passport/knowledge_skills

National Network of Business and Industry Associations (2014). *Common employability skills: A foundation for success in the workforce.* Retrieved from http://businessroundtable.org/sites/default/files/CommonEmployability_asingle_fm.pdf

Soares, L., & Tyszko, J. (2015). *How to navigate the credentialing maze.* Washington, DC: U.S Chamber of Commerce Center for Education and Workforce.

REFERENCES

Accrediting Commission for Community and Junior Colleges. (2015, April). *Special edition: Featuring SLO projects at 16 member institutions.* Novato, CA: Author.

Achieving the Dream, American Association of Community Colleges, Charles A. Dana Center, Complete College America, the Education Commission of the States, and Jobs for the Future. (2015). *Core principles for transforming remediation within a comprehensive student success strategy.* Washington, DC: Authors.

Adelman, C. (2009). *The Bologna process for U.S. eyes: Re-learning higher education in the age of convergence.* Washington, DC: Institute for Higher Education Policy.

Adelman, C. (2015, February). *To imagine a verb: The language and syntax of learning outcome statements* (NILOA Occasional Paper No. 24). Urbana, IL: University of Illinois and Indiana University, National Institute for Learning Outcomes Assessment.

Ajinkya, J., Brabender, L., Chen, E., & Moreland, M. (2015). *Ensuring college readiness and academic system alignment for all students.* Washington, DC: Institute for Higher Education Policy.

Albone, K. R. (2015). Assessment of a small group semester-long project. *Assessment Update, 27*(1), 1–2, 15–16.

Alvarez, L. (2012, December 10). To steer students toward jobs, Florida may reduce tuition for select majors. *The New York Times,* p. A14.

American Association of College Registrars and Administrative Officers. (n.d.). *Comprehensive student records project.* Retrieved from http://www.aacrao.org/resources/record

American Association of Collegiate Registrars and Admissions Officers and NASPA. (2016). *Summary of comprehensive student records project convening.* Washington, DC: Authors.

Anderson, L. W. (2002). Curricular alignment: A re-examination. *Theory into Practice, 41*(4), 255–260.

Angelo, T. (2014, June). *A conversation with Tom Angelo re: assessment* [TLT Friday-Live! Event, Oxford, OH]. Retrieved from https://blogs.miamioh.edu/cte/2014/06/25/tlt-fridaylive-event-a-conversation-with-tom-angelo-re-assessment/

Arum, R., & Roksa, J. (2011). *Academically adrift: Limited learning on college campuses.* Chicago, IL: University of Chicago Press.

Ashford, E. (2015, April). Redesigning for student pathways [Online news]. *ccDaily* (American Association of Community Colleges). Retrieved from http://www.ccdaily.com/Pages/Campus-Issues/Redesigning-colleges-to-focus-on-student-success.aspx

Association of American Colleges & Universities. (n.d.a). *Essential learning outcomes.* Retrieved from https://www.aacu.org/leap/essential-learning-outcomes

Association of American Colleges & Universities. (n.d.b). *What is a 21st century liberal education?* Retrieved from https://www.aacu.org/leap/what-is-a-liberal-education

Association of American Colleges & Universities. (2015a). *The LEAP challenge: Education for a world of unscripted problems.* Washington, DC: Author.

Association of American Colleges & Universities. (2015b). *General education maps and markers: Designing meaningful pathways to student achievement.* Washington, DC: Author.

Association of American Colleges & Universities. (2017). *On solid ground: VALUE report.* Washington, DC: Author.

Bailey, T., Jaggars, S. S., & Jenkins, D. (2015a). *Implementing guided pathways: Tips and tools.* New York, NY: Columbia University, Teachers College, Community College Research Center.

Bailey, T., Jaggars, S. S., & Jenkins, D. (2015b). *What we know about guided pathways.* New York, NY: Columbia University, Teachers College, Community College Research Center.

Bain, K. (2004). *What the best college teachers do.* Cambridge, MA: Harvard University Press.

Baker, R. B. (2015, June). *The student experience: How competency-based education providers serve students.* Washington, DC: Center for Higher Education Reform, American Enterprise Institute.

Baldridge, J. V., Curtis, D. V., Ecker, G. P., & Riley, G. L. (1974). *Alternative models of governance in higher education* (Research and Development Memorandum No. 129). Washington, DC: National Institute of Education.

Barr, R. B., & Tagg, J. (1995). From teaching to learning: A new paradigm for undergraduate education. *Change: The Magazine of Higher Learning, 27*(6), 12–25.

Bial, D., & Gandara, P. C. (2001). *Paving the way to postsecondary education: K-12 intervention programs for underrepresented youth: Report of the National Postsecondary Education Cooperative Working Group on Access to Postsecondary Education.* Collingdale, PA: DIANE Publishing.

Biggs, J. (1996). Enhancing teaching through constructive alignment. *Higher Education, 32,* 347–364.

Biggs, J., & Tang, C. (2011). *Teaching for quality learning at university* (4th ed.). New York, NY: Open University Press.

Birnbaum, R. (1988). *How colleges work: The cybernetics of academic organization and leadership.* San Francisco, CA: Jossey-Bass.

Birnbaum, R. (2000). *Management fads in higher education.* Hoboken, NJ: John Wiley & Sons.

Black, P., & William, D. (1998). Assessment and classroom learning. *Assessment in Education: Principles, Policy and Practice, 5*(1), 7–74.

Blaich, C., Wise, K., Pascarella, E. T., & Roksa, J. (2016). Instructional clarity and organization: It's not new or fancy but it matters. *Change: The Magazine of Higher Learning, 48*(4), 6–12.

Bortman, L. (2013, April). *Meaningful assessment: The benefits of institutional alignment.* Paper presentation at the WASC Academic Resource Conference, San Diego, CA.

Bowman, N. A., & Bastedo, M. N. (2009). Getting on the front page: Organizational reputation, status signals, and the impact of U.S. News and World Report rankings on student decisions. *Research in Higher Education, 50*, 415–436.

Brakke, K., Hite, M. S., Mbughuni, A., Moore, O., Wade, B. H., & Phillips, M. T. (2014). Our beloved journey: Using storytelling to foster faculty community. *Peer Review, 16*(4), 7–9.

Brandt, R. (1993). On outcome-based education: A conversation with Bill Spady. *Students at Risk, 50*(4), 66–70.

Brau, M., Breaden, B., Herburger, L., McGrail, A. B., Newton, A., Parthemer, M., & Ulerick, S. (2013). Lane's GPS guide to student learning, engagement, and navigation. *Peer Review, 15*(2), 10–11.

Briggs, C. L. (2007). Curriculum collaboration: A key to continuous program renewal. *The Journal of Higher Education, 78*(6), 676–711.

Brizee, A. H. (2008). Stasis theory as a strategy for workplace teaming and decision making. *Journal of Technical Writing and Communication*, 38(4), 363–385.

Broad, B. (2003). *What we really value: Beyond rubrics in teaching and assessing writing.* Logan, UT: Utah State University Press.

Brown, G. R., & Rhodes, T. L. (2016). *Assessment practices for advancing transfer student success: Collaborating for educational change.* Washington, DC: Association of American Colleges and Universities.

Brown, K., & Malenfant, K. J. (2015). *Academic library contributions to student success: Documented practices from the field.* Chicago, IL: Association of College and Research Libraries.

Burns, J. S. (Writer), & Haaland, B. (Director). (1999). Mars University [Television Series Episode]. In M. Groening (Executive producer), *Futurama.* New York, NY: Fox Broadcasting.

Buttner, A. C. (2015, September). *Finding the way in the assessment landscape: Developing an effective assessment map.* Urbana, IL: University of Illinois and Indiana University, National Institute for Learning Outcomes Assessment.

Carman, J. G. (2010). The accountability movement: What is wrong with this theory of change? *Nonprofit and Voluntary Sector Quarterly, 39*(2), 256–274.

Center for Postsecondary and Economic Success (CLASP). (2013, February). *A framework for measuring career pathways innovation: A working paper.* Washington, DC: The Alliance for Quality Career Pathways.

Chacon, R. (2014). Mining faculty complaints for valuable assessment clues. *Assessment Update, 26*(5), 5–6, 12.

Community College Research Center (CCRC). (2015). *Implementing guided pathways at Miami Dade College: A case study.* New York, NY: Columbia University, Teachers College, Community College Research Center.

Competency-Based Education Network. (2015, December). *Faculty and staff roles and responsibilities in the design and delivery of competency-based programs: A C-BEN snapshot.* Brooklyn, NY: Public Agenda.

Competency-Based Education Network. (2016). *Quality standards for competency-based educational programs.* San Francisco, CA: Author.

Conley, D. T., & Gaston, P. L. (2013). *A path to alignment: Connecting K–12 and higher education via the Common Core and Degree Qualifications Profile.* Indianapolis, IN: Lumina Foundation for Education.

Cook-Sather, A., Bovill, C., & Felten, P. (2014). *Engaging students as partners in learning and teaching: A guide for faculty.* San Francisco, CA: Jossey-Bass.

Council for Adult and Experiential Learning (CAEL). (n.d.). *Higher education for adult student success.* Retrieved from http://www.cael.org/higher-education-adult-student-success

Crosson, P., & Orcutt, B. (2014). A Massachusetts and multi-state approach to statewide assessment of student learning. *Change: The Magazine of Higher Learning, 46*(3), 24–33.

Cuevas, N. M., Matveev, A. G., & Miller, K. O. (2010). Mapping general education outcomes in the major: Intentionality and transparency. *Peer Review, 12*(1), 10–15.

Cutrufello, G. (2013). *The core curriculum: Justice matters. Report on faculty and student focus groups.* Radnor, PA: Cabrini University.

Dannels, D. P. (2015). More than verbs: Behind the scenes of the learning outcomes in communication project. *Spectra, 51*(4), 10–15.

Dastrup, A. (2015, May 20). How can a degree qualifications profile create a better geosciences workforce? *Directions Magazine.* Retrieved from http://www.directionsmag.com/entry/how-can-degree-qualifications-profiles-create-a-better-geosciences-wor/442779

Dean, K. E., & Dagan, K. A. (2011). *Il-LUMINA-ting the curriculum: Turning the spotlight on civic learning.* Jacksonville, IL: Illinois College.

Dill, D. D. (2014). Ensuring academic standards in US higher education. *Change: The Magazine of Higher Learning, 46*(3), 53–59.

Dolinsky, R., Rhodes, T. L., & McCambly, H. (2016). *Action steps for advancing transfer student success: Lessons learned from cross-institutional collaborations.* Washington, DC: Association of American Colleges & Universities.

Dunlosky, J., Rawson, K. A., Marsh, E. J., Nathan, M. J., & Willingham, D. T. (2013). Improving students' learning with effective learning techniques: Promising directions from cognitive and educational psychology. *Psychological Science in the Public Interest, 14*(1), 4–58.

Education Design Lab. (2016, April 5). *12 promising non-traditional college pathways to attainment.* Retrieved from http://eddesignlab.org/2016/04/12-promising-non-traditional-college-pathways-to-attainment/

Educational Policy Improvement Center. (2011). *Valencia College: Curriculum alignment contributes to award-winning results.* Eugene, OR: Author.

Eisenmann, L., Brumberg-Kraus, J., Gavigan, L., & Morgan, K. (2014). Creating "Connections 3.0." *Peer Review, 16*(4), 16–18.

Elon University. (n.d.). *Elon experiences transcript.* Retrieved from http://www.elon.edu/e-web/students/elon_experiences/VisualEXP.xhtml

Elrod, S. (2014). Quantitative reasoning: The next "across the curriculum" movement. *Peer Review, 16*(3), 4–8.

Evans, C. (2013). Making sense of assessment feedback in higher education. *Review of Educational Research, 83*(1), 70–120.

Ewell, P. T. (1997). Organizing for learning: A new imperative. *AAHE Bulletin, 61,* 52–55.

Ewell, P. T. (2009, November). *Assessment, accountability, and improvement: Revisiting the tension* (NILOA Occasional Paper No. 1). Urbana, IL: University of Illinois and Indiana University, National Institute for Learning Outcomes Assessment.

Ewell, P. T. (2013, January). *The Lumina Degree Qualifications Profile (DQP): Implications for assessment* (NILOA Occasional Paper No. 16). Urbana, IL: University of Illinois and Indiana University, National Institute for Learning Outcomes Assessment.

Ewell, P. (2016, April 7). Essay on value of student learning outcomes in measuring and ensuring academic quality. *Inside Higher Ed.* Retrieved from https://www.insidehighered.com/views/2016/04/07/essay-value-student-learning-outcomes-measuring-and-ensuring-academic-quality

Ewell, P. T., & Jankowski, N. A. (2015). Accreditation as opportunity: Serving two purposes with assessment. In G. D. Kuh, S. O. Ikenberry, N. A. Jankowski, T. R. Cain, P. T. Ewell, P. Hutchings, & J. Kinzie. *Using evidence of student learning to improve higher education* (pp. 146–159). San Francisco, CA: Jossey-Bass.

Ewell, P. T., Jones, D. P., & Kelly, P. J. (2003). *Conceptualizing and researching the educational pipeline.* Boulder, CO: National Center for Higher Education Management Systems.

Félix, A. (2017). *A college where adjuncts are not just add-ons* (NILOA Assessment in Practice). Urbana, IL: University of Illinois and Indiana University, National Institute for Learning Outcomes Assessment.

Felski, R. (2008). *Uses of literature.* Hoboken, NJ: Wiley-Blackwell.

Ferren, A. S., Anderson, C., & Hovland, K. (2014). Interrogating integrative learning. *Peer Review, 16*(4), 4–6.

Ferren, A. S., Dolinksy, R., & McCambly, H. (2014). Collaborative, faculty-led efforts for sustainable change. *Peer Review, 16*(4), 30–32.

Ferren, A. S., & Paris, D. C. (2015). *Faculty leadership for integrative liberal learning.* Washington, DC: Association of American Colleges and Universities.

Finley, A. (2016). Evidence and other eight-letter words: Musings from the national evaluator. *Bringing Theory to Practice* (Winter 2016 Newsletter). Retrieved from http://www.bttop.org/news-events/evidence-and-other-eight-letter-words-musings-national-evaluator

Ford, K. (2016). *Let's "face it": Striving for fair, accurate and transparent assessment.* Urbana, IL: University of Illinois and Indiana University, National Institute for Learning Outcomes Assessment.

Foy, J., Phillips, C., Muir, H., James, P., Robinson, J., & Rome, D. (2014, January). *Quality Collaboratives project* [Quality Collaboratives project meeting presentation]. Retrieved from http://degreeprofile.org/press_four/wp-content/uploads/2016/11/QC_presentation_Jan2014.pdf

Gallup. (2014, February). *What America needs to know about higher education redesign.* Washington, DC: Author.

Gaston, P. L. (2015). *General education transformed: How we can, why we must.* Washington, DC: Association of American Colleges and Universities.

Giffin, L. (2016, October). *DQP case study: Daemen College.* Urbana, IL: University of Illinois and Indiana University, National Institute for Learning Outcomes Assessment.

Graff, G. (1991, February 13). Colleges are depriving students of a connected view of scholarship. *The Chronicle of Higher Education*, p. 48.

Graff, G. (1993). *Beyond the culture wars: How teaching the conflicts can revitalize American education.* New York, NY: W. W. Norton & Company.

Hart Research Associates. (2013). *It takes more than a major: Employer priorities for college learning and student success.* Washington, DC: Association of American Colleges & Universities.

Hart Research Associates. (2015a). *Bringing equity and quality learning together: Institutional priorities for tracking and advancing underserved student success.* Washington, DC: Association of American Colleges & Universities.

Hart Research Associates. (2015b). *Falling short? College learning and career success.* Washington, DC: Association of American Colleges & Universities.

Hart Research Associates. (2016). *Recent trends in general education design, learning outcomes, and teaching approaches.* Washington, DC: Association of American Colleges & Universities.

Heileman, G. L., Babbitt, T. H., & Abdallah, C. (2015). Visualizing student flows: Busting myths about student movement and success. *Change: The Magazine of Higher Learning, 47*(3), 30–39.

Higher education: Not what it used to be. (2012, December 1). *The Economist.* Retrieved from http://www.economist.com/node/21567373/print

Hill, R. (2009). "Why should I do this?" Making the information systems curriculum relevant to strategic learners. *Innovation in Teaching and Learning in Information and Computer Sciences, 8*(2), 14–23.

Horst, S. J., Ghant, W. A., & Whetsone, D. H. (2015). Enhancing assessment through use of mixed methods. *Assessment Update, 27*(1), 4–5, 13–14.

Hossler, D., Shapiro, D., Dundar, A., Ziskin, M., Chen, J., Zerquera, D., & Torres, V. (2012, February). *Transfer and mobility: A national view of pre-degree student movement in postsecondary institutions.* Bloomington, IN: National Student Clearinghouse Research Center.

Huber, M. T., & Hutchings, P. (2004). *Integrative learning: Mapping the terrain.* Washington, DC: Association of American Colleges & Universities, Carnegie Foundation for the Advancement of Teaching.

Humphreys, D., McCambly, H., & Ramaley, J. (2015). *The quality of a college degree: Toward new frameworks, evidence, and interventions.* Washington, DC: Association of American Colleges & Universities.

Hutchings, P. (2014, July). *DQP case study: Kansas City Kansas Community College.* Urbana, IL: University of Illinois and Indiana University, National Institute for Learning Outcomes Assessment.

Hutchings, P. (2016, January). *Aligning education outcomes and practices* (NILOA Occasional Paper No. 26). Urbana, IL: University of Illinois and Indiana University, National Institute for Learning Outcomes Assessment.

Hutchings, P., & Jankowski, N. (2015). Rethinking boundaries: Bringing general education and the discipline together. *Spectra, 51*(4), 24–27.

Hutchings, P., Jankowski, N. A., & Ewell, P. T. (2014). *Catalyzing assignment design activity on your own campus: Lessons from NILOA's assignment library initiative.* Urbana, IL: University of Illinois and Indiana University, National Institute for Learning Outcomes Assessment.

Hutchings, P., Jankowski, N. A., & Schultz, K. E. (2016). Designing effective classroom assignments: Intellectual work worth sharing. *Change, 48*(1), 6–15.

Hynes, S., Pope, M., Loughlin, P., & Watkins, S. (2015, October). *The student transformative learning record at the University of Central Oklahoma: A commitment to improving student learning.* Urbana, IL: University of Illinois and Indiana University, National Institute for Learning Outcomes Assessment.

Jacobson, M. J., & Kapur, M. (2012). Learning environment as emergent phenomena: Theoretical and methodological implications of complexity. In D. Jonassen & S. Land (Eds.), *Theoretical foundations of learning environments* (2nd ed.; pp. 303–334). New York, NY: Routledge.

Jankowski, N. A. (2015). *Evaluation report for AAC&U Quality Collaboratives (QC) project.* Urbana, IL: University of Illinois and Indiana University, National Institute for Learning Outcomes Assessment. Retrieved from http://www.aacu.org/sites/default/lcs/les/qc/EvaluationReportFinal.pdf

Jankowski, N. A. (2017). *Unpacking relationships: Instruction and student outcomes.* Washington, DC: American Council on Education.

Jankowski, N. A., & Giffin, L. (2016a). *Degree Qualifications Profile impact study: Framing and connecting initiatives to strengthen student learning.* Urbana, IL: University of Illinois and Indiana University, National Institute for Learning Outcomes Assessment.

Jankowski, N. A., & Giffin, L. (2016b). *Using the Degree Qualifications Profile to foster meaningful change.* Urbana, IL: University of Illinois and Indiana University, National Institute for Learning Outcomes Assessment.

Jankowski, N. A., & Jones, N. (2016). *DQP/Tuning case study: Utah State University, Bringing it all together to foster intentional learners.* Urbana, IL: University of Illinois and Indiana University, National Institute for Learning Outcomes Assessment.

Jankowski, N. A., & Kinzie, J. (2015). The role of institutional research in institutional engagement with DQP and Tuning. *New Directions for Institutional Research, 165,* 15–26.

Jankowski, N. A., & Marshall, D. W. (2014, October). *Roadmap to enhanced student learning: Implementing the DQP and Tuning.* Urbana, IL: National Institute for Learning Outcomes Assessment (NILOA) and Institute for Evidence-Based Change (IEBC).

Jankowski, N. A., & Marshall, D. W. (Eds.). (2015a). Partners in advancing student learning: Degree Qualifications Profile and Tuning. *New Directions for Institutional Research, 165,* 1–89.

Jankowski, N. A., & Marshall, D. W. (2015b). Degree Qualifications Profile (DQP) and Tuning: What are they and why do they matter? *New Directions for Institutional Research, 165,* 3–14.

Jankowski, N. A., & Marshall, D. W. (2015c). New Directions for IR, the DQP, and Tuning. *New Directions for Institutional Research, 165,* 77–88.

Jankowski, N. A., & Slotnick, R. C. (2015). The five essential roles of assessment practitioners. *Journal of Assessment and Institutional Effectiveness, 5*(1), 78–100.

Jardeleza, S., Cognato, A., Gottfried, M., Kimbirauskas, R., Libarkin, J., Olson, R., . . . Thomas, S. (2013). The value of community building: One center's story of how the VALUE rubrics provided common ground. *Liberal Education, 99*(3), 52–57.

Jobs for the Future. (2014, June). *The pathways to prosperity network: A state progress report, 2012–2014.* Washington, DC: Author.

Johnson, K. E., & Schuck, C. (2014). Using dynamic criteria mapping to improve curricular alignment across institutions. *Higher Learning Commission 2014 Collection of Papers.* Chicago, IL: Higher Learning Commission.

Johnston, R. (2015, November). *Guided pathways demystified: Exploring ten commonly asked questions about implementing pathways.* San Mateo, CA: National Center for Inquiry and Improvement.

Jones, G. R. (2010). *Organizational theory, design, and change.* Upper Saddle River, NJ: Prentice Hall.

Jones, N. (2012). "Tuning" the disciplines. *Liberal Education, 98*(4), 52–59.

Jones, N., & McInerney, D. (2016). *Faculty and the Degree Qualifications Profile: Questions of learning.* Urbana, IL: University of Illinois and Indiana University, National Institute for Learning Outcomes Assessment. Retrieved from http://degreeprofile.org/press_four/wp-content/uploads/2016/08/Thinking-professors-guide-to-DQP.pdf

Jones, S. (2015). The game changers: Strategies to boost college completion and close attainment gaps. *Change: The Magazine of Higher Learning, 47*(2), 24–29.

Jordan-Fleming, M. K. (2015). Unexplored variables in course-embedded assignments: Is there an elephant in the room? *Assessment Update, 27*(4), 7, 12.

Kerrigan, M., Headington, R., & Walker, S. (2011, September). *Visualising the holistic assessment experience—The use of Google tools to support effective design.* Presentation at the 18th International Conference, Association for Learning Technology, Leeds, United Kingdom.

Kezar, A. (2015). *Scaling and sustaining change and innovation: Lessons learned from the Teagle Foundation's "Faculty work and student learning" initiative.* New York, NY: The Teagle Foundation.

Kidd, N. (2015). Reflecting on experience: The heart of NCA's learning outcomes in communication project. *Spectra, 51*(4), 5–8.

Kim, D. H. (1993). The link between individual and organizational learning. *Sloan Management Review, 35*(1), 37–50.

Kinzie, J., Hinds, T. L., Jankowski, N. A., & Rhodes, T. L. (2017). Recognizing Excellence in Assessment. *Assessment Update, 29*(1), 1–16.

Kinzie, J., & Jankowski, N. A. (2015). Making assessment consequential: Organizing to yield results. In G. D. Kuh, S. O. Ikenberry, N. A. Jankowski, T. R. Cain, P. T. Ewell, P. Hutchings, & J. Kinzie (Eds.), *Using evidence of student learning to improve higher education* (pp. 73–94). San Francisco, CA: Jossey-Bass.

Kirkpatrick, K. (2014, September). *DePauw University: Co-curricular inventory* [DQP in Practice]. Urbana, IL: University of Illinois and Indiana University, National Institute for Learning Outcomes Assessment.

Kluger, A. N., & DeNisi, A. (1996). The effects of feedback interventions on performance: A historical review, a meta-analysis, and a preliminary feedback intervention theory. *Psychological Bulletin, 119*(2), 254–284.

Kolb, D. A. (1984). *Experiential learning: Experience as the source of learning and development.* Upper Saddle River, NJ: Prentice Hall.

Kolowich, S. (2011, March 1). How to train your draconian. *Inside Higher Ed.* Retrieved from https://www.insidehighered.com/news/2011/03/01/gates_tells_ governors_they_might_determine_public_university_program_funding_based_ on_job_creation

Kuh, G. D. (1996a). Guiding principles for creating seamless learning environments for undergraduates. *Journal of College Student Development, 37*(2), 135–148.

Kuh, G. D. (1996b). Some things we should forget. *About Campus, 1*(4), 10–15.

Kuh, G. D. (2008). *High-impact educational practices: What they are, who has access to them, and why they matter.* Washington, DC: Association of American Colleges and Universities.

Kuh, G. D., & Hutchings, P. (2015). Assessment and initiative fatigue: Keeping the focus on learning. In G. D. Kuh, S. O. Ikenberry, N. A. Jankowski, T. R. Cain, P. T. Ewell, P. Hutchings, & J. Kinzie (Eds.), *Using evidence of student learning to improve higher education* (pp. 183–200). San Francisco, CA: Jossey-Bass.

Kuh, G., & Ikenberry, S. (2009). *More than you think, less than we need: Learning outcomes assessment in American higher education.* Urbana, IL: University of Illinois and Indiana University, National Institute for Learning Outcomes Assessment.

Kuh, G. D., Ikenberry, S. O., Jankowski, N. A., Cain, T. R., Ewell, P. T., Hutchings, P., & Kinzie, J. (Eds.). (2015). *Using evidence of student learning to improve higher education.* San Francisco, CA: Jossey-Bass.

Kuh, G. D., Jankowski, N., Ikenberry, S. O., & Kinzie, J. (2014). *Knowing what students know and can do: The current state of student learning outcomes assessment in US colleges and universities.* Urbana, IL: University of Illinois and Indiana University, National Institute for Learning Outcomes Assessment.

Kuhn, T. S. (1996). *The structure of scientific revolutions* (3rd ed.). Chicago, IL: University of Chicago Press.

Kurzweil, M. (2015, January 29). Making assessment work: Lessons from the University of Pittsburgh. New York, NY: ITHAKA S+R.

Lancaster, J. S. (2015). Rubric-based mapping for institutional curriculum development projects. *Assessment Update, 27*(1), 8–9, 12.

Land, S. M., Hannafin, M. J., & Oliver, K. (2012). Student-centered learning environments: Foundations, assumptions and design. In D. Jonassen & S. Land

(Eds.), *Theoretical foundations of learning environments* (2nd ed.; pp. 3–26). New York, NY: Routledge.

Lave, J. (2011, February 22). *Learning as a socially situated activity—Graduate student instructors teaching and resource center.* Retrieved from https://vimeo.com/22409249

LePeau, L. (2015). A grounded theory of academic affairs and student affairs partnerships for diversity and inclusion aims. *The Review of Higher Education, 39*(1), 97–122.

Levin, J. S., & Hernandez, V. M. (2014). Divided identity: Part-time faculty in public colleges and universities. *The Review of Higher Education, 37*(4), 531–558.

Liu, Q. (2015). *Outcomes-based education initiatives in Ontario postsecondary education: Case studies.* Toronto: Higher Education Quality Council of Ontario.

Long, T. (2013). Mt. San Antonio College—Roadmap to student success project. *Peer Review, 15*(2), 16–17.

Lumina Foundation for Education. (2011). *The Degree Qualifications Profile.* Indianapolis, IN: Author.

Lumina Foundation for Education. (2014). *The Degree Qualifications Profile.* Indianapolis, IN: Author.

Lumina Foundation for Education. (2016, January). *Connecting credentials: Lessons from the national summit on credentialing and next steps in the national dialogue.* Indianapolis, IN: Author.

Maffly, B. (2011, February 4). Lawmaker laments "degrees to nowhere." *The Salt Lake Tribune.* Retrieved from http://archive.sltrib.com/story.php?ref=/sltrib/home/51183443-76/education-utah-science-degrees.html.csp

Maki, P. L. (2015). *Assessment that works: A national call, a twenty-first century response.* Washington, DC: Association of American Colleges & Universities.

Maki, P. L. (2017). *Real-time student assessment: Meeting the imperative for improved time to degree, closing the opportunity gap, and assuring student competencies for 21st-century needs.* Sterling, VA: Stylus.

Marshall, D. W. (2015). "He said they've already got one!" Strategies for engaging with the LOCs. *Spectra, 51*(4), 18–23.

Marshall, D. W. (2017). *Tuning: A guide for creating discipline-specific frameworks to foster meaningful change.* Urbana, IL: University of Illinois and Indiana University, National Institute for Learning Outcomes Assessment.

Marshall, D. W., Jankowski, N. A., & Vaughan, T., III. (2017). *Tuning impact study: Developing faculty consensus to strengthen student learning.* Urbana, IL: University of Illinois and Indiana University, National Institute for Learning Outcomes Assessment.

Mathematica Policy Research. (2015, May). *Best practices in competency-based education: Lessons from three colleges.* Princeton, NJ: Author.

McClarty, K. L., & Gaertner, M. N. (2015, April). *Measuring mastery: Best practices for assessment in competency-based education.* Washington, DC: Center for Higher Education Reform, American Enterprise Institute.

McCullough, C. A., & Jones, E. (2014). Creating a culture of faculty participation in assessment: Factors that promote and impede satisfaction. *Journal of Assessment and Institutional Effectiveness, 4*(1), 85–101.

McInerney, D. (2017, February). *Eight years on: Early—and continuing—lessons from the Tuning project* (NILOA Viewpoint). Urbana, IL: University of Illinois and Indiana University, National Institute for Learning Outcomes Assessment.

McMahon, T., & O'Riordan, D. (2006). Introducing constructive alignment into a curriculum: Some preliminary results from a pilot study. *Journal of Higher Education and Lifelong Learning, 14,* 11–20.

McNair, T. (2013). Creating community college roadmaps for success. *Peer Review, 15*(2), 3–4.

McNay, M. (2009). *Western guide to curriculum review.* London, Ontario: The University of Western Ontario Teaching Support Center.

McNeill, K. L., Lizotte, D. J., Krajcik, J., & Marx, R. W. (2006). Supporting students' construction of scientific explanation by fading scaffolds in instructional materials. *Journal of the Learning Sciences, 15,* 153–191.

Methvin, P., & Markham, P. N. (2015). Turning the page: Addressing the challenge of remediation. *Change: The Magazine of Higher Learning, 47*(4), 50–56.

Miknavich, M. (2016). Maps and the search for the buried treasure of assessment. *Emerging Dialogues in Assessment* (Association for the Assessment of Learning in Higher Education). Retrieved from http://www.aalhe.org/blogpost/1533254/263882/Maps-and-the-Search-for-the-Buried-Treasure-of-Assessment

Minnesota State Colleges and Universities System. (2002). *A summary of "Best Practices" for recruitment and retention of students of color.* Retrieved from http://www.academicaffairs.mnscu.edu/studentaffairs/documents/BestPractices.pdf

Monaghan, D. B., & Attewell, P. (2015). The community college route to the bachelor's degree. *Educational Evaluation and Policy Analysis, 37*(1), 70–91.

Montenegro, E., & Jankowski, N. A. (2017, January). *Equity and assessment: Moving towards culturally responsive assessment* (Occasional Paper No. 29). Urbana, IL: University of Illinois and Indiana University, National Institute for Learning Outcomes Assessment.

Mordica, J., & Nicholson-Tosh, K. (2013). *Curriculum alignment module.* Champaign, IL: Office of Community College Research and Leadership, University of Illinois Urbana-Champaign.

National Communication Association (NCA). (2015). *Drawing learning outcomes in communication into meaningful practice.* Washington, DC: Author.

National Institute for Learning Outcomes Assessment (NILOA). (2011). *Transparency framework.* Urbana, IL: University of Illinois and Indiana University, Author.

National Institute for Learning Outcomes Assessment (NILOA). (2014). *DQP assignment library.* Retrieved from www.assignmentlibrary.org.

National Institute for Learning Outcomes Assessment (NILOA). (2016a). *Revision and alignment of learning outcomes.* Urbana, IL: University of Illinois and Indiana University, Author.

National Institute for Learning Outcomes Assessment (NILOA). (2016b, May). *Organizing assignment-design work on your campus: A tool kit of resources and materials*. Urbana, IL: University of Illinois and Indiana University, Author.

National Institute for Learning Outcomes Assessment (NILOA). (2016c, May). *Higher education quality: Why documenting learning matters*. Urbana, IL: University of Illinois and Indiana University, Author.

National Institute for Learning Outcomes Assessment (NILOA). (2016d). *Organizing assignment-design work on your campus: Unfacilitated Guide, a toolkit of resources and materials*. Urbana, IL: University of Illinois and Indiana University, Author.

National Network of Business Industry Associations. (2014). *Common employability skills: A foundation for success in the workplace*. Washington, DC: Author.

Newman, L. E., Carpenter, S., Grawe, N., & Jaret-McKinstry, S. (2014). Creating a culture conducive to integrative learning. *Peer Review, 16*(4), 14–15.

Norton, L. (2004). Using assessment criteria as learning criteria: A case study in psychology. *Assessment & Evaluation in Higher Education, 29*(6), 687–702.

Nussbaum, E. M. (2012). Argumentation and student-centered learning environments. In D. Jonassen & S. Land (Eds.), *Theoretical foundations of learning environments* (2nd ed.; pp. 114–141). New York, NY: Routledge.

Nussbaum, M. C. (2010). *Not for profit: Why democracy needs the humanities*. Princeton, NJ: Princteon University Press.

Ohlemacher, J. (2015). Fostering meaningful dialogue can improve success in learning. *Assessment Update, 27*(2), 5, 5–13.

Ozdemir, D., & Stebbins, C. (2015). Curriculum mapping for the utilization of a learning analytics system in an online competency-based master of health care administration program: A case study. *The Journal of Health Administration Education, 32*(4), 543–562.

Ployhart, R. E., & Vandenberg, R. J. (2010). Longitudinal research: The theory, design, and analysis of change. *Journal of Management, 36*(1), 94–120.

Pollock, S. (2014). Interactive engagement in upper-division physics. *Change: The Magazine of Higher Learning, 46*(3), 34–36.

Porter, S. R., & Reilly, K. (2014, July). *Competency-based education as a potential strategy to increase learning and lower costs*. Retrieved from http://www.cbenetwork.org/sites/457/uploaded/files/MaximizingResources_CBE.pdf

Provezis, S. (2010, October). *Regional accreditation and student learning outcomes: Mapping the territory* (NILOA Occasional Paper No. 6). Urbana, IL: University of Illinois and Indiana University, National Institute for Learning Outcomes Assessment.

Public Agenda. (2015). *Shared design elements and emerging practices of competency-based education programs*. Brooklyn, NY: Author.

Reeves, T. C. (2006). How do you know they are learning? The importance of alignment in higher education. *International Journal of Learning Technology, 2*(4), 294–309.

Rhodes, T. L. (2015). Assessment: Growing up is a many-splendored thing. *Journal of Assessment and Institutional Effectiveness, 5*(2), 101–116.

Rhodes, T. L., Albertine, S., Brown, G. R., Ramaley, J., Dolinsky, R., & McCambly, H. (2016). *Collaboration for student transfer: A nationwide Degree Qualifications*

Profile experiment. Washington, DC: Association of American Colleges & Universities.

The role of higher education in career development: Employer perceptions. (2013). *Marketplace & Chronicle of Higher Education.* Retrieved from http://www .chronicle.com/items/biz/pdf/Employers%20Survey.pdf

Rooney, J. J., & Heuvel, L. N. V. (2004). Root cause analysis for beginners. *Quality progress, 37*(7), 45–56.

Rutschow, E. Z., & Diamond, J. (2015). *Laying the foundations: Early findings from the new mathways project.* New York, NY: MDRC.

Samuel Merritt University. (n.d.). *Assessment approaches.* Retrieved from https:// www.samuelmerritt.edu/assessment/goals.

Sanchez, E. R. H. (n.d.). *General education: University-wide faculty inclusion and innovation.* Retrieved from https://www.jmu.edu/assessment/FacultyStaff/ GeneralEducation/example2.shtml

Schleifer, D., & Silliman, R. (2016, October). *What's the payoff? Americans consider problems and promises of higher education.* Brooklyn, NY: Public Agenda.

Shapiro, D., Dundar, A., Chen, J., Ziskin, M., Park, E., Torres, V., & Chiang, Y. (2012, November). *Completing college: A national view of student attainment rates* (Signature Report No. 4). Herndon, VA: National Student Clearinghouse Research Center.

Shapiro, D., Dunbar, A., Wakhungu, P. K., Yuan, X., & Harrell, A. (2015, July). *Transfer and mobility: A national view of student movement in postsecondary institutions, fall 2008 cohort* (Signature Report No. 9). Herndon, VA: National Student Clearinghouse Research Center.

Shireman, R. (2016, April 7). Essay on how fixation on "inane" student learning outcomes fails to ensure academic quality. *Inside Higher Ed.* Retrieved from https://www.insidehighered.com/views/2016/04/07/essay-how-fixation-inane-student-learning-outcomes-fails-ensure-academic-quality

Signorini, A. (2014). Involving undergraduates in assessment: Assisting peers to provide constructive feedback. *Assessment Update, 26*(6), 3–4, 13.

Silva, E., & White, T. (2015). The Carnegie Unit: Past, present, and future. *Change: The Magazine of Higher Learning, 47*(2), 68–72.

Singer, N. (2015, September 5). A sharing economy where teachers win. *New York Times.* Retrieved from http://nyti.ms/1KxLNEH

Singer-Freeman, K., & Bastone, L. (2016, July). *Pedagogical choices make large classes feel small* (NILOA Occasional Paper No. 27). Urbana, IL: University of Illinois and Indiana University, National Institute for Learning Outcomes Assessment.

Skinner, M. F., & Prager, E. K. (2015). Strategic partnerships: Leveraging the center for teaching and learning to garner support for assessment of student learning. *Assessment Update, 27*(3), 4, 12–13.

Smith, A. A. (2016, April 1). Florida's Indian River State College sees significant improvements in remediation. *Inside Higher Ed.* Retrieved from https://www .insidehighered.com/news/2016/04/01/floridas-indian-river-state-college-sees-significant-improvements-remediation

Smith, C. A., Baldwin, C., & Schmidt, G. (2015). Student success centers: Leading the charge for change at community colleges. *Change: The Magazine of Higher Learning, 47*(2), 30–39.

Soricone, L., Pleasants McDonnell, R., Couturier, L., Endel, B., & Freeman, J. (2016). *Scaling innovation in community colleges: A guide to action.* Washington, DC: Jobs for the Future.

Spady, W. G. (1994). *Outcome-based education: Critical issues and answers.* Arlington, VA: American Association of School Administrators.

Spady, W. G., & Marshall, K. J. (1991). Beyond traditional outcome-based education. *Educational Leadership, 49*(2), 67–72.

Steiner, H. H. (2016). The strategy project: Promoting self-regulated learning through an authentic assignment. *International Journal of Teaching and Learning in Higher Education, 28*(2), 271–282.

Studley, J. S. (2016, April). Career readiness meets institution-wide outcomes measures. *NACE Journal.* Retrieved from http://www.naceweb.org/knowledge/career-readiness-and-institution-wide-outcomes-measures.aspx

Sumsion, J., & Goodfellow, J. (2004). Identifying generic skills through curriculum mapping: A critical evaluation. *Higher Education Research & Development, 23*(3), 329–346.

Tagg, J. (2003). *The learning paradigm college.* San Francisco, CA: Anker Publishing.

Taitz, J., Genn, K., Brooks, V., Ross, D., Ryan, K., Shumack, B., . . . Kennedy, P. (2010). System-wide learning from root cause analysis: A report from the New South Wales root cause analysis review committee. *Quality and Safety in Health Care, 19,* e63.

Taylor, P., Parker, K., Fry, R., Cohn, D., Wang, W., Velasco, G., & Dockterman, D. (2011). *Is college worth it? College presidents, public assess value, quality and mission of higher education.* Washington, DC: Pew Research Center.

Teater, B. A. (2011). Maximizing student learning: A case example of applying teaching and learning theory in social work education. *Social Work Education, 30*(5), 571–585.

Tepe, L. (2014). *Common Core goes to college: Building better connections between high school and higher education.* Washington, DC: New America.

Terry, P. (2015). Assessment: Learning by doing. *Assessment Update, 27*(4), 1–2, 16.

Teitelbaum, E., & Schultz, K. (2016, June). *DQP case study: McKendree University.* Urbana, IL: University of Illinois and Indiana University, National Institute for Learning Outcomes Assessment.

Tierney, W. G. (2008). *The impact of culture on organizational decision-making: Theory and practice in higher education.* Sterling, VA: Stylus Publishing.

Tolkien, J. R. R. (1954). *The fellowship of the ring.* Boston, MA: Houghton Mifflin.

Toomey Zimmerman, H., & Bell, P. (2012). Everyday expertise: Learning within and across formal and informal settings. In D. Jonassen & S. Land (Eds.), *Theoretical foundations of learning environments* (2nd ed.; pp. 224–241). New York, NY: Routledge.

Toulmin, S. E. (2003). *The uses of argument* (2nd ed.). New York, NY: Cambridge University Press.

Tuckman, B. (1965). Developmental sequence in small groups. *Psychological Bulletin, 63*(6), 384–399.

Tyszko, J. A., & Sheets, R. G. (2016). *Changing the debate on quality assurance in higher education: The case for employer leadership and a roadmap for change.* Washington, DC: U.S. Chamber of Commerce Foundation.

University of Greenwich. (n.d.). *Map My Programme.* Retrieved from https://sites.google.com/site/mapmyprogramme/home

University of Iowa Vice President for Student Life. (2017). *Iowa Grow.* Retrieved from vp.studentlife.uiowa.edu/initiatives/grow

University of Wisconsin–Madison. (n.d.). *Learning and talent development.* Retrieved from ohrd.wisc.edu/home/Hide-a-tab/WiGrow/tabid/418/Default.aspx

U.S. Department of Education, Office of Vocational and Adult Education. (2012, January). *Aligning secondary and postsecondary education: Experiences from career and technical education.* Washington, DC: Author.

Voss, J. L., Gonsalves, B. D., Federmeier, K. D., Tranel, D., & Cohen, N. J. (2011). Hippocampal brain-network coordination during volitional exploratory behavior enhances learning. *Nature Neuroscience, 14*(1), 115–120.

Wang, X., Su, Y., Cheung, S., Wong, E., & Kwong, T. (2013). An exploration of Biggs' constructive alignment in course design and its impact on students' learning approaches. *Assessment & Evaluation in Higher Education, 38*(4), 477–491.

Wax, D. (2015, November 5). Does your CBE program look like this? *Competency Works.* Vienna, VA: International Association for K-12 Online Learning. Retrieved from http://www.competencyworks.org/higher-education-2/does-your-cbe-program-look-like-this/

Weick, K. E. (1976). Educational organizations as loosely coupled systems. *Administrative Science Quarterly, 21*(1), 1–19.

Wenger, E. (1998). *Communities of practice: Learning, meaning, and identity.* Cambridge, UK: Cambridge University Press.

Western Interstate Commission for Higher Education (WICHE). (n.d.). *Interstate passport.* Retrieved from http://www.wiche.edu/passport/about

White, L. (2015, September 24). Connecting the dots: Helping students develop "transferable" skills. *Toronto Sun.* Retrieved from http://www.torontosun.com/2015/09/24/connecting-the-dots

Wiggins, G., & McTighe, J. (2005). *Understanding by design* (2nd ed.). Alexandria, VA: Association for Supervision and Curriculum Development.

Winkelmes, M., Bernack, M., Butler, J., Zochowski, M., Golanics, J., & Harriss Weavil, K. (2016). A teaching intervention that increased underserved college students' success. *Peer Review, 18*(1/2), 31–36.

Witham, K., Malcom-Piqueux, L. E., Dowd, A. C., & Bensimon, E. M. (2015). *America's unmet promise: The imperative for equity in higher education.* Washington, DC: Association of American Colleges and Universities.

Wolk, R. A. (2015, March). Competency-based education is working. *Education Week, 34*(24), 28–30.

Natasha A. Jankowski serves as director of the National Institute for Learning Outcomes Assessment (NILOA) and research assistant professor with the Department of Education Policy, Organization and Leadership at the University of Illinois Urbana-Champaign. She has presented at numerous national and international conferences and institutional events and written various reports for NILOA. She is a coauthor with her NILOA colleagues of *Using Evidence of Student Learning to Improve Higher Education* (Jossey-Bass, 2015); the reports *Roadmap to Enhanced Student Learning* (National Institute for Learning Outcomes Assessment [NILOA] & Institute for Evidence-Based Change [IEBC], 2014), *Degree Qualifications Profile Impact Study: Framing and Connecting Initiatives to Strengthen Student Learning* (NILOA, 2016), and *Using the Degree Qualifications Profile to Foster Meaningful Change* (NILOA, 2016); and coeditor of a special volume of *New Directions for Institutional Research* on the Degree Qualifications Profile and Tuning's impact on and implications for institutional research. Her main research interests include assessment and evaluation, organizational evidence use, and evidence-based storytelling. She holds a PhD in higher education from the University of Illinois, an MA in higher education administration from Kent State University, and a BA in philosophy from Illinois State University. She previously worked for GEAR UP Learning Centers at Western Michigan University and worked with the Office of Community College Research and Leadership studying community colleges and public policy.

David M. Marshall is a senior scholar with the National Institute of Learning Outcomes Assessment (NILOA) and serves as a professor of English and director of the University Honors Program at California State University, San Bernardino. He facilitated the Lumina Foundation-funded Tuning projects nationally from 2010 to 2016, working with states, regions and national disciplinary associations to identify essential learning within disciplines and develop strategies for campus-based engagement with the resulting learning outcomes. His research, taken from a practitioner lens, explores issues of alignment and curriculum mapping as a complex collaborative process in higher education, both within institutions and across institutions nationally. He is the author of the reports *Tuning American Higher Education: The*

Process (IEBC, 2014) and *Tuning: A Guide for Creating Discipline-Specific Frameworks to Foster Meaningful Change* (NILOA, 2017); coauthor of the report *Roadmap to Enhanced Student Learning: Implementing the DQP and Tuning* (NILOA & IEBC, 2014); coeditor of a special volume of *New Directions for Institutional Research* on the Degree Qualifications Profile (DQP) and Tuning; and editor of *Mass Market Medieval*. In addition to his research interests in student learning, he studies the uses of the medieval in popular culture. A graduate of College of the Holy Cross, he earned his master's degree in Medieval Studies from the University of York, England and his PhD in English from Indiana University.

INDEX

AACRAO. *See* American Association of College Registrars and Administrative Officers

AAC&U. *See* Association of American Colleges & Universities

AALHE. *See* Association for Assessment of Learning in Higher Education

AASCU. *See* American Association of State Colleges and Universities

Abdallah, C., 92

Academically Adrift in America (Arum and Roksa), 2

ACCJC. *See* Accrediting Commission for Community and Junior Colleges

accountability, 4–6, 14, 139

accreditation, 4–5, 130–31
    assessment and, 147–51

Accrediting Commission for Community and Junior Colleges (ACCJC), 9, 66–67

Adelman, Cliff, 8, 10, 106, 118

adjunct faculty, 137–38

administration, 22–23, 136, 140–42

agreement, 82

AHA. *See* American Historical Association

Albone, Kenneth, 120

alignment, 13–14, 77–78, 83

assessment and, 51, 57–58, 90, 95–96, 117–18

assignment design and, 13, 105–6, 124–25

cocurricular programs and, 71–72

collaboration of, 69–71, 74–75, 113

for community colleges, 90–91

consensus in, 70–71, 89

constructive, 57–60, 109–11

descriptions of, 55–57, 69

holistic, 59–60

keys to, 75

learning outcomes and, 56–57, 117–18

in learning systems paradigm, 50–51, 54, 129

in learning systems paradigm application, 117–19, 124–25

in learning systems paradigm curriculum mapping, 89–91

stasis theory in, 71–72

tight, 89–91, 113

workforce and, 90–91

alignment approaches, 59

assessment and, 57–58

embedding, 67–69

integration, 64–67

reinforcement, 62–64

scaffolding, 60–62

alignment building, 69–71

across divisions, 73–74

within programs, 72–73